(SERIOUS)
NEW COOK

(SERIOUS) NEW COOK

RECIPES, TIPS & TECHNIQUES

Leah Su Quiroga and Cammie Kim Lin

FOREWORD BY CAL PETERNELL

Photographs by Molly DeCoudreaux

RIZZOLI
NEW YORK

New York Paris London Milan

For Fina, Oscar, Noie, and Kai

CONTENTS ———

Mains

POT PIES

SUSHI(ISH)

BREADED & PAN-FRIED

FLASH-FRIED CUTLETS

BRICKED

SKEWERED

BRAISED PORK

BULGOGI

Sweets and Treats

DESSERT CUPS

ICE CREAM TREATS

CRISPS & COBBLERS

CAKES

COLD DRINKS

Foreword

I've met a lot of different sorts of cooks over my three plus decades in restaurant kitchens. Different techniques, different characters, different backgrounds. But one thing that they've all had in common is that they love to eat. It's why they cook: to eat delicious food. Or at least it starts that way. Sometimes the grind of a restaurant can crush the joy right out of a cook and cause them to forget that it's not about kitchen cries of ORDER UP! HOT FOOD! YES CHEF!—or even at-the-table *wows*! It's about the in-your-mouth *yum*! Some do survive with yumminess intact, and my friend Leah is one of them. With *(Serious) New Cook*, Leah and her sister Cammie are here to show us the steps to making *seriously* good food: how to do it the right way, why it's the right way, and when to do it your own way—all without ever losing sight (smell, taste, embrace) of the *yum*!

When Leah joined us at Chez Panisse, she was just out of culinary school and ready to learn it all. I like to think that I was able to teach her some of the house fundamentals, and some of my own tricks, but the truth is that she arrived fully equipped with an eagerness and determination, backed by her family's food culture, that were her secret sauces. In Alice's legendary kitchens, Leah became a great cook, a leader, a mentor, and—lucky me!—my co-chef. We spent some happy years collaborating, but after she left, I feared the world had lost a skilled teacher. At least, I consoled myself as she started a family, her kids will learn some sweet savory skills. Turns out, I needn't have worried—Leah and Cammie were busy preparing a cookbook, *this* cookbook! They've filled it with dishes that are delightful, familiar, and new, for all ages. There are puff daddies for breakfast, kimbap for lunch, three different pot pies for dinner! Breaded and pan-fried has *its own section*. Flash-fried same. Inner (hungry) child, meet satisfaction. You hold in your hands the operation manual and that was step one so . . . check.

Step two. Stop reading this introduction right now, open *(Serious) New Cook* and start cooking. You can come back and read the rest later, while you're eating, maybe.

Step three. Use *(Serious) New Cook* as it's meant to be used: often and vigorously. The magic of recipes is that they only get *better* the more you use them. They increase in value and never wear out, never lose potency. Does it take some work to get it right? Sure, but, as they say, it's nice work and you get to eat the results. "Delicious bricked duck breast lettuce wraps *again*?!" said no one ever.

Which brings us to step four and the other magic of cooking the *(Serious) New Cook* way—sharing the love. I am a lifelong witness to the power that cooking and eating have to bring people together. Food evokes memories and passes along knowledge. Leah and Cammie have seen it too: when they are in the kitchen with their kids, seasoning and conjuring and making, maybe, frittery bindaeduk pancakes, tucking in the sprouts along the edges like Cammie and *her* mom did at the little Korean market she had when the sisters were growing up. And they know it when they are with family around the table and the aroma of the pot pie is casting its spell and Leah's husband Martín is remembering and telling about his abuela and the salteña pie she made when he was a kid in Bolivia.

I said before that this cookbook is an operation manual, but maybe that's not quite right. *(Serious) New Cook* is more like a spell book, carefully and lovingly made with clear instructions and illustrations, for creating the delicious concoctions that will feed you, feed your family and friends, and work all sorts of magic along the way.

—*Cal Peternell*

INTRODUCTION ———

CHANCES ARE, the fact that you're reading this right now indicates you've got a thing for good food. Maybe you're lucky enough to have a family that makes a lot of delicious meals, or you've eaten in the homes of other people who do. Perhaps you've had the chance to travel and eat all kinds of new foods or dine at terrific restaurants that have left their mark on you, or you find yourself drawn toward food shows and your social media feed is filled with mouth-watering posts. And maybe you've exhausted the kids' cookbooks or beginner cookbooks that top out at quesadillas and chocolate chip cookies, yet all the gorgeous, more advanced cookbooks you want to use just don't offer enough guidance to get the job done.

We've written this book just for you!

Coming of Age with Good Food

We were lucky enough to grow up in a family that's really serious about good food. And by serious, we don't mean snobby. We mean really serious about it being really good, whether it was homemade nachos or burgers, bibimbap or bouillabaisse, fresh fruit salad or blueberry cheesecake. Our mom cooked it all. That's how the foundation for our own cooking was laid.

Everything about food, from the stories that accompanied it to the preparation and sharing of it, defined our childhoods. Mom cooked the food of America alongside the traditional Korean dishes of her own upbringing, teaching us both. Before every big gathering, we stayed up late sitting around the kitchen counter, making hundreds of *mandu* (Korean "eggrolls," as the relatives and neighbors insisted on calling them). The next day, those *mandu* would be fried up and served alongside our neighbor's homemade spaghetti Bolognese, our grandpa's Lithuanian ham buns, our aunts' German potato salad, and our cousins' ambrosia salad (Jell-O, shredded coconut, mini-marshmallows, and canned mandarin oranges—yum, we kid you not). All of this food was a weird mix, sure, but it represented our family, which was, in every sense that mattered, as American as it could get.

Leah (the older sister in our duo) grew up and became a professional chef, eventually running the kitchen in one of the most famous and influential restaurants in America, Chez Panisse. It was started by Alice Waters, the pioneer of America's farm-to-table movement, and pretty much launched the modern American foodie movement. Leah was just a young cook when she started out as an intern there, but she quickly worked her way up, becoming one of the youngest head chefs in the restaurant's history. She got

to know, work with, and teach many amazing cooks along the way, including quite a few who have gone on to make big names for themselves in the food world. (A handful of those folks have even contributed recipes here! Look for the "guest recipes" throughout the book.) She also got to cook for a bunch of important and influential people, including the Prince Charles, and President Barack Obama and First Lady Michelle Obama, to name just a few. After an incredible ten years, she left Chez Panisse to start a family and a small farm where she could teach other people—including kids like her own little ones, Oscar and Fina—how to grow food and cook their own meals.

Cammie (the younger sister in our duo) started out as a cook but eventually became a teacher and a writer. Food regularly makes its way into her work as a college professor, from reading and writing about how food shapes who we are, to engaging with students in cooking projects and food tours, to working with students to run a campus food pantry. Her own kids, Kai and Noie, are impressive young cooks themselves, and it's been a riot watching them grow up in the kitchen. Kai learned to make shrimp tempura, light-as-air, at age ten and perfected his chicken pot pie recipe not long after. He discovered that bringing homemade English toffee and petite meringues to his school's bake sales was a surefire way to turn heads, and when he made goat cheese and garlicky kale crostini for a middle school class project—strategically calling it *crostini with greens and cheese*—his classmates devoured them. He even interned at Chez Panisse when he was fourteen. Noie makes her fair share of family dinners, but her real specialty is sweets. Pretty early on, she realized if she wanted to eat more than Cammie was offering, the solution was to start making it herself. No one can say no to her homemade ice cream and wonderfully chewy cookies and molten chocolate cakes.

A Book Idea Forms

As Kai and Noie were growing up, we noticed something interesting: They constantly dog-eared recipes in our cookbooks, yet they rarely cooked them. Instead, they tended to stick with the recipes they'd already mastered. Why? Because recipes in more advanced cookbooks often *look* and *sound* awesome, but they don't actually *show* you what to do. That meant that if Kai or Noie wanted to try something new, they had to be sure one of us was close by to answer their nagging questions: "What does 'fold it in' mean again?!" "This doesn't look right! Does it?!" We never minded, but let's be real: Sometimes you just want to do it on your own, don't you?

What they needed—what every new cook needs—was a book full of sophisticated, drool-worthy recipes that illustrates what to do so clearly that no parent, no adult, and certainly no professional chef is necessary. That's the cookbook Kai and Noie were desperate for, but it didn't exist. So, we set about making it ourselves: A cookbook for beginner—and even intermediate—cooks just like them. And you! A cookbook with inspiring—yet totally doable—recipes for young people with advanced palates and a sense of adventure.

Some cookbooks inspire, some teach, and some give you all the tools you need to get it done. *(Serious) New Cook* aims to do all three, all at the same time. The recipes are written so you can follow them time and again, but they're also packed with interesting and important information that will help you to learn and grow as a cook. And with loads of step-by-step photos, we actually *show* you what to do to nail each and every one of them.

The recipes in this cookbook reflect the backgrounds, tastes, and experiences of our family, and—just like the whole country—our family is quite diverse. The recipes also reflect the kind of flexibility you need when you're trying to feed a group of people that may include someone with food allergies, another with gluten and dairy intolerances, some who avoid grains, another who's vegan, and so on. (That describes lots of folks—we're guessing in your circle, too!) To that end, we offer recipes and modifications that can work for many diets without sacrificing taste. Sometimes this is intentional from the get-go. (Weekend mornings just wouldn't be the same if we didn't develop a formidable gluten-free recipe for our Puff Daddy pancake!) But more often, we simply point out natural variations of our recipes that allow you to easily cut or substitute ingredients in order to accommodate dietary restrictions, seasonal availability, personal preferences, or simply what's in your fridge when you feel like cooking.

Many of the recipes in *(Serious) New Cook* are quick and simple. You'll notice, though, that some of them are kinda long. It's not that they're typically complicated (though *some* of them are; consider those extra challenges!). It's that we want you to not only have the instructions to make any given dish but to learn about the ingredients and techniques and nuances of every dish (see also "Extra Credit," page 21!) so that you can apply that knowledge to all of your cooking. Through that process, you'll become the kind of cook who can tweak and vary and level up any recipe, fix things that aren't working, and make a habit of pulling off a killer meal or a swoon-worthy treat without making (or *becoming*) a hot mess.

How *(Serious) New Cook* Is Organized

A Great Start

This might just be everyone's favorite section. It's full of recipes you can make for a great start to your day or a great start to a meal—or an anytime snack or light lunch. There are breakfasts, appetizers, snacks, sides, light meals, and party foods—all as fun to make as they are to eat.

Mains

The mains offered here range from quick and easy to more involved and challenging, all drawing on a wide variety of cuisines and traditions. Some of the dishes will be familiar to you, and, most likely, some will introduce you to new techniques and flavors. Try them all, expand your palate, and maybe even discover a new favorite.

Sweets and Treats

If you're looking for a way to get more sweets into your home, turning into a dessert master is a pretty good move. Who can say no to homemade Buttermilk Panna Cotta Cups (page 208) or bubbling fruit crisps and cobblers (pages 221 through 226), or (Double) Dalgona Coffee Milkshakes (page 217)? These recipes are perfect for satisfying your own sweet tooth, topping off an excellent dinner, or quenching your thirst for something out of the ordinary.

Extra Credit

You'll also notice that some words throughout the book are <u>underlined</u>. This indicates there's an entry for those words in the Extra Credit section. Think of it like a glossary: If you're already very familiar with the term, you can just gloss over it. But, if you aren't quite sure what it means or want some extra info (because you're a food geek, just admit it), flip to the Extra Credit section in the front of the book and read a little more about it.

Special Menus

Composing a complete meal from appetizers to dessert is a special challenge. One approach is to simply pick your favorite recipes (or your friend's or parent's or whomever you're cooking for). But another approach is to put together a menu of dishes that really complement one another, whether it's about regional flavors, what's in season, or a careful balance of ingredients and techniques. When Leah was head chef at Chez Panisse, menu planning was one of the most challenging and exciting parts of the job. She would come up with a new menu every single day based on the ingredients that were delivered each morning. It took a *lot* of practice. Designing a menu at home can be challenging and exciting, too; it involves taking into account personal desires, dietary restrictions, what's fresh from the garden or farm, and what looks incredible at the grocery store. To help you get the hang of menu planning, we offer some ideas for special menus so you can see what recipes we think work well together. Take a look, try a few, and then start composing your own!

Tips for Using This Book

The recipes are arranged in trios, with one core recipe that introduces a dish or concept, followed by two recipes that present variations or different approaches. You can start with any recipe, but we recommend trying the core recipe first so you can cook it with the guidance of step-by-step photos.

You'll notice that in addition to the ingredient list and instructions, the recipes contain sidebars with helpful information like:

- Detailed **Ingredient Notes**
- **Optional Prep** suggestions, in case you want to prepare part of the recipe ahead of time
- **Variations**, for when you want to mix it up a bit
- **Equipment**, when a recipe calls for something specialized, such as a waffle iron, muffin tin, ramekins, or specific sizes of baking dishes
- **Tips** where you'll learn more about the art and science behind the recipe so you can better understand not only *what* you're doing but *why* you're doing it. That'll help you master the recipe and also transfer the skills and knowledge to all of your other cooking, too.

Most of the recipes serve about four people, but that of course varies depending on appetite and what else, if anything, you serve with it. In rare cases, a recipe will serve only one or two (like the drinks, which you might prefer to make just for yourself and a friend) or may serve up to eight (like more involved recipes where, if you're going to take the time to make it, you really want leftovers to use for a second meal!).

Almost all of the recipes can be made gluten free, if they aren't already, and a lot of them are or can be made vegetarian or even vegan. We've highlighted many places where this can be done easily, but we encourage you to experiment and tweak the recipes even more in order to fit your dietary needs and desires and those of the folks you feed. Substituting or leaving out ingredients will often result in a pretty different outcome, but sometimes it's a surprisingly terrific one. Figuring that out is what cooking is all about.

We think it's usually impossible to say the amount of time a recipe will take to make.

For reasons we think are obvious, what takes one cook 30 minutes can easily take another 60. On average, the recipes here take a pretty typical amount of time, ranging anywhere from 20 minutes to 1 hour. We've only noted the expected preparation and cooking time on recipes that are especially quick or that require some planning (such as those that involve time for marinating or braising or resting).

We encourage you to keep a little bowl of salt—preferably something pinchable like kosher or sea salt—on the counter as you cook. It will make it easier to "season as you go," an important *(Serious) New Cook* Principle (see opposite page!). The recipes were written with kosher salt in mind, as it is the preferred cooking salt of most serious cooks (because it's reliable—always uniform in size and salinity, with a usefully pinchable texture, making it easy to see and sprinkle). If you are using fine table salt, you'll need to slightly reduce the amount you use; if a recipe calls for 1 teaspoon, use about ¾ teaspoon instead.

Getting Started

Have you ever followed a recipe to a T, only to end up with a dish that looked *nothing* like the photo in the cookbook? We have, and we are here to tell you why. Sure, sometimes it's because we screwed something up. And sometimes it's because there's something screwed up in the recipe. Sometimes, it's because we aren't as experienced or skilled as the cook who made the dish in the photo (well, not *we* … just Cammie. Leah's dishes pretty much always look *better* than the photo). A lot of times, it's because the

dish in the photo has been doctored up—think glue and lacquer and makeup sponges and loads of photo editing. You won't find that here in *(Serious) New Cook!* But more often, it's because the whole follow-a-recipe-to-a-T thing is a bit of a farce. We realize it's a little risky to say this in a cookbook. But we're saying it anyway because what we really want is for good cooking to take root in you, and the only way for that to happen is to tell you the truth.

The reality is, there's cooking as science (basically a chemistry experiment), and there's cooking as improvisational art. And when you're working with food, it's sometimes impossible to replicate the scientific experiment that is a recipe. Because unlike a science lab, it's impossible to control for every variable in a kitchen: the exact material and thickness and size of your frying pan, the precise temperature of your stovetop, the moisture content of your tomatoes or rice, the specific variety or maturity or freshness of your cucumbers, the amount of fat in your particular steak or ground beef or butter, the size of your potatoes or apples or even your salt granules, and believe it or not, even the exact amount of sodium in the particular brand of salt you use. The more sophisticated the recipe, the more variables you introduce into the equation.

So, what's a new cook to do? Follow these basic principles, and soon you'll become not only someone who can replicate a recipe but a cook who knows their way around the kitchen so well that recipes aren't even needed to turn out great dishes. Eventually your cookbooks will become tools for inspiration more than instruction.

(Serious) New Cook Principles

1. USE GOOD INGREDIENTS. Whenever you can, start with ingredients that have been grown locally (which usually means seasonally, too) and with respect: for how they're grown (organically, if possible), respect for the people who grow them (organically, if possible), and appreciation for how they're produced (naturally and authentically, preferably). Doing so will result in better-tasting food that's better for the environment, for your health, and for the people who have grown or produced it for you. Shopping at farmers' markets and local, independent markets is a good start. There, you can ask about the products and learn from people who know and care deeply about what they're selling.

2. TASTE AND ADJUST. Most recipes indicate precisely how much of each ingredient, including seasonings, you need. That's helpful, of course, but it's a little misleading. The saltiness of different salts varies, as does the acidity of different vinegars or lemons, or the depth of flavor in different olive oils. And don't even get us started on the variation in soy sauces and hot sauces! With this in mind, it's crucial that you do what all great cooks do: taste and adjust. Constantly. (Professional cooks even have little jacket pockets for tasting spoons, which they use constantly as they cook, taste, and adjust!) And we don't just mean taste and adjust at the end. We also mean, season as you go! Except in rare circumstances, don't wait until the end to add seasoning. Build flavor and depth by seasoning as you go.

3. EXPERIMENT. Try, pay attention, develop theories, test, try again! Take your time. Make mistakes. Take notes. Try every recipe at least twice.

4. SHARE. Definitely cook for yourself. You're worth the effort. But also share! What you make doesn't have to be perfect to be appreciated. So make enough to share. Gifts of food are gifts of nourishment and love and joy. (Plus, people who cook are cool, so don't be shy about that!)

5. HAVE FUN! Enough said.

EXTRA CREDIT ————

THIS SECTION CONTAINS all kinds of geeky, extra info to help you master the recipes and deepen your knowledge so you become a better, more serious cook. In the recipes, you'll see words that have been <u>underlined</u>, indicating there's a corresponding entry for each of them here. So, use this section for reference, kind of like an old-school glossary, or read it through for extra credit.

Aioli is a terrific fancy-but-not-fancy kind of sauce. It's basically a lemony, garlicky mayonnaise that's marvelous on so many things: Crispy Fried Potato Cubes (page 72) and Crispy Smashed Potatoes with Fried Herbs (page 69), Breaded and Pan-Fried Vegetable Platter (page 147), steamed vegetables (especially asparagus and broccoli!), grilled fish, and more. The easy way to make it is to add a little spoonful of pounded or minced garlic, a squeeze of lemon juice, and a little drizzle of olive oil to your favorite store-bought mayonnaise (bonus points for organic!). For extra, extra credit, make the fully homemade version: Separate a room temperature egg by cracking it into one (very clean!) hand, keeping your fingers together enough to hold the yolk and just open enough to let the whites fall through to the bowl below—or, with a little experience, use the shell to separate it. (Don't use a straight-outta-the-fridge egg. It won't emulsify—or, come together

into a seemingly unified, thickened mixture—the way it needs to for aioli. Save the egg whites for a different use; they can be frozen and later defrosted to make meringue or something else that calls for egg whites only.) Place the yolk in a small bowl, and add one small clove of pounded, finely minced or pressed garlic. Whisk together for a minute or two, until it starts to turn a pale yellow color. Very, very slowly, drop-by-drop, begin drizzling in your best extra-virgin olive oil. After you've added a tablespoon or so, continue drizzling the oil in a slow, steady stream. (This is an exercise in patience. If you're in a rush, it will "break," separating into a gross mess of oil and egg yolk that won't emulsify.) After adding about ½ cup oil, add a squeeze of lemon juice with a sprinkle of salt on top of it. Landing the salt on the juice helps it dissolve more quickly. Whisk a bit more and then continue whisking in up to another ½ cup olive oil.

Anchovies are awesome. If you think you don't like them, set this thought aside. Chances are, you're basing your reaction on *bad* anchovies, the mushy-pasty, freakishly salty things that come cheap in a little tin. Good anchovies, on the other hand (which, yes, sometimes come in a little tin, but more often come in a jar) are tiny little flavor miracles. A secret ingredient in many a marvelous dish, they impart massive *umami*—that

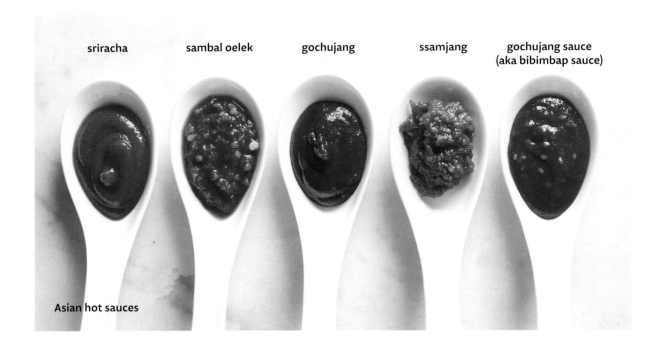

sriracha   sambal oelek   gochujang   ssamjang   gochujang sauce
(aka bibimbap sauce)

Asian hot sauces

hard-to-describe, mouth-filling, savory "fifth flavor." Indeed, *umami* means "essence of flavor" in Japanese. For the full effect, we highly recommend getting the best anchovies you can. But if the cheap ones are all you have, they will still add depth and complexity to the dish. Usually, no one will even guess they're in there. They'll just taste that delicious umami-ness and ask, "Whoa! What's your secret?" You don't have to answer. Quick tip: If you don't have anchovies, but you do have Asian fish sauce, you can substitute with a splash of that!

Applesauce is easy to make and way better than the store-bought kind. Peel, cut, and core 4 or 5 apples. Place in a pot with a splash of apple juice, water, or lemon juice and a few tablespoons of sugar to taste. Cover and cook for about 15 minutes. If they're a soft-fleshed variety, they will naturally break down into applesauce. If they're a very firm-fleshed variety, you may need to

cook them longer or give them a whir in a food processor or with a stick (immersion) blender. (If you know you're going to blend it, you can leave the peel on, which will impart additional flavor and cut down your prep time.)

Asian hot sauces usually impart more flavor than just heat. Good examples include *sriracha*, a spicy, tangy Thai/Vietnamese-style hot sauce popularized by the American brand Huy Fong Foods (aka Rooster Sauce); the similarly flavored *sambal oelek*, which has whole flecks of chiles and garlic, making it a great choice for stirring into soy dipping sauces; *gochujang* sauce, a sweet, spicy, tangy Korean hot sauce used to dress bibimbap; and *ssamjang*, a garlicky, salty, just-slightly-spicy Korean hot sauce typically eaten with grilled meats and lettuce wraps. All can be found online, at Asian markets, and at grocery stores that stock international foods. (Extra, extra credit: Gochujang itself is a Korean hot pepper

breadcrumbs

fine dry (toasted)

fresh (untoasted)

panko

paste. To make gochujang *sauce*—also known as bibimbap sauce—stir together 3 tablespoons of gochujang with 1 teaspoon sesame seeds and 1 tablespoon each of sugar, sesame oil, rice vinegar, and water.)

Berries are often called superfoods, and it's no surprise why. What else is so incredibly healthy and so flavorful and delicious at the same time? Just remember that the intensity of their flavors—mellow, sweet, or tart—can vary dramatically based on many factors, such as their particular variety and growing conditions. If you can, spring for local, organic varieties, which are better for the environment, the people who grow and harvest them, and for your health. Like most fruits and vegetables, if you buy berries that have traveled long and far, it's likely they'll be a variety selected more for their heartiness than their flavor and were picked a little underripe so they could withstand the trip. The result: less

time under the sun developing exquisite berry flavors. If you can't get fresh, ripe, local berries, it's often best to head to the freezer aisle, where they were more likely picked ripe and frozen immediately. In recipes, you can generally swap any type of berry for another. The longer you cook them, the more concentrated their flavors will be. That said, some types—such as strawberries—are best enjoyed super fresh and barely cooked (as in Fresh Berry Compote, page 57) or cooked down until they are nice and jammy; in their in-between stage, they can be a little weird, having let off their flavor and color before their moisture.

Breadcrumbs can be purchased at any supermarket, but homemade is almost always better. Making them allows you to control the ingredients, flavor, texture, and quantity. There are many types of breadcrumbs, and you can typically substitute one for another, though they do cook up slightly differently. *Fine dry crumbs* are great for flash-frying because they are already golden and crispy. To make them, just toast some sliced bread (with crusts on) in the oven at 250°F until it's bone dry and light golden brown, about 20 minutes. After it has cooled completely, process it in a food processor or roll it with a rolling pin, little by little, until you have a big bowlful of fine, toasted crumbs. *Fresh breadcrumbs* are untoasted. They create a thick coating and are great for the three-step breading process (see page 146). To make them, begin with a loaf of white bread (some white gluten-free sliced bread loaves will work, though they may get a little gummy). You can remove some of the crusts if you want a finer, more tender crumb. Cut the bread into cubes, then place a few handfuls into a food processor and pulse until you get evenly sized, but not superfine, crumbs. Continue cutting and blitzing until you're done with the whole loaf or have made as much as you need. *Panko* are flaky, all-white, Asian-style breadcrumbs used for creating a super crispy coating. Japanese in origin, they are now widely available (look for Japanese and Korean brands, which tend to be the lightest and crispiest). To make them at home, follow the same process as for fresh breadcrumbs (detailed above), then gently dry them out in the oven at 200°F, just until dry and crispy but still white, about 15 minutes. All breadcrumbs can be stored in an airtight bag in the freezer. When you use them to coat raw meat, be sure to use only as much as you need. You can always add more breadcrumbs to your breading plate, but for food safety reasons, you shouldn't return leftovers from the breading plate back into the freezer bag.

Brine is a salt soak—usually a saltwater bath with a few other elements, like herbs, sugar, and sometimes baking soda—used to impregnate something with flavor. It is used for improving the texture and flavor of meat and seafood (as in our Frittery Shrimp and Scallion Pancakes on page 80), as well as pickling vegetables.

Buttermilk is the liquid that separates from the fat when you make butter. If you want to make your own butter and buttermilk, pour some heavy cream into a jar and shake it until you have gobs of delicious butter and a thin, slightly acidic liquid—buttermilk! That said, you'd have to shake an awful lot of heavy cream and make an awful lot of butter to get enough buttermilk to cook with. An easier approach, if you don't have any buttermilk on hand, is to combine some liquid dairy (milk, cream, half-and-half, or a combo of all three) with a little lemon juice and, if you have it, a bit of plain yogurt. To make 1 cup, just squeeze 1 tablespoon of lemon juice and/or 1 tablespoon of plain yogurt into a glass measuring cup. Add enough milk to bring it up to 1 cup and stir together. You could even use apple cider vinegar instead of lemon juice. The idea is to reproduce the slightly tangy flavor of buttermilk and to add a bit of acid, which interacts with baking powder and baking soda to help baked goods rise.

Chicory—a cousin to lettuce—is a type of hearty salad green that has a lot of texture and flavor. On their own, chicories are a bit bitter (more or less, depending on variety), but they are super delicious when paired with a strong dressing such as Chef Russell Moore's Broken Caesar Vinaigrette (page 112) or our Gorgeous Green Goddess (page 99). There are many types of chicories—endive, radicchio, puntarelle, escarole, and sugarloaf, to name a few. Use a couple different varieties if you can find them. They will

chicories

impart beautiful colors, textures, and flavors to your dishes. Escarole, which is one of the easiest to find, pairs marvelously with red radicchio.

Chocolate is super confusing, when it really comes down to it. It doesn't matter much when it just comes to eating it straight—either you prefer milk or dark or super dark! But cooking with it is a different story. What you might not realize is that one brand of 70% dark may be much sweeter or smoother than another brand of 70% dark. This nuance creates a little difference in taste but a big difference in the way they cook. When it comes to baking, the differences between various types and brands can really affect the end product. Surprisingly, even the differences between semisweet and bittersweet are not standardized across brands. That leaves it to preference and experimentation—*(Serious)*

New Cook Principle #3!—no matter what one recipe might say. If what you're making requires melting the chocolate, look for couverture chocolate, which is a particularly high-quality chocolate that contains a greater percentage of cocoa butter relative to the other ingredients in it. If you're using cocoa powder, note that there's red cocoa, black cocoa, and Dutch-processed cocoa, to name just a few. The difference will be seen (and tasted) in your dessert. So, try every recipe a few times, pay attention to the different effects of using different types and brands of chocolate, and figure out what you think works best and what you enjoy most.

Coleslaw can add great brightness and zing to tacos, sandwiches , and arepas. To make a quick and simple tangy coleslaw, start by macerating some thinly sliced red onion in a few tablespoons of lime juice (or lemon juice or vinegar) and a big pinch of salt. Massage some thinly sliced red or green cabbage with a big pinch of salt and let it sit for a few minutes. Meanwhile, slice or grate a carrot, thinly slice a jalapeño or sweet red pepper, and chop a half bunch of cilantro. Combine everything together, taste, and add more salt and lime juice, if needed.

Cutting boards are essential cooks' tools. Ideally, they are hard enough to take some abuse, but soft enough to allow your knife to cut into it just slightly, so the food is properly sliced through without damaging the knife's blade. Wood is ideal for these reasons, and also because it's natural and long-lasting, though it does take a bit of extra care. There are a lot of other synthetic options available, the most popular being white plastic that mimics the knife feel you get with wood. (We avoid glass and other solid-surface cutting boards because we find that they slip around, damage knives, and make for an all-around more difficult and less satisfying cooking experience.) Some cooks like to designate specific cutting boards for proteins (especially raw meat and poultry) and produce (fruits and vegetables). When you're dealing with raw meat, you don't want to then use the same cutting board for a salad, for example, without thoroughly cleaning it first; some people just prefer to maintain multiple boards for that reason. Another thing to be careful of is the flavor that can be left behind on a cutting board. Sometimes it's not easy to scrub the garlic (or onion or shallot) flavor out of your cutting board, which is a real bummer if what you use it for next is slicing oranges or strawberries! So, always clean them thoroughly, and if you have a spent lemon half laying around, try rubbing it all over the board to help clean and deodorize it.

dusting

Dusting is what you call the process of applying an even layer of powder—such as flour or powdered sugar—to something. Sometimes bakers will grease their pans with butter, then dust the butter with flour in order to create a nonstick surface. To do so, you can put a tablespoon or two of flour into a fine-mesh strainer, then tap it on the sides, allowing the flour to sprinkle down evenly. Then, just tip the pan upside down and tap out any excess flour. For a perfect dusting of powdered sugar, use the technique described above, allowing a lovely layer to snow down on top of whatever you're trying to decorate, like our Chocolate Air Cake (page 234).

Five-spice powder is a classic Chinese seasoning typically comprising cinnamon, star anise, black pepper, fennel seeds, and cloves. It can be found in the spice aisle of most grocery stores, but it can also be made at home by grinding a spoonful of each in an electric spice grinder (such as a designated coffee grinder) or pounding it to a fine powder with a mortar and pestle.

Flavor profiles are a great concept to master, as they'll provide you with a foundation for numerous recipe creations. For Latin American flavors, you can use a combination of garlic, cilantro, cumin, oregano, chili powder, orange, lime, bay leaf, and black pepper.

For Asian flavors, you can use garlic, ginger, soy sauce, and/or five-spice powder. You could also use *garam masala*, which is somewhat similar to five spice-powder, but also includes cardamom and mace.

For Mediterranean flavors, you might use garlic, parsley, thyme, and/or bay leaf.

For Middle Eastern flavors, use Chef Russell Moore's spice mix (see his Lamb Skewers recipe, page 176): 2 teaspoons cumin, 1 teaspoon coriander, 1 teaspoon caraway, 1 teaspoon fennel seeds, ½ teaspoon cardamom seeds (more if whole in the pod). Toast all of these in a dry pan until they turn a shade darker and smell great, then grind them in a designated electric spice grinder or a mortar and pestle.

Folding is an essential baking technique used to combine something that's been whipped up (think light and airy, like whipped cream or whipped egg whites) with other ingredients (like flour or liquid batter) without deflating the airy, whipped part. Just think, if you beautifully whipped up some egg whites, then combined them with an egg yolk mixture by stirring the heck out of it, all those lovely, miniscule bubbles forming the whipped egg whites would be broken, undoing all your hard work and resulting in a less airy, less fluffy baked thing. Instead, fold them together: Add just a small portion of the whipped

ginger

ingredient(s) to the other ingredients. Using a rubber spatula, very gently mix them together by scooping up the batter from the bottom of the bowl and turning it over onto itself. Repeat this process only until no large streaks of the whipped ingredient(s) are visible.

Ginger is easy to peel but a little tricky to mince or grate. To peel, just scrape the skin with the edge of a regular spoon. For mincing, some people use a dedicated grating device to grate off the meat while separating out the stringy fibers, but ours has been in the back of the random utensil drawer for years because it's so inefficient and difficult to clean. We find there are two good alternatives: grating it (on its side, rather than across the grain) on a super sharp, extra-fine microplane grater, or smashing and mincing it with a good, sharp chef's knife. A sharp microplane grater does a nice job cutting through the fibers while straining out the toughest of them.

If you have enough experience with big, sharp knives, use a chef's knife to smash and mince ginger. Cut it into ¼-inch-thick slices across the grain (in other words, make short slices across it, not long, lengthwise slices) and then carefully use the flat side of the knife to smash it to bits. Then use the sharp blade to chop it like crazy. Don't stop until it's minced very finely; an unexpected little chunk of ginger in your mouth is rarely a pleasant surprise.

Hoisin sauce is a thick, sweet, salty, dark sauce made primarily from fermented soybean paste and sugar (or corn syrup). It can be found in most Asian grocery stores and many American supermarkets, but if you have a gluten intolerance, you may need to make your own, as the store-bought kinds typically contain wheat. Making your own also allows you to control the ingredients, including the level of sweetness and spice, since some store-bought brands taste more like corn syrup than anything else. The amounts in this recipe are very flexible, and you can even omit something if you don't have it. To make your own: Whisk together 2 tablespoons molasses, 2 tablespoons honey, 2 tablespoons nut butter (any kind), 2 tablespoons miso, 1 clove minced garlic, 1 teaspoon five-spice powder, 2 tablespoons rice vinegar, 2 tablespoons sesame oil, and 2 tablespoons soy sauce or tamari. It should be thick, sweet, and super savory.

Knives are among the most important—and often beloved—tools in a good cook's kitchen. If you can only have two, they should be a chef's knife and a paring knife. Two other frequently used types are a serrated knife, used to cut through items with tender flesh and/or a tough skin or crust (like tomatoes or bread) and a

macerating

fillet knife, used to cut fish or debone chicken. Good knife skills take practice and are well worth learning. (And as you are learning, always remember to slightly curl the fingers that are holding and guiding the food you're chopping, slicing, or dicing; that way, you'll keep your fingertips out of the blade's path. See onion photos, page 30, for an example.) Taking care of your knives (including sharpening them) is also worth learning. Quality knives should never be washed in the dishwasher. (In case you're curious, Leah's handmade carbon steel knives, pictured throughout the book, illustrate the surface staining that occurs when you allow carbon steel to air dry. It's only superficial and does not affect performance—but people who don't know better think it looks pretty weird!) Keeping your knives nice and sharp makes prepping feel more effortless and graceful. It can also decrease accidents because you won't have to exert as much pressure as you would with a dull knife. For brand and size

mandoline

matchstick cutting

recommendations, ask the knife expert at your favorite local kitchen shop. And following the (brilliant!) norm of Korean cooks, make frequent and creative use of one of our favorite "knives" ever: a great pair of kitchen shears (aka scissors).

Macerating is a brilliant technique that means soaking in a liquid to soften and encourage an exchange of flavors. It's the key to many delicious salad dressings because it allows you to use alliums, like onion, garlic, and shallot, without experiencing the sharp, pungent flavors that come through in their natural, raw state. When macerated with salt and acid (like lemon or vinegar), they become pickle-y and perfect for a vinaigrette, while flavoring the acid at the same time. Strawberries are also commonly macerated, usually in sugar and lemon juice, resulting in berries that become more sweet and tart with juice that becomes a lemony strawberry delight—perfect for spooning over yogurt or making

strawberry shortcake (which you can make with some whipped cream and biscuits, which we have a great base recipe for on page 224!).

Mandolines are specialty slicers that can produce exceptionally thin, perfectly even slices of just about anything. They are marvelous, but because they are razor sharp, there's hardly a cook who hasn't had a gnarly accident with one. Use them with extreme caution: Stop before the thing you're slicing gets too small; otherwise your fingers may be next. Then use a knife to hand slice any remaining chunks.

Matchstick cutting (also called julienning) is a knife technique used to create skinny, even little "matchsticks." To matchstick cut something long and cylindrical like a carrot or zucchini, first cut a thin, lengthwise slice (¼ inch thick, at most) off one side. Then set it flat on that side so it won't roll around. Cut the rest into long slices no more than ¼ inch thick. Stack a few of the slices, then

onion slicing

onion dicing

cut through the stacks, creating long, thin strips. Finally, cut the long, thin strips into 2- to 3-inch-long segments, leaving you with a pile of evenly cut "matchsticks."

Neutral oil is what we call oils that cook without imparting a particular flavor, allowing the flavor of the food itself to come through without interference. Examples include avocado, grapeseed, canola, corn, and "vegetable" (which is usually made from soybeans) oil. In addition to being neutral in flavor, they tend to have a high heat tolerance, which means you can fry at high temperatures without the oil smoking. In contrast, there are more flavorful oils, like olive, sesame, and coconut. Some, like extra-virgin olive oil, are healthier than others, but their health benefits start to dwindle once you heat up the oil to frying temperature. Flavorful oils tend to have a lower smoke point, which means they burn more easily. Nonetheless, you can actually fry in just about any oil, including a combination of them.

So, for frying, think a little about flavor (a little coconuttiness might be delicious if you're frying shrimp but probably not as much if you're frying beef or potatoes, which might be better complemented by olive oil or a neutral oil), and consider cost (save the extra-tasty, extra-spendy olive oil for salads or drizzling over vegetables). Other than that, use what you have!

Olive oil is one of the most versatile and important ingredients in a good cook's kitchen. It's made from the flesh of fresh olives and is incredibly healthful. At its best, it's unadulterated (which means totally pure) olivey goodness—smooth and fresh-tasting, with a hint of natural spiciness, and somehow managing to taste rich without tasting oily. That's what makes it so perfect for most salads and other raw "drizzling" applications. It has a slightly lower smoke point than most neutral oils, but it's a misconception that it's impossible to fry with. Olive oil—especially the highest grade,

parchment paper cartouche

extra-virgin olive oil—is more expensive than most neutral oils, and since the health benefits and flavor diminish when it's heated to high temps, many cooks reserve it for dishes where its subtle flavor (and sometimes fairly bold flavor, depending on the particular bottle you get your hands on!) can really shine.

Onions form the foundation of dishes in countless cultures around the world. In general, the various types—sweet, white, yellow, red—are interchangeable, though some recipes might favor one over the other because of the desired color or level of sweetness. To *slice* an onion, cut off the bottom/root and the top/stem, then peel it, removing the papery outer layer (along with the first layer if it has any dry or papery parts). Cut it in half along the axis (that means in half from the bottom end to the top end). Then, lay it on the flat side and thinly slice from pole to pole—top to bottom—not across the equator! (Earth metaphors come in handy when describing bulbous vegetables!) Slicing from pole to pole means you're slicing along the onion's fibers, rather than across them; this helps the onions hold their shape, even when caramelized or macerated. If you slice across the equator, the onions will have a slightly different mouthfeel and will be more likely to get mushy when cooked. To *chop* an onion, make the slices a little wider, then give them a chop until you have a bunch of rough squares. To *dice* an onion means something a bit more precise, resulting in tiny, even squares. Dicing is a little tricky: Cut off the top/stem end, but leave the bottom/root end intact. Slice in half along the axis, then remove the papery outer layer. Lay one half flat-side down. Turn your knife sideways and carefully make two or three horizontal cuts, parallel with the table, stopping before you hit the root end. Then, using a sharp, pointy knife, make vertical cuts into the onion—pole to pole, but *not through* the bottom stem—as narrow as you want the pieces diced. Finally, hold the onion together (so it doesn't bloom like a flower!) and slice it finely across the cuts, creating a dice.

Parchment paper is terrific for almost every application involving your oven. It's commonly used to line baking pans because it creates a natural nonstick coating (and easy cleanup) while allowing the food (like cookies or roasted vegetables) to brown nicely on the bottom. You can also make little packets in which you can poach delicate food like fish, a technique called *en papillote* (French for "enveloped in paper"), or cut it into a round (called a cartouche) to be used as a makeshift lid or a liner for a cake pan. Bakers use them to prevent delicate batters from sticking. To cut a cartouche to line the bottom of a cake pan, you can either trace the pan and cut along

soft peak

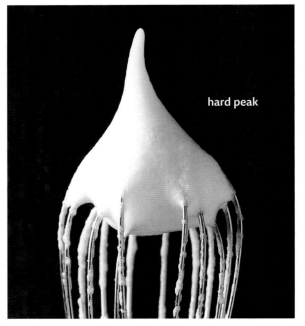

hard peak

the marking, or use the snowflake method: Cut a square that is larger than your pan. Then, fold in half diagonally, then in half again, creating smaller and smaller triangles. Keep folding like you would to make a paper snowflake, making a skinny triangle that resembles a paper airplane. Hold the tip in the middle of your pan and mark the paper where it meets the edge of the pan, basically measuring the radius. Cut the triangle at the marking, then unfold and—voilà!—you'll have a perfectly sized cartouche.

Parsley comes in a couple varieties. When we say parsley, we always mean flat-leaf parsley. It's sometimes called Italian flat-leaf parsley or just Italian parsley. But as far as we're concerned, it's the only parsley that belongs in food. We don't use "curly" parsley—ever, for anything. It's dry and weird and feels yucky in your mouth, which is why we recommend limiting it to symbolic or nostalgic uses.

Peaks refer to the consistency of whipped egg whites or whipped cream. They're typically described as soft peaks (when you lift up the whisk, the egg whites have enough body to form little mounds, but they are soft enough that the tops of those mounds fall over softly), medium peaks (the mounds have good structure and the peaks stand up pretty tall, but fall over at the tips when you hold the whisk upside down), and stiff/firm/hard peaks (the peaks stick straight up and don't fall over when you hold the whisk upside down). If you don't stop as soon as they get to stiff/firm/hard (more or less interchangeable terms), they will break down and become overbeaten and sudsy looking. Broken and overbeaten egg whites can sometimes be fixed by adding one more egg white and slowly beating a little more, and likewise, overbeaten cream can often be fixed with a slow drizzle of a few more tablespoons of cream. Like most things, their fixability just depends on how broken they are. If you are able to fix it with additional cream or egg white, remember that the volume will have increased. That's fine if you're just making whipped cream to dollop on something, but the change in volume may screw things up if you're incorporating it into a recipe. In that case, it may be better to start fresh, if you have enough ingredients. As for technique, there are lots of variables. First of all, choose your tool: a large glass or metal bowl (stainless steel works, but copper is best, if you're so lucky!) with a hand whisk is the most reliable choice because you can control it the most precisely, though it takes a little muscle and time. A stand mixer is super convenient, but that convenience makes it easy to overbeat egg whites. An electric hand mixer is a great in-between tool. Always make sure your bowl and whisk are squeaky clean. Many folks say it's useful to move your whisk quickly and in big circles, lifting it out of the cream/egg white in order to incorporate as much air as possible. Leah's preference is to keep the whisk more or less in the cream/egg white for most of the time, incorporating less air more slowly, in order to produce finer bubbles and, therefore, a smoother and less foamy whipped cream or egg white. Finally, consider whether to add anything to the whip: A few drops of lemon juice or vinegar, or ⅛ teaspoon cream of tartar per egg white will help them hold their shape when whipping. As for heavy cream (or whipping cream, which is similar and interchangeable), nothing additional is needed but a tiny bit of sugar and a couple drops of vanilla. Just remember: If you're serving it dolloped on a dessert that is already quite sweet, unsweetened or barely sweetened whipped cream will better allow the dessert to shine.

Pie crust is easier to make than most new cooks realize. Here's a basic all-butter crust that can be used for sweet or savory dishes: In a large bowl, sprinkle ¼ teaspoon salt and 1 teaspoon sugar over 1½ cups all-purpose flour, then whisk to combine. Cut a stick (8 tablespoons) of cold butter into about 16 pieces, and add about 8 of them to the flour mix. Rub the butter and flour between your fingers until it resembles wet sand and the butter is mostly mixed in. Add the rest of the butter, pinching and rubbing it a bit more, this time leaving some large pieces of butter, which will help make the pie crust flakier. Continue mixing and tossing the dough with one hand while drizzling in up to 6 tablespoons ice-cold water, 1 tablespoon at a time, tossing the flour around to combine after each addition. The dough should not be too wet and sticky, nor too dry and floury. Without squeezing or kneading it, keep lifting and tossing the dough until it forms a loose ball. Wrap the dough ball in plastic wrap and press it down to form a round 1-inch-thick disc. Chill for at least 30 minutes (or overnight) in the refrigerator. When ready to use, let the dough sit at room temperature for about 20 minutes. Then unwrap it and roll it out on a lightly floured surface. Lightly flour the top, especially any visible butter spots, and use a rolling pin to roll out the dough until the crust is about ⅛ inch thick. Now it is ready to top a pie or cut to top several ramekins.

Pink sauce can refer to a few different things, but when we say it, we typically mean the condiment that's delicious on a freakishly wide variety of things: french fries and other fried potatoes, sandwiches, fried meats, rice plates, sliced cabbage and lettuce, eggs, shrimp, and

Yukon Gold potatoes

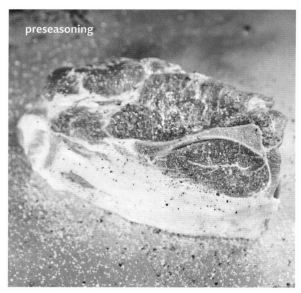
preseasoning

more. It's basically good on anything that's good with ketchup or mayo (no surprise, since those are the main ingredients)! To make it, simply add a few squeezes of ketchup (and/or sriracha, see page 22) to a little bowl of mayonnaise, along with a little splash of vinegar or lemon juice. To turn it into a bona fide diner salad dressing, add a spoonful of pickle relish and, if you have it, a little bit of horseradish. Voilà! Thousand Island dressing.

Ponzu sauce is a Japanese citrus-soy dipping sauce that can be used on a wide variety of dishes, including grilled meats and vegetables, dumplings, noodles, and even salads or simple raw vegetables. To make it, combine 1 tablespoon each of rice wine vinegar, lemon and/or lime juice (or, more traditionally, yuzu, which is a very aromatic lemon-lime-like citrus fruit), and tamari or soy sauce, with ½ teaspoon sugar, and (optionally) a smidgen of minced ginger. To flavor it more deeply, Japanese cooks will typically steep it with some kombu (thick seaweed) and/or bonito flakes (dried fish shavings). If you add a

bit of sesame oil and a sprinkling of pounded sesame seeds to it, you'll have a terrific Asian-style salad dressing.

Potatoes come in many varieties, and they aren't necessarily interchangeable. On one end of the potato spectrum you've got starchy varieties like russets (known in some parts as Idaho potatoes). They tend to have a thicker, rougher skin that's perfect for baked potatoes and a drier flesh, making them good for fluffy mashed potatoes and twice-fried french fries. On the other end of the spectrum are waxy varieties like white and red "boiling potatoes," which tend to have a thin skin and a super moist flesh that makes them harder to fry. In the middle, you have yellow varieties like Yukon Golds and Yellow Finns, which are delicious and truly all-purpose. Aside from the variety, the age of your potatoes will also influence cooking and taste. So, if you ever follow a potato recipe to a T and wonder why it comes out differently each time, it's likely due to one of these factors: variety, age, or size.

Powdered sugar is also called confectioners' sugar, a confectioner being a person who makes sweets. It's sugar that has been pulverized to a fine powder, and it usually has a bit of cornstarch added to it as an anticaking agent (in other words, the cornstarch prevents the powdered sugar from clumping). If you want to make your own, you can pulverize regular sugar in a bullet-style blender; if you need it to remain nonclumping (as for dusting a donut or cake), add 1 tablespoon of cornstarch per 1 cup of sugar.

Preseasoning is one of the most important skills for a cook to learn. It's a useful way to gauge the amount of salt needed to season a raw ingredient, and it provides time for the salt or other flavorings to seep in. In the case of preseasoning meat, you have to keep in mind that the salt will, over time, be absorbed *into* the meat. That means the amount of salt you want to sprinkle onto a very thin cut is quite different from the amount you want to sprinkle onto a very thick cut. You really have to use your eyes, your logic, and your intuition. In the case of a large roast, sprinkle the salt liberally and evenly, understanding that as it rests in the refrigerator overnight (or up to a couple days, assuming it's a fresh piece of meat), the salt will be deeply absorbed.

Puff pastry usually comes frozen in a standard-size box (approximately 14 to 17 ounces). You may only need half for a recipe (such as the Puff Pastry–Topped Mushroom Pot Pie on page 131), but once you thaw the whole box, you'll need to use it all up. So, use half for your recipe, then have some fun with the other half, (*Serious) New Cook* Principle #5! While your pot pie bakes, you can prep some quick and easy desserts to pop in the oven while you eat: To make little turnovers, cut the puff pastry into three- or four-inch squares, spoon in some jam or Any Berry Compote (page 53), fold them over, crimp the edges, and bake. Or, dream up something else! The possibilities are endless, so experiment, (*Serious) New Cook* Principle #3!

Quick-pickled cucumbers are an easy, refreshing addition to many meals, especially those that include fried or grilled meats and rice. They provide a nice crunch, along with a sweet and tangy bite, making them a delicious accompaniment. To make, simply sprinkle 1 teaspoon salt over 4 or 5 diced or sliced cucumbers in a bowl. Let them sit for a few minutes while the salt draws out liquid and the cucumbers draw in the salt. Then drain off the liquid and sprinkle 2 tablespoons sugar over the top, along with ½ cup rice wine vinegar (or apple cider vinegar) and (optionally) a diced fresh chili pepper. Refrigerate for at least 30 minutes. Serve cold. For extra flavor, stir in ½ bunch chopped fresh mint or cilantro.

Rice comes in countless varieties. (Duh.) In our recipes, we typically use short- or medium-grain white rice, both of which cook up into plump, sticky, glossy grains sometimes referred to as sticky rice or sushi rice. It is the preferred rice in much of East Asia (like Korea, where our mom was born, as well as Japan, Taiwan, and parts of China). Maybe because it's the rice we grew up with, we feel pretty strongly it's the best, most versatile and satisfying rice. Cooked well, each grain is distinct, shiny, and plump—perfect for absorbing sauces and stews or bathing the palate in unadulterated rice-iness. Especially when it's fresh ("new crop"), it's Just. So. Good. Like most recipes and techniques people are passionate

salsa verde

about, many will argue there is only one right way to make it, with only one correct proportion of rice to water. We'd argue that's not *quite* correct. Like everything in the kitchen, there are too many variables to account for! In this case, the grains themselves are more variable than many folks realize. They might be truly short grain or more of a medium grain. They might be really fresh, requiring a bit less water, or a bit drier, requiring more. And they might cook up a bit more quickly or slowly, depending on your cooking vessel and stove.

That said, the basic recipe is this: Wash the rice in several changes of water. Then, after draining the rinsing water, add 1¼ cups water for every 1 cup of rice. Bring to a boil in a saucepan over high heat, then turn down to low, cover, and simmer for 20 minutes. Be gentle scooping out the rice, taking care not to break the grains. The rice should be sticky but not goopy. If it's too wet and sticky, simmer it with

the lid off for a few minutes—and next time, use slightly less water. If it's too dry, add a few tablespoons of water and simmer, covered, for a couple more minutes—and next time, use slightly more water.

Roux is a butter and flour mixture that acts as a velvety thickener for sauces and stews (such as the stews inside of our pot pies; see pages 125 and 131). It is called a roux until you add stock, and then it's called a velouté. If you add milk instead of stock, it's called a béchamel.

Salsa verde (Italian style) is the most versatile, useful sauce, added to many foods to brighten them up (as in our Flash-Fried Cutlets, page 160). Akin to chimichurri (which is sometimes called Argentinian pesto), it's basically chopped green herbs bathed in olive oil with a splash of lemon juice or vinegar for brightening. We love it on everything from meats to vegetables and eggs, and even stirred into soups or yogurt. Here's our basic recipe: Finely chop 1 bunch parsley and a few sprigs of some other fresh herb like thyme, dill, cilantro, basil, or chives. Combine it in a bowl with a few tablespoons diced, macerated shallot or red onion, a few fillets chopped anchovy, a big pinch of salt, and enough olive oil to cover. If you'd like to vary things a bit, try adding chopped capers, olives, or cornichons (tiny pickles); lemon zest; minced garlic or hot chiles; or diced tomatoes.

Salt is the most fundamental seasoning in almost every culture around the world. It preserves food and enhances flavor dramatically. There are several kinds of salt, not all created equally! Table salt has tiny granules, is highly processed, and usually has numerous additives;

kosher salt

coarse pink rock salt

table salt

fine pink rock salt

flaky sea salt

its saltiness sometimes tastes harsh rather than full and clean. Kosher salt typically has larger, more flaky granules than table salt, making it ideal for cooks to pinch with their fingers and sprinkle evenly over foods; it tends to be moderately processed, and only some brands include additives. Because it is so easy to use and control, and it's fairly inexpensive, it is the choice of many chefs. Sea salt, which is made simply by solar evaporation of seawater, is the least processed and, by and large, the most delicious. There's also rock salt, which is sea salt so ancient it has turned to rock (not all of which is suitable for cooking, but some of which is delicious). There is great variation among the different types of rock and sea salts, owing to the different minerals that naturally occur in the particular bodies of water they come (or came) from. They also vary dramatically in granule size and

structure, as well as price. We like to use sea salt or high-quality rock salt whenever possible. Just note that if your granules are coarse, they will take time to dissolve, making it difficult to taste and adjust as you cook and easy to oversalt your food. For balanced flavor, convenience, and a good price, use kosher salt for cooking and flaky sea salt for finishing (that is, when you want a little hit of salt to top something off—like fresh, sliced tomatoes or crispy fried potatoes or a chocolate chip cookie)!

Sesame sprinkle is a terrific way to add flavor and crunch to many dishes. A beloved sesame sprinkle most Americans know is found on the everything bagel, which is usually made from sesame seeds, dried garlic and onion flakes, salt, and poppy seeds. To take it in an Asian direction, use a combination of toasted black or white sesame

skillets

seeds, dried chili flakes, dried garlic flakes, poppy seeds, and crumbled nori—or use *furikake* or *shichimi togarashi* (pictured on page 93), two types of Japanese sesame sprinkles you can find in Asian grocery stores and specialty markets.

Sifting is a technique used to eliminate lumps from flours and other dry ingredients, such as salt, baking powder, and sugar. It also combines and lightens the dry ingredients, which can contribute to a finer texture in your baked good. There are sifters designed specifically for this purpose, but a fine-mesh strainer works just as well. Set the strainer over a bowl, spoon in the dry ingredients, and gently tap its sides to let everything pass through and "snow" down into the bowl. If necessary, use a spoon to break up and press through any lumps. If you don't have a fine-mesh strainer or a sifter, simply whisk the dry ingredients together, combining and fluffing them up.

Skillets are—in American parlance—also known as frying pans. Some people get more specific and call a frying pan with curved sides a skillet and one with straight sides a sauté pan (ironic, since curved sides actually make it easier to do a fancy sauté-flip maneuver). Except for a few very distinct applications, they're more or less interchangeable. Everyone has their favorites, and many cooks, when asked about theirs, get real geeky, real fast. It's no wonder: There are definitely some awesome pans and some pretty awful ones. We avoid thin pans, which don't hold heat well and easily lead to burned and uneven food. We also avoid most pans with nonstick coatings because most are coated in chemicals, and as a general rule, we avoid chemicals in or near our food. In recent years, some manufacturers have started producing eco-friendly nonstick pans, but we're already pretty attached to our old pans, especially our cast iron, which is naturally nonstick. Some people are super geeky about "seasoning" their cast iron and never using soap on it; we're a little more relaxed about this. In our experience, if you reserve your cast iron for cooking that involves browning things in oil or butter (such as shallow-fried frittery pancakes and fried cutlets, and even pancakes and fried eggs), and you clean it by giving it a scrub with hot water (though a little soap on the scrubber won't hurt it), it stays reliably nonstick, time after time. You may notice we often say to use a "reliably nonstick pan." What we mean is a pan you know you can cook on without food sticking like crazy, whether it's a well-seasoned cast-iron pan or your favorite nonstick. Acids and liquids leech the oils out of cast iron, ruining their "seasoning." So, for things where the nonstick quality of a cast-iron pan is not needed—particularly acidic and wet things like tomato sauce, vegetables that let out a lot of moisture, and braised meats and vegetables—we prefer heavyish stainless steel pots and pans that cook evenly and are easy to clean. That said, if you ruin the seasoning and things start sticking, take that as a sign it's time to naturally reseason it by making something fried—like our flash-fried cutlets (pages 153–160), frittery pancakes (pages 75–80), or breaded and pan-fried things (pages 145–150).

Soy dipping sauce is great with dumplings, but it's also great with potato pancakes and other lightly fried things, including Mom's Frittery Bindaeduk Pancakes (page 75) and Frittery Shrimp and Scallion Pancakes (page 80). To make it, simply combine equal parts soy sauce (or tamari) and rice vinegar (or use white or apple cider vinegar). If you want to be fancy and add a little extra flavor, texture, and color, top it with some finely sliced scallions, a pinch of sesame seeds, and/or a pinch of chili flakes or little spoonful of Asian hot sauce (especially *sambal oelek*).

Soy sauce, probably the most well-known Asian condiment, is a dark, salty seasoning liquid made from fermented soybeans. It's super common, but surprisingly complicated. After we grew up and started cooking in our own kitchens, one thing that perplexed us the most when trying to replicate our mom's Korean cooking was why our dishes often came out so much saltier or darker or just-not-the-right-*sohn-mat* as hers. (Sohn-mat means "taste of the hands" and refers to the specific taste of the maker—in this case, our mom.) Eventually, we realized it was in part because of the soy sauce we were using. One of the key ingredients in Asian cooking, soy sauce comes in just two varieties (regular and low sodium), and typically in just one brand at American supermarkets;

Asian markets often have dozens of different types and brands. They have dramatically different sodium levels, different ingredients, different fermentation processes, and most importantly, different flavor profiles. One of our favorites is Korean *joseon ganjang*, which is traditionally used to flavor soups but is versatile enough to be used for any recipe or dipping sauce. It's lighter colored, with a clean, savory, and not-so-bracingly-salty flavor. Most soy sauce is made with wheat, but there are some gluten-free options, including tamari, which is a Japanese sauce—usually made without wheat—that's typically interchangeable with soy sauce; there are also some traditionally brewed and fermented Korean varieties of soy sauce that are made without wheat. If your options are limited to plain and low-sodium soy sauce, though, go for the low-sodium version, if possible. And err on the side of less than a recipe calls for, then add more, if needed, as you taste and adjust.

Stock refers to the "broth" made from cooking bones (often with additions like vegetables and herbs), which is used as the base in many soups and stews. (Technically, the word broth refers to the "broth" made from meat—as opposed to bones—and vegetables, though many people use the terms interchangeably.) Chicken stock (or a good vegetable stock, if you lean vegetarian) is one of those things a good cook always has in the fridge or freezer. In fact, it's one of the best reasons to buy chicken with the bone in, raw or roasted! You can cut off the meat you need and toss the bones in a pot—along with some vegetables and aromatics to round out the flavor, if you'd like—and voilà! You have the base of innumerable dishes. Store it in the fridge in a large, clean glass jar for up to four days. Or, freeze it for

stock

Chicken Pot Pie (page 125)!—and toss the carcass back into the pot of water to continue cooking. Occasionally skim any gunk that rises to the top. For a lighter broth, keep the simmer very low and remove from the heat after no more than 2 hours. For a richer broth, simmer for longer—up to 6 hours for a large batch. When it's done, let it cool a bit, then pour it through a fine-mesh strainer into a plastic or glass storage container (1 quart yogurt containers and Ball jars are our favorites), and freeze or refrigerate until ready to use.

Tomatoes are the kind of vegetable (er … fruit) that can be extraordinarily delicious or not even worth eating. When we say tomatoes, we mean delicious (and preferably organic) tomatoes only—none of the mealy, mushy things many supermarkets carry. Tomatoes are meant to be juicy and marvelous, but they are delicate and don't travel well. That's why so many supermarket tomatoes are terrible. They are often picked green, when they are firm and easy to transport across the country (or continent), refrigerated (which results in the mealy, weird texture), and then set out to ripen (poorly) before purchase. That's not a bad technique for pears, but it's awful for tomatoes, which should not be refrigerated at all. Cherry tomatoes are usually packed in a plastic clamshell container, which makes it possible to pick them ripe and transport them without harm. But to really increase your chances of tomato deliciousness, limit your fresh tomato eating to summertime, when they're freshly picked, and buy them from farmers' markets or local shops that support local growers. Or, best yet, try growing your own!

up to six months. (Clean yogurt containers make perfect vessels for freezing!) We always have at least a couple quarts in the freezer. Some cooks even freeze it in ice cube trays so they can use just a cube or two when they need just a bit for a sauce, for heating up leftovers, or even sautéing vegetables.

To make chicken stock, put 1 whole chicken or the equivalent amount in bones and/or meat into a large stockpot. Cover by a few inches with cold water, add 1 peeled and halved onion, 1 peeled and halved carrot, and 1 rib celery, and bring to a boil. (Or, for a more Asian-leaning stock, leave out the vegetables, instead tossing in a couple of scallions and a knob of ginger in the final 30 minutes of cooking.) We sometimes poach a whole chicken, then cut off the nice hunks of meat after it's just cooked, reserving it for other uses—such as Biscuit-Topped

Yogurt whipped cream is a brilliant alternative to typical whipped cream. It's still fluffy and rich and indulgent, but the yogurt gives it a slight tang that offsets and complements the sweetness of many desserts and sweets. To make it, simply whip together 2 parts heavy cream and 1 part whole milk Greek yogurt, with a bit of sugar to taste. Stop whipping when it reaches soft peaks.

Whipped cream can be made by whisking together heavy cream with a small amount of sugar (and a couple drops of vanilla extract, if you'd like), until you have soft peaks. It's best to use less sugar so it doesn't interfere with the flavor of the dish you're serving it with.

A Great Start

Classic Puff Daddy

Maybe you've heard some people call this a Dutch baby, and others a German pancake. As the story goes, the young daughter of a German restaurateur in Seattle couldn't pronounce the word "*Deutsch*" (which actually means "German"!) and instead said "Dutch." The restaurant served individual-size pancakes, calling them "babies." Hence, Dutch baby. You can use the same basic recipe to make Dutch babies, using tiny frying pans, if you have them. Or, make a giant one, as we do here, and call it what you like! Our name of choice? Puff Daddy.

This pancake is traditionally served for breakfast or brunch, but it's equally good for dessert or with dinner. It has lots of cousins—or siblings, more like: think popover, Yorkshire pudding, or even cream puffs. The variations depend mostly on the vessel you cook it in and what you serve it with. It can be served simply with a squeeze of fresh lemon and sprinkle of powdered sugar—like its cousin, the crepe, which is as flat as this daddy is puffy!—and fresh berries, or with whatever genius toppings you can dream of. (Ice cream, anyone?)

The recipe illustrates a key *(Serious) New Cook* principle: Understand the inherently experimental nature of baking. You can read a hundred different recipes that claim their exact technique or exact ratio of eggs to milk to flour will yield the puffiest pancake. This makes sense, since baking is a real science—or maybe it's more of an art . . . we can never decide. Or maybe it's a science, but when we don't exactly KNOW the science, we call it art.

At any rate, what most recipes don't tell you is that every tweak has an effect, including subtle variations in pan shapes, sizes, and materials, the exact size of your eggs, the temperature of the raw ingredients, the size and type of your salt granules, the precise amount of flour, the way your oven heats up, and so forth. Puff Daddies are perfect examples. Using really big eggs and cooking the daddy a little less can yield a more tender, more luscious pancake interior, while a couple extra minutes (or slightly smaller eggs) can yield a more impressive puff height. If you're serving it with maple syrup or loads of berries and powdered sugar, maybe achieving a gravity-defying puff is most important to you. But if a silky interior sounds more satisfying, it might be worth

• • •

Serves 2 to 4

For a gluten-free version, use white rice flour

Equipment: Your choice of oven-safe baking vessel, such as a 10-inch cast-iron skillet, a small roasting pan, a stainless-steel sauté pan, a glass or ceramic baking dish, five or six ramekins, or even a muffin tin. If you use a pan that is 12 inches or more in diameter, you might consider increasing the quantities of all the ingredients in this recipe by one third.

Optional Prep

The batter can be made in advance and kept in the refrigerator for a few hours or even overnight. In fact, letting it rest for a few hours improves the Puff Daddy's texture and can increase its height. Just make the batter without the butter and refrigerate, covered, right in the blender jar. When you are ready to bake it, melt the butter in the pan, add half to the batter, and reblend before pouring and baking it. Note that cold batter will require extra baking time, so keep a close eye on it. If you want to reduce that baking time and improve the height even further, warm the blender jar of cold batter in a pan of hot tap water before before pouring it into the buttered pan.

Tips

Ingredient temperatures affect baking considerably. Just imagine the difference between starting with eggs and milk straight out of the fridge at 40°F compared to room temperature at around 70°F or slightly warmed at around 90°F. Baking times will increase or decrease dramatically, and in a recipe like this, the particular puffiness or crispiness or egginess can be affected as well. When we have time, we use the standard professional pastry chef approach and warm our eggs and milk first. This allows all of the ingredients to bond together more easily, resulting in more uniformly textured baked goods. In a Puff Daddy that usually means it will rise a little taller, too. It's easy enough and is good practice, particularly if you want a consistent result. But the truth is, when we're hungry or in a hurry, we sometimes use them cold, and not many people can tell the difference. If you're up for a tiny bit of extra effort, warm your milk for a few minutes by placing it in a glass measuring cup in a pan of hot water, along with your eggs—and see if you can notice the difference! Also try experimenting—*(Serious) New Cook* Principle #3—with oven temperatures. Some cooks start with a blazing hot oven, while others start with a cold one, believe it or not. We lean toward cold, in this case, but the outcome depends on how fast your oven heats up, so . . . experiment!

Here's a trick to the perfect powdered sugar sprinkle. Put the sugar in a sifter or a fine-mesh strainer and "dust it" onto the pancake by tapping the side of the sifter with your hand as the sugar "snows" down beautifully.

sacrificing a tiny bit of height. Using little ramekins yields fun results, too (see the third recipe in this Puff Daddy trio!)—kind of like a popover or even a bit like a cream puff.

When it comes down to it, after testing and tweaking our recipe countless times over the years, we realized that you can get an impressive result with a remarkably wide variety of approaches. This is what works best for us. Try it once, develop your own theory for what's working best and least given the specifics of your own kitchen and your own ingredients, then tweak the recipe just a tad and try again the next weekend! (Or, better yet, try it once for breakfast, then later for dessert!)

The bottom line: This is a really easy, really fun recipe that cooks up a treat as impressive as it is delicious. So, it follows two more *(Serious) New Cook* Principles: Have fun and share!

INGREDIENTS

Butter, 4 tablespoons unsalted (if you only have salted, reduce the salt to just a pinch)

Whole milk, ¾ cup, slightly warmed (15 seconds in the microwave or a few minutes sitting in a measuring cup in a pan of hot water will do the trick)

All-purpose flour, ¾ cup (or ½ cup white rice flour, preferably superfine)

Sugar, 1 tablespoon (if you're going the savory route, feel free to reduce or skip the sugar)

Salt, 1 teaspoon

Eggs, 3 large, at room temperature (warming briefly in a bowl or pan of hot tap water—perhaps alongside the milk—works well)

Your favorite toppings: lemon juice and powdered sugar, fresh berries, Any Berry Compote (page 53), chocolate-hazelnut spread and bananas, ice cream, a fried egg, ham and cheese, a salad, etcetera, etcetera, etcetera

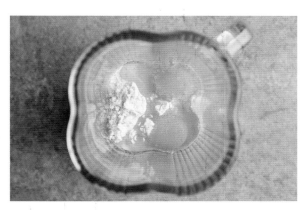

1 **Prep:** Preheat your oven to 400°F. (And if it hasn't come all the way up to temperature by the time the batter is ready, that's okay!) Then, on the stovetop over medium heat, melt the butter in the pan you will bake the pancake in, swirling to coat the bottom and sides. Remove the pan from the heat and start the batter. (If you're using a baking dish or ramekin, pour the melted butter into it and swirl to coat.)

2 **Make the batter:** Spoon out 2 tablespoons of the melted butter and put it into a blender. Then add the milk, flour, sugar, salt, and eggs (in that order, to reduce the amount of flour that gets stuck to the blender cup) and pulse a few times, until nearly smooth. Scrape down the sides to make sure all of the dry ingredients have a chance to blend in, and pulse a few more times. The batter should be thin, frothy, and free of lumps. Alternatively, you can whisk together the ingredients by hand in a large bowl.

3 **Pour the batter and start baking:** Pour the batter into the buttered pan and place it in the oven (even if it hasn't preheated all the way). Resist opening the door to peek for at least 15 minutes (10, if you're using small pans or ramekins).

4 **Finish baking:** Remove from the oven when the puff daddy is super puffy and golden brown all over, 15 to 25 minutes total, depending on your pan and your oven. If you're going for maximum height, let it get nice and brown; if tender deliciousness is your goal, a light golden brown is better. Top as desired and serve immediately.

Caramelized Apple Puff Daddy

This is what you'd get if a Puff Daddy had a baby with a tarte tatin. In other words, it's dessert you can pass off as breakfast. (Unless you add a scoop of vanilla ice cream. Then let's just agree it really is dessert, okay?) Like a classic tarte tatin, the apples are caramelized in butter and sugar before the crust—or, in this case, the Puff Daddy batter—is added to the pan. It bakes up looking rather like a regular Puff Daddy, but as soon as it's done, you flip it upside down onto a plate, which deflates it but allows the caramelized apples to shine. Literally. It's lovely on its own, but our favorite way to serve it is with a dollop of Greek yogurt or with some yogurt whipped cream, which balances out the sweetness of the caramelized apples by bringing out their natural tartness.

● ● ●

Serves 2 to 4

For a gluten-free version, use white rice flour

Time: 45 minutes, though if you have a really hungry crew that can't wait the extra 15 to 20 minutes it takes to caramelize the apples first, you can cheat by making the plain version of the Classic Puff Daddy (page 45), and while it's baking, caramelize the apples in the butter and sugar, then spoon it all over the top of the Puff Daddy.

Equipment: A heavy-bottomed, oven-safe 8- to 10-inch skillet

INGREDIENTS

Butter, 5 tablespoons unsalted (if you only have salted, reduce the salt to just a pinch)

Apples, 2 or 3 large (preferably a firm, tart variety like Pink Lady or Granny Smith), peeled and cut into ⅓-inch-thick slices

Sugar, ½ to ⅔ cup (depending on how sweet or tart your apples are and how strong your sweet tooth is)

Salt, 1 teaspoon plus a pinch

Whole milk, ¾ cup, slightly warmed (15 seconds in the microwave or a few minutes sitting in a measuring cup in a pan of hot water will do the trick)

All-purpose flour, ¾ cup

Eggs, 3 large, at room temperature (warming briefly in a bowl or pan of hot tap water—perhaps alongside the milk—works well)

1 Caramelize the apples: Melt the butter in your skillet over medium-high heat. Then, add the apples, sugar, and a pinch of salt, stirring constantly as the sugar dissolves and the apples begin to release their juices. Continue cooking, stirring frequently, until the apples become soft and translucent, 15 to 20 minutes, depending on your apple variety (see Tips). The consistency of the caramel will change throughout the cooking process. Ultimately, you want it to become a thick, golden-brown syrup. If it gets thicker than that, add a squeeze of lemon juice or a splash of water to loosen it up. Remove from the heat.

2 Make the batter: Preheat your oven to 400°F. (And if it hasn't come all the way up to temperature by the time the batter is ready, that's okay!) Then, into a blender, put the milk, flour, remaining 1 teaspoon salt, and eggs (in that order, to reduce the amount of flour that gets stuck to the blender cup), and pulse a few times, until nearly smooth. Scrape down the sides to make sure all of the dry ingredients have a chance to blend in, and pulse a few more times. The batter should be thin, frothy, and free of lumps. Set it aside to rest for at least a few minutes, until the apples are done.

3 Bake: Slowly and evenly pour the batter over the top of the caramelized apples. Place in the oven (even if it hasn't preheated all the way). Avoid opening the oven door for at least 15 minutes. Then, you can sneak a peek. Keep baking until it is golden brown and puffy all over, about 15 to 25 minutes total, depending on your pan and your oven.

4 Serve: As soon as you remove the Puff Daddy, flip it over onto a large plate or cutting board. If your pan is well-seasoned, it shouldn't stick; if it does, you can use a knife or spatula to help loosen it from the pan. (Another set of hands helps!) Serve warm.

Optional Prep

The batter can be made and refrigerated a day in advance. The apples can be caramelized up to two hours in advance and left in the pan at room temperature. When you are ready, rewarm them over low heat (with a squeeze of lemon juice or splash of water to help loosen them up) before adding the batter and baking.

Tips

Choose your apples wisely. Firm-fleshed varieties like Pink Ladies and Granny Smiths cook differently than soft-fleshed apples like Gravensteins and MacIntoshes, which sometimes turn to applesauce in the pan. The firmer-fleshed varieties are likely to take 15 to 20 minutes to cook through and will puff up before they break down. When you see that puffing start to happen, give them a gentle poke with your spatula or spoon or press them to squeeze the air out. If you don't, the apples will rise to the top (which will be the bottom) of the Puff Daddy. To keep it all caramelly on the bottom (er . . . top), you want the apples to be caramelized, heavy, and free of air. As soon as they become translucent, and before they break down, remove from the heat.

Make it pretty. If your apple slices maintain their shape during caramelization, even after becoming translucent, take a minute to arrange them neatly in the pan (off the heat); use chopsticks, tongs, or a fork to place them in a spiral pattern, which will ensure every single bite has a perfectly balanced sweet-tart flavor. Then, pour over the batter.

Savory Puff Daddy Minis

Puff Daddies aren't only delicious in sweet preparations, and this savory version proves it. You could simply omit the sugar in the Classic Puff Daddy (page 45), and then top it with savory items like cheese, herbs, sautéed vegetables, eggs and bacon, or even a green salad. Or, you could do what we have here, and bake the savory stuff right into it. With shredded Gruyère and fresh herbs, these Savory Puff Daddy Minis could be served as a snack or a side, or even with a green salad for a light brunch.

• • •

Serves 4 to 6

For a gluten-free version, use white rice flour

Equipment: Oven-safe ramekins, 4 to 6, depending on size (or use a muffin tin or popover pan)

INGREDIENTS

Butter, 2 tablespoons unsalted, for greasing (if you only have salted, reduce the salt to just a pinch)

Whole milk, ¾ cup, slightly warmed (15 seconds in the microwave or a few minutes sitting in a measuring cup in a pan of hot water will do the trick)

All-purpose flour, ¾ cup

Salt, ¾ teaspoon

Eggs, 3 large, at room temperature (warming briefly in a bowl or pan of hot tap water—perhaps alongside the milk—works well)

Cheese, 1 to 1½ ounces Gruyère, cheddar, goat cheese, or Parmesan, finely grated

Fresh herbs, 1 tablespoon finely chopped (chives, garlic chives, thyme leaves, and savory—alone or in combination—are great options)

1 Prep: Preheat your oven to 400°F. (And if it hasn't come all the way up to temperature by the time the batter is ready, that's okay!) Then, use your fingers to butter the bottom and sides of each ramekin fairly heavily. Place all of the ramekins on a baking sheet and set aside.

2 Make the batter: Into a blender, put the milk, flour, salt, and eggs (in that order, to reduce the amount of flour that gets stuck to the blender cup) and pulse a few times, until nearly smooth. Scrape down the sides to make sure all of the dry ingredients have a chance to blend in, and pulse a few more times. The batter should be thin, frothy, and free of lumps. Pour it into a 4-cup measuring cup or pitcher. Add the grated cheese and chopped herbs, and whisk or stir to combine.

3 Bake it: Carefully pour the batter into the buttered ramekins, dividing it equally, and place them in the oven (even if it hasn't preheated all the way). Resist opening the door to peek for at least the first 10 minutes. At that point, start peeking for doneness (but make sure your peeks are quick!). It will probably take somewhere between 15 to 25 minutes total, depending on your oven, your ramekins, and the temperature of your ingredients. Remove the mini Puff Daddies from the oven when they are super puffy and golden brown all over. If you're lucky, some of them will have "popped," or levitated out of the ramekin. Serve immediately—either directly in the ramekins (easiest!) or carefully remove each one after running a knife around the inside edge of the ramekin to loosen it.

Tip

Preheating your oven is usually essential for baking. In this case, surprisingly, it can go either way! Some cooks start with a blazing hot oven and others with a cold one. We tend to favor a cold one for our Puff Daddies, resulting in a slower, longer rise in the oven, but the truth is, both work well, and the outcome can be dependent on your particular oven. So, we sometimes go with what's convenient (which is usually preheating, but only for as long as it takes to prep the batter). Try to figure out what works best for you! Remember *(Serious) New Cook Principle #3*: Experiment!

SUPER CRISPY WAFFLES
WITH ANY BERRY COMPOTE

Making compote—a fruity, jammy sauce made with little more than fruit, a sweetener, and a little time to concentrate the flavors—is a simple thing with a big return. Learn how to make this simple Any Berry Compote recipe, and you'll be thinking up endless ways to eat it: over pancakes (page 55), crepes (page 57), or puff daddies (page 45), on ice cream (page 211), with panna cotta (page 209), in a glass of seltzer, or on a giant spoon with peanut butter. Literally, limitless options. Here we've paired it with a recipe for Super Crispy Waffles, which are as buttery as they are light.

INGREDIENTS

ANY BERRY COMPOTE

Berries, 2 cups any type, fresh and/or frozen

Sugar, about ¼ cup (use slightly more or less, depending on how sweet your berries are)

Lemon zest (optional) a big pinch, grated

Cornstarch, 1 teaspoon (or substitute tapioca starch)

Lemon juice (optional), a few drops, freshly squeezed (helpful if your berries are not super delicious)

WAFFLES

Buttermilk, 2 cups, slightly warmed in a measuring cup, in a pan of hot water for a few minutes, or in the microwave for 15 seconds (or substitute regular milk plus 1 tablespoon lemon juice)

Butter, ½ cup (8 tablespoons) unsalted, melted (plus a bit more for the waffle iron, if your waffles tend to stick)

Eggs, 2 large, at room temperature (warming them in a bowl or pan of hot water—perhaps alongside the buttermilk—for a few minutes does the trick)

White rice flour, 1 cup (or substitute all-purpose flour or a gluten-free white flour blend)

Heartier flour, ½ cup total (almond, fine cornmeal, oat, or buckwheat, in any combination)

Cornstarch, ½ cup

Baking powder, 2 teaspoons

Baking soda, 1 teaspoon

Salt, 1 teaspoon

Sugar (optional), 2 tablespoons, white or brown

Greek yogurt (optional), plain or vanilla, for serving

• • •

Serves 3 to 4 (Because the batter is thin and the waffles cook up super light and crispy, folks might eat a surprising number of waffles in one sitting, particularly if you use a classic-style waffle maker, as opposed to the deeper Belgian-style.)

Gluten free, depending on the flour used

Equipment: A waffle iron. The type of waffle iron—size, shape, material—will dramatically affect the number of waffles you make, as well as how light or thick or crispy they are.

Optional Prep

The compote can be made up to 1 week ahead and stored in the refrigerator. (Go ahead and make a triple batch, as you're likely to find many reasons and ways to eat it!)

Tip

Mix up your flours. The base recipe here is naturally gluten free. The heartier flour provides texture and flavor, and the rice flour, the traditional choice for waffles in much of the American South, makes them especially light and crispy. Using primarily all-purpose or a gluten-free white flour mix works well, too, though you won't get the exceptional crispiness of a rice waffle. For your mix of heartier flours, avoid using more than ¼ cup of any one, as it will shift the flavors too far in a single direction.

1 Start the compote: In a small saucepan, stir together the berries and sugar (and zest, if using) over medium-high. If all or most of your berries are frozen, start cooking without adding water, as frozen berries release their juices as they defrost. If all or most are fresh, add a tiny splash of water, which will help the berries transform into a sauce. Cover the saucepan for about 1 minute, until the berries have released some juices, keeping a close eye (and nose) on them to be sure they don't burn. If they aren't releasing enough juice to start getting syrupy, add another tablespoon of water to help them along.

2 Cook the compote: Once the berries have released their juices and started to break down into a syrup, cook them uncovered over low for a few minutes, stirring occasionally. When they have broken down and become syrupy, make a cornstarch slurry, which will help thicken the compote: In a small bowl or cup, stir together 1 teaspoon cornstarch with 1 teaspoon water. Stir the slurry into the compote, and allow it to cook for another 1 to 2 minutes, until it is glossy and slightly thickened.

4 Make the waffles: Preheat your waffle iron. Whisk together the buttermilk and melted butter in a large bowl. Add the eggs and whisk well. In a separate bowl, whisk together the flours, cornstarch, baking powder, baking soda, salt, and sugar (if using). Then, add the flour mixture to the buttermilk-butter mixture, whisking until combined. You want the consistency of a smoothie that is neither too thick nor too thin. Add a little dribble of water or a touch more buttermilk if it's too thick.

When your iron is hot, cook up your first waffle. Sometimes the first one sticks. If yours does, carefully remove it, butter the waffle iron a bit, then try again. After you get a good one, you won't likely need to re-butter the iron in between waffles. If you're cooking for a crowd, you can keep the waffles warm in a hot oven as you cook up all the batter. Or, do what we do: Make everyone share the first one or two, then watch them sit in anticipation as you make the rest one by one. Serve with your warm Any Berry Compote and a big dollop of Greek yogurt (if you like).

3 Finish the compote: When you've got a beautiful, glossy sauce, taste and adjust. Does it need more sugar? A little squeeze of lemon juice to add another layer of flavor? More berries to dilute the sweetness or thin it out a bit? A bit more cornstarch slurry to thicken it up a bit more? When it's just how you like it, take it off the heat until you're ready to serve it, at which time you can carefully pour it into a serving bowl.

Pillowy Silver Dollar Pancakes WITH Maple-Berry Compote

While Any Berry Compote is made thick and jammy by cooking down fruit with sugar, this Maple-Berry Compote is more of a berry syrup—and it's great with just about any breakfast pancake or waffle.

Many traditional pancake recipes claim to make the fluffiest stack, but this recipe owns the claim to something a little different: the most delicate, pillowy little pancakes. These aren't stacking pancakes. They're melt-in-your-mouth little clouds. The recipe is adapted from Marion Cunningham's recipe for Bridge Creek Restaurant Heavenly Hots, published in *The Breakfast Book*. She was an adored American food writer, authoring revisions of the iconic *Fannie Farmer Cookbook*, *The Supper Book*, and *Cooking with Children*, in addition to countless articles and columns for notable newspapers and food magazines.

* * *

Serves 2 to 4

For a gluten-free version, use GF flour

Equipment: A reliably nonstick skillet or griddle and the thinnest spatula you have (provided it's not too floppy!)

Optional Prep

The batter can be made and refrigerated up to 3 days in advance.

Tips

Be systematic. If you keep your griddle at the right temperature, these pancakes cook very quickly. So, be systematic about how you spoon out the batter: If your griddle is square or rectangular, for example, start at the top and spoon the batter out in neat rows. When you get to the last one, the first will probably be about ready to flip. If their color turns darker than a very light gold, they'll be overcooked.

Keep the pancakes small. These delicate pancakes are perfect for making true silver-dollar size, allowing them to be cooked quickly, flipped (more) easily, and devoured more efficiently.

Mix in broken-down and still-whole berries. That is, if you'd like multiple textures in your compote. If you're using fresh blueberries, you can toss in a handful after the mixture has cooked down, allowing them to remain plump and juicy amid all that thick berry-liciousness.

Warm your serving platter. You can do this by running the platter under hot water, microwaving it for a minute or two, or heating it on a warming rack above your stove.

INGREDIENTS

PANCAKES

Eggs, 4 large

Salt, ½ teaspoon

Baking soda, ½ teaspoon

Flour, ⅓ cup (cake or all-purpose)

Sour cream, 2 cups

Sugar, 3 tablespoons

Butter, a few tablespoons for frying (or substitute neutral oil, or half butter and half oil)

MAPLE-BERRY COMPOTE

Berries, 3 cups, fresh or frozen (blueberries are particularly good here, but any variety—or combination of varieties—will work)

Maple syrup, ½ cup

Lemon zest (optional) a big pinch, grated

1 Make the pancake batter: Whisk together all of the pancake ingredients except the butter. Allow the batter to rest, covered, in the refrigerator while you make the compote (or rest in the refrigerator overnight—or even up to a few days). Keeping the batter cold helps them cook up well. In fact, if you're pausing in between batches, be sure to pop the batter back in the fridge.

2 Make the maple-berry compote: Combine the compote ingredients in a medium saucepan. Bring to a boil over medium-high, then reduce to low and simmer for 5 to 10 minutes. Keep an eye on the berries to be sure the liquid doesn't reduce (evaporate) and thicken so much that it scorches. This maple-berry syrup is delicious runny and thin—as real maple syrup is. As the mixture cooks and reduces, it will thicken into a true compote. Taste it and see what you prefer! Transfer to a serving bowl.

3 Cook them up: Heat a nonstick skillet or griddle over medium heat. Drop a pat of butter on it and spread it around evenly. As soon as the butter starts to sizzle, reduce the heat to medium-low and start spooning out the batter using a soup spoon. Keep them small—no larger than 2 inches in diameter. When the edges of the pancakes just start to firm up and there are a couple bubbles on the surface, flip them very carefully. (Don't wait until they are covered with bubbles; if you cook them a moment too long, they will lose the delectable, creamy centers that make them so special.) Flip carefully and cook the second side for less than 1 minute. If you have trouble flipping them, make the rest smaller and, if necessary, cook the first side slightly longer.

4 Serve: The second the pancakes have a lovely, very light golden color on the bottom, transfer them to the serving platter—or directly onto the plates of your eager eaters—with a little bowl of maple-berry compote on the side.

CRAVABLE CREPES
WITH FRESH BERRY COMPOTE

While Any Berry Compote is cooked down over a long period of time until jammy, Fresh Berry Compote is made quickly to preserve the bright, juicy flavors of fresh berries, keeping it closer to <u>macerated</u> berries than a jammy compote. Strawberries are particularly well-suited for it, as they tend to shine when eaten fresh, keeping their juices and texture intact, or slow roasted, concentrating their juices and, in a way, their pulp. They don't do quite so well in between, when they've just let out their juices and leave behind a somewhat mushy pulp. But no matter the berry you choose, Fresh Berry Compote is a bright and juicy version that can be used in nearly as wide a variety of applications as its predecessors—including strawberry shortcake!

● ● ●

Serves 4-ish

For a gluten-free version, use GF flour

Time: 15 minutes if you want them quick, but they are even better if you let the batter rest for an hour—or up to two days—in the fridge.

Equipment: A small, slope-sided <u>skillet</u> that is reliably nonstick. We always use a smooth, well-seasoned cast-iron pan, but you could also use a pan with a nonstick coating or a stainless-steel pan (which may benefit from a spritz of nonstick cooking spray).

Crepes, as we know them in the U.S., are related to a wide variety of thin pancakes found throughout the world: perhaps especially, French *crêpes* and Breton *galettes*, but also Jewish *blintzes*, Russian *blini*, Italian *crespelle*, South African *pannekoek*, Taiwanese *dan bing*, Chinese *jian bing*—to name just a handful!

Fresh Berry Compote—or any type of compote, really—makes a perfect filling for crepes, but they are so versatile, the serving possibilities are really limitless. A squeeze of fresh lemon and a <u>dusting</u> of <u>powdered sugar</u> is classic. So is a slice of ham and melted Swiss cheese—sometimes with an egg broken right in the crepe to gently cook as the cheese melts. Also terrific is a spoonful of cottage cheese or ricotta with the compote. And then there are dessert crepes. If you're a fan of chocolate-hazelnut spread (think Nutella or, better yet, Nocciolata), you won't believe how good they are with a hearty smear and some sliced bananas. And not to be outdone: crepes with ice cream and compote! Since the batter can keep in the refrigerator for a couple days, you could always make a couple kinds for brunch, then whip up dessert crepes after dinner!

INGREDIENTS

FRESH BERRY COMPOTE

<u>Berries</u>, 2 cups, fresh (strawberries and raspberries are particularly good here, but any variety—or combination of varieties—will work)

Lemon juice, about 1 teaspoon, freshly squeezed

Sugar, about ¼ cup (use slightly more or less, depending on how sweet your berries are)

CREPES

All-purpose flour, 1¼ cups (or gluten-free flour—see Ingredient Note)

Buckwheat flour, ¼ cup (or use only all-purpose or a gluten-free flour for a total of 1½ cups flour)

Milk, 1 cup (preferably whole milk, but lowfat and skim will work, too)

Water, 1 cup

Melted butter or <u>neutral oil</u>, 1 tablespoon, plus more for cooking (if you only have salted, reduce the salt in the batter to ¼ teaspoon)

Eggs, 2 large

Sugar (optional), 1 to 2 tablespoons

<u>Salt</u>, ½ teaspoon

FOR SERVING

Yogurt or <u>yogurt whipped cream</u> (see page 41) or Homemade Ice Cream (page 211; optional)

Additional fillings/toppings of your choice (optional; see above for suggestions)

Optional Prep

Both the compote and the batter can be made ahead and stored in the refrigerator for up to 2 days.

Ingredient Note

Gluten-free flour mixes that contain xanthan gum don't work well for crepes because the xanthan gum causes the batter to thicken quite quickly. This makes it difficult to keep the batter nice and runny, which is necessary in order to make thin crepes.

1 **Make the fresh berry compote:** Combine the berries with the lemon juice and sugar in a small saucepan over medium heat. Stir frequently and gently while the mixture heats up, the sugar dissolves, and the berries release their juices. Taste and adjust. Does it need more lemon juice or sugar? Don't cook for more than 2 minutes, as you want to preserve the natural texture and fresh flavors of the berries. Carefully pour the compote into a serving bowl (as soon as it is ready, immediately transfer it out of the hot saucepan in order to stop the cooking).

2 **Make the crepe batter:** Dump all the crepe ingredients into a blender (in the order listed, to reduce clumping on the sides of the blender jar), and pulse several times. Scrape down the sides and blend again, this time for a full 30 seconds. Alternatively, if you whisk by hand, place the ingredients in a large bowl, and keep whisking until the batter is completely smooth. It should be quite runny—about the consistency of heavy cream; if it's thicker than this, add a bit more water and remix. Transfer the batter to a large liquid measuring cup, if you have one, or a bowl. Allow it to rest for at least 30 minutes, time permitting. (If you're resting it for longer than that, cover and keep in the fridge.) Resting the batter will make the crepes easier to flip and less likely to tear. If you don't have time to let the batter rest, it's okay; just be extra careful when flipping.

3 **Cook the crepes:** Gently stir the batter, just to remix it. (You don't want to reintroduce air.) If it has thickened up (this sometimes happens when the flour absorbs the liquid), add a tiny bit more water, stirring gently to combine. Heat your pan over medium-high heat, then drop in a tiny pat of butter (or a drizzle of oil), swirling to coat. If there's not enough butter to coat the pan with a thin layer, add a bit more. The heat should be high enough for the butter to bubble slightly, but not to brown or smoke. Gently pour or ladle in a couple tablespoons of batter, swirling the pan at the same time in order to create a thin, even layer on the bottom. Let it cook over medium or medium-high heat until the edges start to brown, 30 to 60 seconds. Then, carefully slip a thin spatula underneath and flip it to cook the other side. The first crepe of the day is often sacrificial; it may stick and fall apart in the pan, making you worry that the whole endeavor is a mistake. But don't worry: It's not you, it's the pan. It just needs a little warm-up round. Toss the first one, if necessary, and try again. Usually, the second crepe comes out beautifully.

4 **Serve:** We like to serve them DIY-style, with a bowl of compote on the table along with a little bowl of yogurt for dolloping. For each crepe, spoon some compote onto one half, fold it over once, then again, making a triangle. Alternatively, spoon some compote into a wide stripe across the center, then roll it up like a log. Give it a dollop of yogurt or yogurt whipped cream (or ice cream, if you're going there!), and enjoy.

Variation

For fun—or to impress someone—try making a crepe layer cake. The trick is to first make a big stack of crepes (at least twelve, but as many as twenty-five) and then allow them to cool. Then, spread an extremely thin layer of compote and yogurt whipped cream in between each one, repeating until you have a "'cake" of stacked crepes. Top with a spoonful of compote and a big dollop of yogurt whipped cream.

Simple Handmade Arepas

Arepas are a staple in many Central and South American countries and are especially prominent in Colombian and Venezuelan cuisine. Sometimes compared to the soft corn tortillas that are a staple of Mexican cuisine, they are incredibly versatile. Fun and simple to make, arepas use a specially prepared corn flour, are shaped by hand into discs, then cooked on a griddle. Particularly good when served warm, arepas can be eaten plain or as a snack or side dish (rather like bread). They can also be stuffed like a sandwich, as in the recipe that follows, or sweetened and filled, as in the one after that. Master this Simple Handmade Arepa recipe first, then try the rest.

• • •

Makes 6 to 8 arepas

Gluten free and vegan

Ingredients

Salt, 1 teaspoon

Hot water, 2 cups

Olive oil, 1 tablespoon, plus more for frying

Arepa flour, 2 cups (see Ingredient Note)

Tip **The particular technique for cooking arepas can vary**, depending on the particular region, variation, or cook. They can be made with varying amounts of oil: in a fairly dry skillet with just a touch of oil, shallow- or deep-fried in more oil, or somewhere in between using a moderate amount of oil. We like the somewhere-in-between approach: just enough oil for them to char a bit while developing a crispy outside, but not so much oil that they become heavy and greasy.

Ingredient Note

The corn flour (also known as fine cornmeal) commonly used for arepas has been precooked, then dehydrated, which allows it to cook very quickly. Popular Latin American brands include P.A.N. (often referred to as Harina PAN) and Goya (which calls theirs Masarepa). Arepa flour comes in a white corn and a yellow corn variety, both of which work well.

1 Make the dough: Add the salt to a large mixing bowl and pour the hot water over it, mixing to dissolve. Stir in 1 tablespoon of olive oil, followed by the arepa flour. Using a spoon or one hand, mix thoroughly until the consistency is even. Cover the dough with a clean, damp dish towel or plastic wrap, and let it rest for 5 to 10 minutes.

2 Shape the arepas: Using a spoon or your hand, scoop out some dough and roll it between your palms until you have a ball about 2 inches in diameter (about halfway between the size of a ping-pong ball and a tennis ball). Then, gently flatten it into an even disc ½ to ¾ inch thick (thinner if you're serving them plain; thicker if you're going to slice and stuff them). Continue until you've used all the dough.

3 Pan-fry them: Heat a light drizzle of oil on a skillet or griddle over medium-high heat. Once it is hot but not smoking, carefully place the arepas in the pan. Cook for 5 to 7 minutes per side, until they are golden brown; if you like, cook them a little longer until they are charred lightly on each side. They need long enough for the centers to cook through. (If they are browning too quickly, turn down the heat and flip them over; you can flip them back and forth as necessary.)

4 Remove from heat and serve: After 10 to 14 minutes of total cooking time, test one for doneness by breaking or cutting a piece off, examining the inside, and tasting it. If it seems unevenly cooked or if it tastes like raw dough, give the arepas a few more minutes in the pan. If eating them plain, serve immediately. If splitting for sandwiches, let them rest on a cooling rack for 10 minutes before using.

HANDMADE AREPA SANDWICHES

While arepas can be served plain, they also make brilliant sandwiches—or, stuffed arepas. You can fill them with whatever you please, but Latin American flavors should be your first go-to. Our fillings are inspired by the offerings at Venezuelan arepa spots in New York City. Our favorite is a breakfast arepa with a delectably runny egg.

• • •

Serves as many as you make

Gluten free; can be made vegetarian or vegan (see breakfast and lunch arepas; omit the cheese for vegan version)

INGREDIENTS

Simple Handmade Arepas (page 61)

For a breakfast arepa: goat cheese, salt, tomato, avocado, egg

For a lunch arepa: black beans, cotija, avocado, macerated onions, fresh cilantro

For a dinner arepa: braised pork (page 181), macerated onions, fresh cilantro

1 Prepare the arepa: Carefully slide a knife into the side of a warm arepa (rewarm it on a hot griddle first, if necessary), slicing it almost but not quite all the way through, so you can stuff ingredients in it (like a split-open pita pocket), rather than on it (like a sandwich).

2 Stuff and serve: For a breakfast arepa, spread 1 tablespoon goat cheese on the bottom. Sprinkle a little salt and pepper on some tomato and avocado slices, *(Serious) New Cook* Principle #2: Taste and adjust—and season as you go!—then layer them in over the goat cheese. Heat a drizzle of olive oil or pat of butter in a reliably nonstick skillet, and fry up your egg the way you like, seasoned with a little salt and pepper. Slip the egg into the arepa and serve warm. For lunch or dinner arepas, layer in your selected ingredients similarly. Arepa sandwiches can be served cold or at room temperature, depending on the fillings, but they are best served warm (especially the egg sandwich!), with lots of napkins.

Sweet and Cheesy Handmade Arepas

These incredibly snackable arepas satisfy a hankering for something sweet and salty. No surprise, especially if you consider how satisfying kettle corn and sweet corn muffins are. In the area of Cotoca, Santa Cruz in Bolivia, known for its beautiful ceramics and extensive sugarcane production, you can find a sweet arepa made with cheese mixed into the dough. Colombians also make *arepas dulces con queso* (sweet arepas with cheese), and *arepas de choclo* (arepas with fresh Incan sweet corn). Our version is akin to the popular NYC street fair arepas, which—so the story goes—started with Colombian immigrants selling their version of *arepas de choclo* at New York City's annual Feast of San Gennaro festival in Little Italy and evolved into the sweet, melted-mozzarella-filled delight now ubiquitous at New York City street fairs.

• • •

Makes about 8 arepas

Gluten free and vegetarian

INGREDIENTS

Sugar, 3 tablespoons, plus an optional pinch for serving

Salt, 1 teaspoon

Milk, 2¾ cups, warm (whole, lowfat, skim, or a combination of milk and water)

Arepa flour, 2 cups (see Ingredient Note, page 61)

Butter, about 3 tablespoons for frying (or you could use a combination of butter and neutral oil)

Mozzarella cheese, about 4 to 6 ounces, cut into slices about ⅓ inch thick (or, for a more authentic version, use *queso fresco*)

Flaky sea salt (optional), for finishing

1 Make the batter: Combine the sugar and salt in a large bowl, and pour the warm milk over it, stirring to dissolve. Add the arepa flour, stirring until the ingredients are well combined and the batter is an even consistency. Cover and set aside to rest for about 10 minutes; the batter thickens as it sits. Check the consistency: if it is firm and dry, mix in a couple more tablespoons of milk or water until it is neither runny like a smoothie nor thick like cookie dough—somewhere around Greek yogurt consistency. You should be able to easily spread it with the back of a spoon.

2 Cook them up: Melt 1 tablespoon of the butter in a cast-iron skillet or other reliably nonstick skillet over medium heat. When it begins to sizzle, spoon about 2 tablespoons of the batter into it, carefully spreading it into a pancake-like disc. If you are using a large pan, make a few at once, allowing room for the spatula to get in between them. Add a thick slice of cheese (or a few smaller bits, depending on how it's sliced) to the center of each arepa, avoiding the edges. Then, spoon another tablespoon or two of batter on top, spreading it out as evenly as possible. Reduce the heat to medium-low and cook for 3 to 4 minutes, until the bottoms are golden brown. (The heat should be high enough to gently cook the dough but low enough to not burn the bottoms.) Carefully flip them over and cook the other side for 3 to 4 minutes. If the pan is dry at any point, add more butter. After 6 to 8 minutes of cooking, the cheese should be melted and the dough should be cooked through.

3 Brown and serve: All that's left is to brown them up nicely, if they aren't already. Add a little more butter, if needed, and crank up the heat to medium-high. Once they are brown and a bit crisp on both sides, serve 'em up! If you'd like, add a pinch of sea salt and a tiny sprinkle of sugar on top. Serve them on a plate with a fork, which makes sense given the oozy cheese, or wrap them in a piece of parchment paper and eat them out of your hand, cheese oozing and stretching unimaginably far (that's definitely street-fair style).

Tips

Clean up while you wait. One of the most important skills of a good cook is staying organized, and that's much easier to do when you clean as you go. Plus, it's nice not to have a giant mess in the kitchen after you've just finished enjoying something delicious. So, whenever there is a bit of cooking downtime—like while you wait for the dough to rest for 10 minutes—get a jump on the cleanup!

These arepas are made with a thick batter rather than a dough. That means they need to be spooned into the pan (because batter is pourable, by definition), rather than formed by hand as you do with the arepa dough in the preceding recipes.

Variation

The Bolivian version of cheesy arepas, *arepas de Cotoca*, is made with the cheese grated or diced and then mixed right into the batter. To reduce the steps and simplify things, you could do something similar: instead of adding the sliced cheese to the bottom layer of arepa batter, grate the cheese and mix it right into the batter. The melted cheese won't stretch out an arm's length this way, but it'll still be sweet and cheesy and delicious.

CRISPY POTATO PANCAKES

Easy and addictive, these crispy potato pancakes turn ordinary potatoes into thin, devourable rounds in a matter of minutes. They are delicious morning, noon, and night—an instant favorite for everyone who tries them! Clearly, they could fit in our frittery pancake trio, as that's just what they are—crispy, frittery pancakes. But the truth is, despite their pancake-like shape, their familiar fried potato-ness is so indelible, we couldn't justify prying them away from their crispy potato siblings.

We can never agree whether our version of these originates from our paternal grandparents' German and Lithuanian cooking, the pancake house restaurant we frequented as kids in suburban Detroit, or the Korean *gamja-jeon* our mom made when we were growing up. The remarkable thing: all three are quite the same. That must be why, when we make them for breakfast, we serve them with three accompaniments: applesauce and sour cream (Eastern European style) and soy dipping sauce (Korean style). In fact, we won't even make them if we don't have all three! (Sounds weird, we know, but don't knock it 'til you try it.)

• • •

Serves 4

For gluten free, substitute rice flour; for vegan, omit the sour cream

Tip

If the pancakes are crispy enough, they'll be delicious even after they've cooled. But if you want to serve and eat them blazing hot, you can do what we do: Take turns at the stove.

Variation

To us and many others around the world, potato pancakes are classic comfort food, but they can also be served up as a fancy appetizer: Potato Blinis with Crème Fraîche and Smoked Salmon. Just blend the potato batter extra smooth and add an extra tablespoon of flour. Make the blinis (pancakes) small—about 1½ inches in diameter. After they have cooled, top with a dollop of crème fraîche (or sour cream, which is quite similar), a little piece of smoked salmon (or caviar, if you want to be *extra* fancy), and a pinch of finely chopped chives or red onion.

INGREDIENTS

Potatoes, 4 large russets or Yukon Golds (or a combination), peeled and diced into large chunks

White onion, ½ small, peeled and roughly chopped

Egg, 1 large

All-purpose flour, 1 tablespoon

Salt, 1 teaspoon

Neutral oil, for frying

Applesauce, 1 to 2 cups, for serving (see page 22)

Sour cream or plain yogurt, about 1 cup, for serving

Soy dipping sauce, about ½ cup (optional; see page 39)

1 **Make the potato batter:** Place the potatoes, onion, egg, flour, and salt into a blender. Pulse or blend until everything is fine and even but not completely smooth. Pour into a large bowl (it will be easier to spoon out the batter from a bowl than the blender).

2 **Fry 'em up:** Heat 2 tablespoons oil in a large frying pan. Test the oil by dropping in a tiny bit of the potato batter. If it sizzles, you're ready to fry up the first batch. Use a long-handled spoon to carefully place small spoonfuls of the batter in the hot oil, spreading each out into a thin circle and leaving a bit of room in between each one so they don't stick together. Let them sizzle for about 1 minute.

3 **Flip and fry:** When the edges of the potato pancakes are brown, check the bottom of one. If it's nicely browned, flip them all over, being careful to avoid splashing the oil. Add extra oil as necessary so the pancakes continue to sizzle and can slide around. To achieve maximum crispiness, flip the pancakes one more time, giving the first side a second fry. Remove them to a platter.

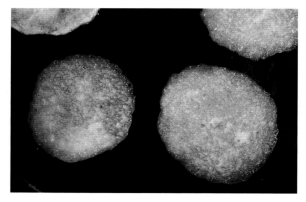

4 **Adjust, finish, and serve:** Before starting the second batch, taste one. Is it delicious? If it's not crispy enough, cook the second batch a bit longer. Is it salty enough? If not, add a bit more salt to the potato batter. Too salty? Toss in another chopped potato and a bit more flour, and blend together again before frying up the rest. When you have a platter full of potato pancakes, serve them with a bowl of applesauce and a bowl of sour cream or yogurt on the side. (And, if you want to go full-on multicultural style, also serve with a small bowl of soy dipping sauce.)

CRISPY SMASHED POTATOES WITH FRIED HERBS

We've never, ever met someone who didn't fall in love with Crispy Smashed Potatoes. They're like french fries, but easier and more interesting, and the fried herbs, though not strictly necessary, elevate them considerably with very little extra effort. These potatoes can do it all—partner up with some fried eggs, sidle up to a steak and a little lemon wedge, or get devoured on their own—ketchup optional.

• • •

Serves 4

Gluten free and vegan

INGREDIENTS

Yellow potatoes (such as Yukon Golds), about 10 ping-pong-ball-size ones

Salt

Olive oil, for frying (or substitute neutral oil)

Rosemary (optional), leaves picked from 1 to 2 fresh sprigs (dry, not damp!)

Sage (optional), a handful of fresh leaves (dry, not damp!)

Flaky sea salt (optional), for finishing (or substitute any sea salt or kosher salt)

Ketchup or aioli (optional; see page 21), for serving

Ingredient Note

The best potatoes for Crispy Smashed Potatoes are ping-pong-ball-size Yukon Golds, which smash and fry beautifully. While yellow (sometimes called gold) varieties fry up the best, you can substitute many other varieties—you'll just get slightly different results and the cooking time may vary. Use whatever size you have: for this recipe, about 10, if they are the size of ping-pong balls; 8, if they are a little larger; 5 or 6, if they are like limes; 2 to 3, if they're quite large. You get the idea. If they are bigger than limes, you'll want to cut them into large chunks before boiling. If you have a mix of sizes, you should cut the larger ones so they are all around the same size, which allows them to cook more evenly.

1 Boil the potatoes: Place them into a medium pot, cover with water, and add a hefty sprinkle of salt. (After it dissolves, taste the water; it should be just a little less salty than a nice bowl of brothy soup.) Bring to a boil over high heat, then turn down to low and continue cooking for about 15 minutes. Carefully stick a fork, knife, or skewer into a potato. If it slides in easily, they are done. If it still feels firm, continue cooking for 2 minutes, then check again.

This recipe works really well if you boil the potatoes ahead of time—which you can do a day or two before. You could also use leftover boiled potatoes, of course! When they are cold, they are much easier to smash.

Tip

Fry carefully. This recipe is pretty easy in one sense: there aren't many ingredients. But the frying part takes a little practice. Be sure the potatoes and herbs are dry before you fry them, which will decrease your risk of getting burned when you put them in the hot oil. Also take care to flip them gently. Hot oil is scary, and cooking burns hurt. That said, it's something that happens to all cooks occassionally. When it does, remember: Soak the burn in or under cool water for way longer than you'd think (dinner can wait) and apply burn cream (which works like a miracle for pain and speeds up healing).

2 Cool and smash: When the potatoes are cooked, use a slotted spoon to scoop them out and place them on your cutting board to cool for at least 5 minutes—or preferably 10 or more. You want them to be cool enough to handle and dry enough to prevent the dreaded (and dangerous) water-in-hot-oil popping effect. Place a flat-bottomed cup, mug, or ramekin on top of one potato. Press down, smashing it to about half its original height. It should split open and some pieces may break off. (Those broken pieces will be the crispy bits everyone fights for!) Run a knife or spatula across the bottom of the cup if the potato sticks and needs to be gently scraped off. Repeat with all the potatoes until you have a gorgeous mess of smashed potatoes and bits.

3 Fry 'em up: Into a large cast-iron skillet or large shallow frying pan, pour enough olive oil to cover the bottom. Heat over medium-high for 1 minute, then add the potatoes. (If your skillet is large enough to fit all of them with a tiny bit of space in between each one, fry them all at once; if not, fry them in two batches.) You should hear and see a nice sizzle. If you don't, turn up the heat to high; then, when the oil is sizzling, reduce the heat to medium-high. When the potatoes are brown on one side, flip them and brown the other side. It should take 6 to 8 minutes per side. You want to maintain a steady sizzle in the pan, so use your eyes and your ears! The slower that steady sizzle, the crispier they will be. Add a bit more oil, as necessary, if the pan becomes dry. When they are irresistibly brown and crispy, scoop them out of the pan with a slotted spoon, letting the excess oil drain off, and place on a warm serving platter.

4 Fry the herbs (optional): Set out a cooling rack or a paper towel on a plate or cutting board. Then, carefully place the fresh rosemary and sage into the sizzling oil. (Be sure the oil is sizzling, but not burning. The herbs may let off some steam as they fry, but take care not to let them burn.) Allow them to crisp up for about 30 seconds, or until they just start to develop dark spots and the tiny bubbles forming around the herbs subside, a signal that the moisture in the herbs has evaporated, leaving them crisp. Ultimately, you want them to be dark green, not brown or tan. (If you smell or see that the herbs or any remaining potato bits are burning, scoop them out immediately.) After the herbs have crisped up, remove to the rack or paper towel, allowing the excess oil to drain off for a minute before topping the crispy smashed potatoes with them.

5 Adjust and serve: Taste a bite of potato with a bit of fried herb; if they need more salt, top them with a little sprinkle of flaky sea salt. Serve them with ketchup or aioli on the side, and you may never crave a french fry again.

CRISPY FRIED POTATO CUBES

We've never, ever met someone who didn't fall in love with these Crispy Fried Potato Cubes. (Wait, didn't we say that about the other potatoes, too? Seriously, though . . . who doesn't love crispy fried potatoes??) They're addictive like the best french fries and are perfect for breakfast, lunch, dinner, or a late-night snack. You can play around with the dipping sauces: Ketchup, obviously. Or aioli, which is a really good garlicky mayo. Or, better yet, ketchup *and* aioli! And speaking of ketchup and mayo, there's always pink sauce—especially great here with the Asian hot sauce called sriracha. You could also try it with Romesco Dip and Sauce (page 101), especially a smooth-blended version, which would make the dish something akin to the Spanish tapas favorite, *patatas bravas*. No matter what you serve them with, though, everyone will wish you'd made more.

• • •

Serves 4

Gluten free and vegan

INGREDIENTS

Potatoes (preferably russets), 3 large, peeled and cut into 1-inch chunks

Salt

Neutral oil, about 1 cup, for frying (or, better yet, a combination of duck fat, olive oil, and neutral oil)

Flaky sea salt (or substitute any sea salt or kosher salt), for finishing

1 Boil: Place the potato chunks in a medium-size saucepan or pot filled with water and 1 teaspoon kosher salt. Bring to a simmer over high heat, and cook until they are *almost*—but not quite!—falling apart, about 10 minutes (if they do fall apart completely, make mashed potatoes instead!). They should taste nicely salted and have shaggy edges and a creamy interior. Remove the potatoes with a slotted spoon or small mesh strainer, draining thoroughly, and gently place them in a single layer on a large plate (if you dump them out instead, they will break up and may turn to mush). If water pools on the plate, drain it off or absorb it with a clean napkin or paper towel. Allow the potatoes to cool and their remaining moisture to evaporate.

2 **Fry the potatoes:** Heat the oil in a large <u>skillet</u>—cast iron works great! (There should be about ½ inch of oil in the pan). Gently slide the potato cubes into the pan, arranging them in a single layer. (If your pan is large enough, they should all fit; if not, fry them in two batches.) Allow the potatoes to fry, without moving them, until the edges start browning, about 6 or 7 minutes. Then, very gently turn them over with a spoon or spatula. Add a bit more oil if the pan becomes dry. Continue frying and turning the potatoes until they are completely golden brown on all sides, about 12 to 15 minutes total.

3 **Serve:** Use a slotted spoon to transfer the golden potato cubes to a platter or individual plates, and sprinkle them with the flaky sea salt. Serve immediately with your choice of dipping sauce.

Mom's Frittery Bindaeduk Pancakes

If you're like most Americans, you probably think *breakfast* when you hear *pancakes*. But pancake batter is a brilliant vehicle for countless ingredients, and pancake making is a technique used in cuisines around the world. Rather than soft and fluffy, these pancakes are frittery—and by that we mean cooked up crispy in hot oil. Technically, fritters are deep-fried things made by dropping thick batter into a pot of hot oil, whereas pancakes are pan-cooked things made by pouring a thin batter onto a lightly greased griddle or pan.

Our frittery pancakes are a hybrid—we make medium-thick batters and shallow-fry them in a heavily oiled pan. Korean *bindaeduk* is a great example. Made with yellow mung beans and spicy kimchi, they're irresistible flavor bombs with crunchy, crispy edges. This recipe, which uses more fillings than most, is our mom's. She and Cammie used to make hundreds of these pancakes every Saturday morning at the little Korean market our mom owned when we were growing up. They got snapped up just as fast back then as they do now, when we make them for guests of all ages and backgrounds. They're very good at room temperature, but *exceptional* when served blazing hot, with a side of vinegary soy dipping sauce.

INGREDIENTS

Mung beans, 1 cup skinless yellow (split)

White sweet rice (aka glutinous rice), ¼ cup (or substitute short-grain white rice)

Bean sprouts, about 2 cups loosely packed

Kimchi, 1 cup (see Ingredient Note)

Scallions, 4 large

Salt, 1½ teaspoons

Neutral oil, for frying

Soy dipping sauce (see page 39), for serving

• • •

Serves 4 to 6 for a snack or appetizer, 2 or 3 for a meal

Gluten free and vegan

Variation

For a non-spicy version, substitute chopped napa cabbage for the kimchi. In this case, you may want to add a bit more seasoning, such as another pinch of salt and maybe some crushed garlic. Or, experiment with whatever vegetables you have. You just might invent a delicious new frittery pancake!

Ingredient Note

Kimchi is ubiquitous in Korean cuisine. It's a spicy fermented pickle made primarily with fresh napa cabbage, salt, and Korean chili flakes. Before refrigeration existed, people needed a way to preserve the summer harvest in order to eat well throughout the winter. To do this, Koreans would make enormous vats full of kimchi, then bury it in the cool earth. Kimchi can be eaten when it's more salad-like and not very sour (or fermented), when it's nicely soured (which is best for *bindaeduk*), or even when it's wildly soured (or really ripe, as some would say). It's super healthy and full of flavor, which is why Koreans eat it with nearly every meal—breakfast, lunch, or dinner.

1 Soak the mung beans and rice: Into a large measuring cup, jar, or medium bowl, add the mung beans, rice, and enough very hot water (simmered in a kettle or pot or from a very hot tap) to cover them by 2 inches. Allow them to soak for at least 20 minutes (or overnight in the fridge) while you prepare the other ingredients.

2 Prep the vegetables: Pick off any brown or very stringy ends on the bean sprouts, then rinse them and toss into a large bowl. Add the kimchi, along with a couple spoonfuls of kimchi juice. Cut the scallions into 1-inch slices on the diagonal and add them to the bowl.

3 Make the mung bean batter: First, carefully pour off most of the water from the soaked beans and rice. Then, scoop it all into a blender and add the salt and enough fresh water to just cover. Start by pulsing it, and blend until it's finely ground. Continue blending on high until the batter is an even consistency with grains no larger than fine sand. If it's not blending so easily, add water a teaspoon at a time until the batter blends smoothly. Pour the batter over the vegetables and mix until well combined.

4 Fry 'em up: Heat a large skillet over over high until hot, but not smoking. Add oil to cover the bottom generously. Once the oil is hot, carefully drop in about a heaping tablespoon of batter, flattening out the vegetables and tucking in the sprouts along the edges. Reduce the heat to medium-high and cook for 3 to 4 minutes. When they are deep golden brown, flip and cook the other sides. Maintain enough heat that the pancakes look, smell, and sound sizzling; if they are starting to burn, turn down the heat. Thoroughly cook and crisp them, moving them around and flipping them back and forth a few times for a total of 7 to 10 minutes, adding oil as necessary to maintain a shallow fry. Repeat with the remaining batter. Serve hot with soy dipping sauce on the side.

CHEF SEAN SHERMAN'S
FRITTERY CORN (PAN)CAKES

The organic, local, "slow" food movement is often described as a modern American approach to cooking and eating that is informed by traditional (mostly Western) cooking techniques. Long left out of this conversation, however, are the *original* locavores: Indigenous peoples around the world. There is nothing more organic, local, and seasonal than eating off the land, as Indigenous people did forever prior to colonization.

Sean Sherman, an Oglala Lakota Sioux chef, activist, and educator, is working to increase awareness of Native foodways and fighting for Indigenous food sovereignty. That means he is fighting for Native people to have control over their own food systems, which includes having access to food that is culturally appropriate, healthy, and sustainable. Chef Sherman, along with his partner, Dana Thompson, a lineal descendant of the Wahpeton-Sisseton and Mdewakanton Dakota tribes, started The Sioux Chef, a team of food professionals committed to revitalizing Native American cuisine, as well as the nonprofit organization NATIFS, which stands for the North American Traditional Indigenous Food Systems. Chef Sherman is the James Beard Award–winning author of *The Sioux Chef's Indigenous Kitchen* and the chef/owner of Owamni, a Minnesota restaurant dedicated to local Indigenous cuisine. His cooking uses indigenous ingredients—which means foods that are native to the land, rather than brought in by people from other parts of the world—cooked in both modern and traditional ways. He advocates for foraging local wild fruits and vegetables, eating meats that existed before colonization, and learning about Native American cooking traditions. In other words, he is spreading awareness of the *original* organic, locavore cuisine while redefining North American cuisine.

These easy corn cakes are versatile and delicious—wonderful on their own, as a side, or topped to make a full meal. They are especially good with a fried egg, braised meat, simmered beans, sautéed greens, or any combination of these toppings. Chef Sherman uses them as the base for many dishes, from simple to fancy. The base of cooked cornmeal can be stored in the refrigerator for up to four days, ready for add-ins like fresh corn and herbs (as he incorporates here), wild greens, dried meat, seeds, nuts, mushrooms, berries, or even maple sugar.

• • •

Serves 4 to 6

Gluten free and vegan

Ingredient Notes

Cornmeal is dried corn that has been ground to a consistency that is between something like very fine and rather coarse sand. Corn, which is native to the land we refer to as the Americas, was first cultivated by Indigenous people some nine thousand years ago. It is the basis for all of the corn goods we know and eat today, including arepas, tortillas, corn on the cob, popcorn, and more. Italians use cornmeal to make a dish called polenta, so sometimes you may find cornmeal labeled "polenta." For this recipe, Chef Sherman recommends coarse cornmeal, which may better approximate what was used by his ancestors, though nearly any cornmeal (or polenta) will do. If you can, look for cornmeal made from native or heirloom varieties of corn, which will provide the most flavor and authenticity. Here we've used the exceptionally delicious Ute Mountain Yellow Cornmeal and Navajo Grown Roasted Blue Cornmeal from Tocabe, an Osage Nation restaurant and online food supplier based in Colorado.

Note that this recipe is similar to Simple Handmade Arepas (page 61), which originates from Native cuisines of South America. Because arepas are made with precooked (then redried) cornmeal, the dough does not need to be cooked before frying the patties. The cornmeal in these corn (pan)cakes, on the other hand, requires cooking before being shaped into patties and fried.

Ingredient Notes (continued)

Sunflower oil, as well as duck fat and oils from indigenous seeds and nuts (like walnuts), keeps this recipe true to its Native roots. If you don't have any, however, you can use olive oil or any neutral oil.

Alliums—such as chives, onions, and garlic—are delicious with fresh corn. While you could use any cultivated variety you find at the market, Chef Sherman recommends using wild varieties. After all, they can be foraged in many parts of North America—perhaps even in your own backyard! Wild chives and wild garlic grow abundantly throughout the spring and summer in many parts of the country. Wild leeks, also called ramps, are especially delicious, though their growing season is quite brief (early spring), and because they are increasingly recognized as a culinary delight, they risk being overharvested. If you can harvest them yourself, you're in for a real treat. Have an experienced forager show you the way—and be sure you leave some to the land (and for others). If you're using fresh corn, you'll need to pair it with something that also grows in the summer, like garlic chives, wild garlic, chives, or even scallions. An alternative would be to use other wild greens (or "weeds"), such as dandelion leaves, which are slightly bitter, providing a great contrast to the sweet corn.

INGREDIENTS

Sea salt, ½ teaspoon

Cornmeal, 1 cup (see Ingredient Notes)

Fresh corn, 1 small ear, kernels removed (see Tip; or 1 cup frozen or canned corn)

Fresh alliums (such as chives), a very small bunch, cleaned and chopped roughly (see Ingredient Notes)

Sunflower or nut oil, for frying (or substitute neutral oil; see Ingredient Notes)

1 Make the cornmeal base: In a medium pot set over high heat, bring 3 cups water and the salt to a boil. Then, whisk in the cornmeal in a slow, steady stream; continue whisking until there are no lumps, a minute or so. Reduce the heat and simmer, occasionally giving the cornmeal a good stir, until the mixture is thick but stirrable and the flavor is rich and corny. This will take about 25 to 45 minutes, depending on the variety of cornmeal you use. Keep tasting it along the way. When it is done, it will be very thick and taste cooked through. (The coarser your cornmeal, the grainier it will be. This is desirable, as long as the grains absorb enough water to become fairly tender. You can add a few more tablespoons of water, if necessary, to keep it a stirrable consistency.)

2 Make the corn cakes: Put the corn kernels and alliums in a large bowl. Then, add the cooked cornmeal and stir to combine. Taste for salt, adding another pinch or two if necessary. Then, dampen your palms and use a spoon to scoop out a handball-size portion (a bit larger than a golf ball but smaller than a tennis ball) into the palm of one hand. Using both hands, shape it into a patty about 3 inches in diameter and ¾ to 1 inch thick, and set it on a platter or cutting board until ready to fry. Repeat with the remaining batter.

3 Fry the corn cakes: Coat the bottom of a large, reliably nonstick skillet with oil and set it over medium-high heat. Once the oil is hot but not smoking, about 30 to 60 seconds, add the patties and fry until they are nicely browned on one side, 5 to 6 minutes (or longer, if the cornmeal is cold from the fridge). Then flip them and brown the other side. Be sure to maintain enough heat and oil for a gentle sizzle as they cook.

4 Serve: The corn (pan)cakes can be enjoyed hot or cold, plain or fancied-up.

Tip Frying fresh corn kernels can be tricky business: If you cut the kernels off whole, you'll end up with some hot-oil-splashing kernels popping right out of the pan (ouch!). If you cut the kernels off the cob more shallowly—essentially slicing the kernels in half as you cut them off—they will become unpoppable, and thus safer for you as the cook. Just hold the cob vertically and slice down shallowly. Then, use the back of the knife to scrape off the rest of the kernels.

Frittery Shrimp and Scallion Pancakes

One of our absolute favorite Korean dishes to eat at home or from a good Korean market or restaurant is *jeon*—which refers to any number of frittery pancakes made with a wheat flour batter. Here we've made a type of *saeu pajeon*, or shrimp and scallion pancake, which is similar to the traditional Korean *haemul pajeon*, the seafood pancake gracing the menu of nearly every Korean BBQ restaurant. For us, *jeon* translates to pan-fried awesomeness, and you can add in pretty much anything you can imagine. Try this recipe first, with shrimp and scallions, then try experimenting with different add-ins. It's so versatile, mastering the basic recipe means you'll be able to come up with infinite varieties of your own pan-fried awesomeness.

• • •

Serves 4 for a snack or appetizer, 2 for a meal (or double the recipe for a crowd)

For a gluten-free version, substitute 1 cup potato starch; for a vegan option, omit the egg and shrimp and replace with more vegetables, if you'd like!

INGREDIENTS

<u>Salt</u>, 1 tablespoon plus ½ teaspoon

Baking soda, ½ teaspoon

Water, 1 cup warm and ⅔ cup very cold

Shrimp, 8 to 12 ounces raw

Egg, 1 large

All-purpose flour, ¾ cup, plus more if needed

Baking powder, ½ teaspoon

Scallions, 1 bunch, sliced into rounds about ⅓ inch long

<u>Neutral oil</u>, for frying

<u>Soy dipping sauce</u> (see page 39), for serving

1 Prep the shrimp: In a medium bowl, make a <u>brine</u> with 1 tablespoon salt, the baking soda, and 1 cup warm water; stir to dissolve the salt and baking soda. Add a cup or so of ice to chill the brine. Peel and clean your shrimp (use a <u>knife</u> to remove the dark vein running along the top, if there is one). Then, cut each shrimp into 4 to 6 small pieces. Drop the shrimp pieces into the chilled saltwater brine, and let them rest at room temperature for 15 to 45 minutes while you clean up a bit and then start the batter.

2 Make the batter: Whisk the egg and ⅔ cup very cold water together in a large bowl. Then, <u>sift</u> the flour, baking powder, and ½ teaspoon salt on top, and whisk it just until no large lumps remain. The batter should be about the consistency of runny yogurt. If it seems too thick and pasty, add another splash of cold water; if it seems too watery, add a tablespoon of flour.

3 Add the shrimp and scallions: Place a paper towel or cloth napkin on a plate. Drain the shrimp using a slotted spoon or colander and transfer to the paper towel–lined plate; pat them dry just a bit. Drop them into the batter, along with the scallions. Stir to fully incorporate.

4 Fry 'em up and serve: Coat the bottom of a <u>skillet</u> (cast-iron works particularly well) with oil and set over medium-high heat. After about 30 seconds, test if the oil is hot enough by dropping a tiny dollop of batter into the pan. If it sizzles, it's ready. Using a soup spoon, wooden spoon, or small serving spoon, drop small rounds of batter into the oil. (If you keep them small, they'll be easier to flip and serve, and they will do a superior job of holding on to their crispiness.) Or, you can do it the Korean restaurant way: Make one giant pancake and serve it cut into wedges, like pizza. When the pancakes are browned around the edges, after 2 to 3 minutes, carefully flip them. Fry the other side for another couple of minutes, until golden brown. Transfer them to a cooling rack or a plate lined with clean paper towels, then fry up the next batch. Serve with soy dipping sauce.

Optional Prep

You can prep your shrimp up to one day ahead of time, but if you <u>brine</u> the shrimp in advance, give them a quick rinse after no more than 45 minutes. (Longer will make them too salty.) Then, refrigerate the rinsed, brined shrimp until you are ready to use them. You can also clean and dice the scallions (or other add-ins) and make the <u>soy dipping sauce</u> in advance. Then, throwing together the batter with your add-ins takes only a few minutes.

Tip

Be sure to keep up the sizzle! If your oil isn't hot enough to maintain a consistent sizzle, your frittery pancakes will absorb too much oil and won't come out light and crispy.

Variation

Jeon batter is so versatile, you can even take it in a non-Asian direction, using the same batter recipe with diced zucchini, sweet <u>onion</u>, and fresh corn—one of our *other* favorite versions.

Prosciutto-Wrapped Stuffed Dates

When we were growing up in Michigan, we lived next door to a lovely older Italian couple. Their stories, wisdom, and gifts of food helped to shape how we eat and cook. They gave us wheels of raw Tuma cheese, teaching us to patiently rub them with olive oil, salt, and black pepper every day for a month, as we eagerly awaited the day we could cut out a precisely ripened hunk. They fed us homemade Italian sweets and pastas and sauces, taught us to grow the most delicious grapes, and helped with our large backyard garden. And perhaps, most memorably, they gave us whole legs of prosciutto—Italian salt-cured pork—to hang from the ceiling in our garage. In the evenings, we loved to take a knife and hack off (not very elegantly, we admit!) a piece to nibble as we watched TV. Delicious on its own, it was even better with a piece of fresh or dried fruit.

These prosciutto-wrapped dates evoke those memories for us. They are the perfect appetizer or hors d'oeuvre—so sophisticated, yet so simple!—or a great late-night snack to satisfy a sweet and salty craving. The creamy goat cheese plays nicely with the salty cured ham and sweet dates. All you need are ten minutes (five if you're extra quick!) and three ingredients (four if you're being extra fancy!).

Ingredients

Medjool dates, 12 (or substitute another variety; see Ingredient Notes)

Goat cheese, 4 ounces (see Ingredient Notes)

Basil (optional), a handful of fresh leaves

Prosciutto, 6 slices, kept cold until ready for use (or use Spanish *jamón serrano*)

• • •

Makes 12 stuffed dates

Gluten free

Ingredient Notes

Goat cheese, also called chèvre, is a creamy, soft cheese made from goat milk. It's typically mild, but sometimes (depending on where it comes from and what the goats have been eating), it can have a flavor some people describe as "barnyard funk." Many people love this, while others prefer a milder flavor. The only way to know which one you're getting is to ask your cheesemonger or try a few kinds yourself. A mild goat cheese is perfect in this recipe, but you could also use creamy mascarpone, cream cheese, a funkier (stronger) one, or even a blue cheese. Try some different versions and see what you like!

Medjool dates, especially when eaten in season, are a marvel. They are dry to the touch, yet moist, rich, and a little bit chewy on the inside. You might think of them as a dried fruit, but they are actually harvested in their beautifully "dried," ripe state, the season running from September through December. The largest date variety, they are perfect for stuffing. If you can't find Medjools, you can use a different variety for this recipe, though the stickiness and smaller size of the more common varieties makes them harder to work with.

1 **Split your dates:** Using a paring <u>knife</u> and/or your thumbs, carefully split one side of each date and remove the pit. Be careful not to rip the whole thing in half. You want it open on only one side, like a hot dog bun. If there is a little stem on one end, remove that, too.

2 **Stuff them:** Using a very small spoon, put a scoop of goat cheese in the middle of each date. If you're using basil, lay a small leaf (or half a leaf if it's large) on the goat cheese before squeezing the date closed.

3 **Halve the prosciutto:** Using your fingers or a pair of scissors, halve each piece of prosciutto lengthwise.

4 **Wrap the dates and serve:** Using your fingers, wrap a piece of prosciutto around each date. Voila! Sweet and savory, fancy little apps.

PROSCIUTTO-WRAPPED MELON WEDGES

This has to be one of the best two-ingredient hors d'oeuvres around. Wedges of juicy, fragrant melon and salty prosciutto partner up brilliantly for this finger-food classic. It makes an elegant starter, but as you can imagine, it's also very nice for breakfast or brunch. Make it in the summer when melon is in season—fragrant and juicy, but firm enough to hold up to being wrapped.

While cantaloupes and honeydews are the most common sweet summer melon (aside from watermelon, of course), you may be fortunate enough to find a wide range of similar varieties at your local farmers' market. The other benefit of buying your melon from a farmers' market or a market that sells local produce is that there's a better chance it was picked ripe, rather than picked green so it could endure being shipped across the country. Seek out the melon with the most intoxicating fragrance and flavor. If possible, ask the seller to recommend the one with the most flavor. If it's not quite ripe when you buy it, store it at room temperature in a paper bag for a few days. And if you want to speed up the process, stick a banana or apple in the bag with it; the natural gases they produce will speed up ripening.

Makes 16 wedges

Gluten free

INGREDIENTS

Cantaloupe, 1 (or muskmelon, honeydew, Crenshaw, or similar; see above)

Prosciutto, 8 slices, kept cold until ready for use (or use Spanish *jamón serrano*)

Fresh mint (optional), for garnish

Variation

The flavors of good prosciutto and good melon are enough to make this a killer two-ingredient appetizer. That said, for a really simply prepared yet complexly flavored starter, you can plate this instead of wrapping it: Cut the melon into bite-size chunks and arrange on a plate with the prosciutto, each slice torn into a few smaller pieces and arranged into a few loose little mounds. Give the melon a tiny drizzle of high-quality olive oil and a pinch of Marash or Aleppo chili flakes or a crack of black pepper, then finish it with a few torn mint leaves. And if you're really going all out, add some fresh, ripe figs alongside the melon. Serve it with a cold drink (like the Lemon-Apple Fizz on page 240!) and you'll be dreaming you're in the Mediterranean, relaxing under an umbrella in the hot sun.

1 **Slice the melon:** Cut off just a bit of the top and bottom of the melon to create flat edges. Stand it up on one end and use a knife to cut off the rest of the rind, following the curve of the melon from top to bottom. Then, slice the melon in half lengthwise (also known as "pole to pole"). Use a spoon to gently scoop out the seeds; discard them. Slice each half into 8 equal wedges. (Use your math! Split in half, then quarters, then eighths, then sixteenths. Approaching it this way will help you cut uniform slices—and make your middle school math teacher proud.)

2 **Wrap the melon and serve:** Wrap one piece of prosciutto around each melon wedge, keeping it as flat as you can. If you want to make it fancy, arrange the wedges on a plate or platter, and add a few fresh mint leaves for garnish.

Prosciutto-Wrapped Asparagus Spears

These crispy asparagus spears make a terrific appetizer or side—or a fancy finger food—and they couldn't be simpler to make. Make them in the spring, when asparagus is in season, to ensure the best flavor and texture.

. . .

Makes 16 to 20 spears

Gluten free

INGREDIENTS

Asparagus, 1 bunch or around 16 to 20 spears (preferably medium-thick spears, rather than pencil-thin or extra fat)

Olive oil, for drizzling

Salt

Black pepper

Prosciutto, 8 to 10 slices (or use Spanish *jamón serrano*)

1 Prep the asparagus: Set the oven rack to its highest level and then preheat your broiler (or your grill, if you prefer). Then, cut off the tough, fibrous bottoms of the asparagus spears (see Tip). Thoroughly rinse and dry the spears, then arrange them in a single layer on a baking sheet, drizzle them lightly with olive oil, and sprinkle on a pinch of salt and pepper, gently rubbing to distribute.

2 Wrap the spears: Cut each piece of prosciutto in half crosswise, resulting in two shorter pieces. Then, holding a piece of prosciutto just below the "flowery" tip of one asparagus spear, wrap it tightly around the length of the asparagus in a spiral motion. Ideally, you'll have an inch or two (max) of asparagus peeking out on both ends. Repeat with the remaining asparagus and prosciutto, and arrange neatly on the baking sheet.

3 Broil them: Under the broiler, broil the wrapped spears for 2 to 3 minutes, until the prosciutto crisps up and the asparagus browns slightly. (Same idea if you're using your grill, but the fire will be underneath instead of over the top.) Remove the baking sheet and use tongs to flip them over. Return the pan to the broiler for another 2 to 3 minutes. Be sure not to overcook the asparagus.

Tip

Prepping asparagus spears can be done a number of ways. They sometimes need a hearty rinse to remove any sand or dirt, and there's a whole geeky cooking thing about how to "snap" or trim the ends. Conventional wisdom says if you hold each end of the asparagus and bend it, the spear will snap in just the right place to separate the too-fibrous, "woody" bottoms from the more tender part of the shoot. We say that kinda works, especially if you have lots of experience doing it (like Leah). But as often as not, folks (like Cammie) end up snapping off far more than necessary with this technique. Use your eyes (how much of the ends look fibrous and tough?), maybe your mouth (take a little nibble; raw asparagus is great), and your knife of choice, and just chop off the tough ends already.

ALICE WATERS'S
GARLICKY KALE CROSTINI

Alice Waters is the acclaimed chef, restaurateur, author, and activist perhaps most associated with the seasonal, local, slow-food movement. Her commitment to these values—that it is best to eat what is grown organically, locally, and seasonally, as often as possible; that traditional cooking methods, which take time and effort, yield the most delicious, nourishing food—has transformed the American food landscape over the last several decades. It all began when she opened her now-iconic Berkeley, California, restaurant, Chez Panisse—where Leah began cooking as an intern, eventually working her way up to head chef of the Cafe. The restaurant has served as a breeding ground for generations of chefs who have gone on to spread Alice's philosophy—and a whole lot of deliciousness—across the country and around the world.

Kale crostini was the first recipe cooked by students at Martin Luther King Jr. Middle School in Berkeley, California, when Alice started the Edible Schoolyard Project there. It was 1995—before kale became "cool," but Alice had a vision: If you got young people to eat what they grow, they would develop a whole new relationship with food. While others might have been skeptical that uber-green, slightly bitter kale would be the vegetable to mark a turning point in kids' relationships with vegetables, Alice knew better. This recipe was a hit back then and has never waned in popularity.

For this version, we've paired creamy goat cheese with Alice's garlicky kale, resulting in complex flavors and textures that have been proven to make a kale lover out of even the most skeptical eater.

INGREDIENTS

Baguette, 1, sliced about ⅓ inch thick on the diagonal (or substitute any other crusty bread)

Olive oil, a few tablespoons for drizzling and sautéing

Kale, 1 bunch (see Ingredient Note; or substitute other hearty greens, such as Swiss chard, collard greens, or broccoli raab)

Garlic, 2 or 3 large cloves, minced

Salt

Chili flakes (optional), a good pinch

Lemon, some zest and a squeeze of juice (or you can substitute a small splash of red wine vinegar)

Goat cheese, about 5 ounces

• • •

Serves 4 to 6 as an appetizer, but it is easy to scale up for a crowd

For a gluten-free version, use GF bread; for a vegan version, skip the goat cheese

Optional Prep

You can prepare the kale and make the toasts up to one day in advance. Store the kale, covered, in the fridge and the toasts in an airtight bag on the counter. When you're almost ready to assemble the crostini, just let the kale come up to room temperature, or warm it in a pan, and then give it a stir and taste it again. Does it need anything? Another pinch of chili flakes or salt? A little squeeze of lemon or a few drops of olive oil?

Ingredient Note

Kale comes in many varieties. Lacinato kale, also known as dinosaur kale or cavolo nero, is one of the most flavorful varieties in the kale family. It is a little tougher and contains less moisture than curly kale, so it often needs a little water in the pan to help it along. If your kale is young and tender, it will cook in as little as 3 to 4 minutes. If it is older and tougher—or if you're using a more robust variety like lacinato kale—it will take longer. In that case, cook it with a lid on for a few minutes at the beginning so the steam can help it along.

1 **Start the toasts:** Preheat your oven to 400°F. (Or you can do this in several batches in a toaster oven.) Arrange the slices on a baking sheet and drizzle or brush some olive oil over them. (This will add flavor and help them stay crisp, even under the goat cheese and sautéed kale.) Toast for 7 to 8 minutes, until golden brown. (Because most ovens have hot spots, it's a good idea to rotate the pan halfway through so they toast evenly.) Let cool. (If they are close to being over toasted, get them off the hot baking sheet as quickly as possible!)

2 **Prep the kale and garlic:** Meanwhile, use your fingers to strip the leafy part of the kale from its stems. Discard the stems and rinse the leaves. (It's okay if they are a little damp before cooking; the water will help it cook.) Chop the kale. Mince the garlic and set aside. Add about 2 tablespoons of olive oil to a large skillet over medium-high heat. Add the kale and sprinkle with a pinch of salt. Move the kale around as it cooks. (If you have too much kale to fit in the pan, add half; it will begin to wilt quickly, making room to add the rest of it.)

3 **Finish and adjust:** Taste for doneness. If it is tough or dry, add a splash of water and cover the pan. When the kale is tender—after 3 to 7 minutes, depending on the age, size, and variety—move it to the sides, leaving a space in the center of the pan. If there's a lot of liquid in the pan, raise the temperature to quickly evaporate it. Over medium heat, add a bit more olive oil to the center, along with the minced garlic and chili flakes. Stir for 30 seconds or so, just until soft and fragrant. Turn off the heat, add a squeeze of lemon juice, and stir. Taste and adjust for salt, spice, and acid (lemon juice).

4 **Assemble the crostini:** If you love garlic and want an added layer of flavor, gently rub a raw garlic clove on each piece of toast. (This is optional.) Spread a thick layer of goat cheese on each slice, then a spoonful of kale. After you've made a platterful, zest a tiny bit of lemon peel on top, and serve!

RADISH AND MISO-BUTTER CROSTINI

This crostini is a total umami bomb. That taste—umami, one of the five core tastes, along with sweet, sour, salty, and bitter—is hard to describe, but with one bite of this miso-butter toast, you'll understand what it means: a mouth-filling savoriness. All of the flavors and textures work together brilliantly, from the creamy miso butter to the clean, crisp radish slices to the crunchy <u>sesame sprinkle</u> and chives. And, it's so simple, it's almost a no-recipe recipe. To serve at a party or delight just yourself with a terrific mid-morning snack, scale it up or down by using the ratio of one part miso to two parts butter.

Makes 4 slices

Vegetarian

INGREDIENTS

Butter, 4 tablespoons, unsalted and softened

Miso, 2 tablespoons (preferably mellow white miso, but try with whatever you have)

Bread, 4 slices, from a handmade loaf of sourdough, levain, rye, or another flavorful, crusty variety

Radishes, 1 to 8, depending on size of the variety (for example, 6 to 8 typical red radishes or 1 watermelon radish)

Sesame sprinkle, a few pinches (Japanese *furikake* or *shichimi togarashi* would be especially good, but you could substitute a simple pinch of sesame seeds, chili flakes, and/or garlic flakes)

Flaky sea <u>salt</u>, a few pinches

Chives or scallions, about 1 tablespoon, very thinly sliced for garnish

furikake

shichimi togarashi

The miso butter can be made in advance and stored, covered, in the refrigerator for up to 2 weeks. Otherwise, you can store it in the freezer—in a freezer-safe container or rolled into a log and wrapped in parchment paper— for longer. It's worth making a large batch because miso-butter is terrific in many different applications: with baked sweet potatoes, fish, and even pasta with Parmesan. However much or little you make, just remember the ratio: one part miso to two parts butter.

The radishes can also be prepped ahead: Clean, slice, and store them in cold water in the fridge for up to 2 hours (longer and they may curl up). Doing so will increase their crispiness terrifically. And, if they are particularly sharp-tasting (which happens when they are grown in high heat with not quite as much water as they'd like), it can mellow out the flavor. To store longer than 2 hours, wrap them in a damp paper towel, place in a plastic bag, and refrigerate for up to 1 week, depending on how fresh they were to start.

1 **Make the miso butter:** In a small bowl, use a fork to smash and stir together the butter and miso until very well combined. Set aside.

2 **Toast the bread:** Toast the bread in a toaster oven until very light golden brown, keeping a close eye on the slices so they don't burn. (If you are doubling the recipe for a crowd, you can do this in a preheated 400°F oven.)

3 **Assemble the toasts:** Wash the radishes and slice them thinly. Spread a layer of miso butter, Goldilocks-style (not too thin, not too thick), onto the toasts. Top with a layer of radishes and a big pinch of sesame sprinkle, along with a small pinch of flaky sea salt and a scattering of chives. Serve immediately, while the toast is still warm and the radishes are still cold.

White Bean and Parsley Pesto Crostini

This is one of those recipes you can quickly throw together, transforming some pretty humble ingredients into a crazy satisfying, deliciously creamy, marvelously crunchy snack or appetizer. It really rides the line between a subtle hors d'oeuvre and a crunchy chip with some tasty bean dip. If you have a can of beans in th e pantry, some herbs and garlic, and some good bread—even good, stale bread!—you're all set. And if you have dried beans and a little more time on your hands, even better.

● ● ●

Serves 5 to 10 as an appetizer (makes 20 to 25 crostini)

Vegan

INGREDIENTS

Baguette, 1, sliced very thinly into rounds (or other crusty bread, or even your favorite crackers)

Olive oil, about ½ cup, plus more for brushing the toast

Nuts, ½ cup walnuts, almonds, or pine nuts

Fresh parsley, 2 bunches (for about 2 cups plucked leaves), washed

Salt, ¼ teaspoon plus a pinch

Parmesan (optional), ¼ cup grated (pecorino works, too)

Lemon juice, 2 to 3 squeezes

White beans, about 30 ounces (two 15-ounce or one 30-ounce can; see Ingredient Notes) , rinsed and drained

Garlic, 2 large cloves

1 Toast the bread: Preheat your oven to 400°F. Lightly brush both sides of the bread slices with some of the olive oil and arrange them on a baking sheet. Toast in the oven until light golden brown, keeping a close eye on them so they don't burn. When they are light and golden, try one. The key is to get them totally crispy without over-browning.

2 Make the parsley pesto: In the still-hot oven, toast the nuts on a baking sheet for about 5 minutes or until fragrant and light golden. Watch them carefully (with your eyes and your nose!), as they can go from under- to over-toasted very quickly. When they're cool to the touch, put them in a food processor (or blender, or even a mortar and pestle) along with the parsley, ¼ cup of the olive oil, ¼ teaspoon salt, the Parmesan (if using), and a small squeeze of lemon juice. Process until well minced and combined. Taste and adjust. Need more salt? Perhaps another little squeeze of lemon to brighten it up? When it tastes just right—bright and savory and full of flavor—scrape it into a bowl and set aside.

3 Prep the beans: Put the beans into the food processor bowl, along with one clove of garlic, the remaining ¼ cup olive oil, and a pinch of salt. Process until smooth. (Alternatively, you could just pulse it a few times or even leave the beans whole for a chunkier version. Just make sure your garlic is finely minced or grated, in that case.) Add a squeeze of lemon juice to brighten the flavor. Taste and adjust. Need more salt? Perhaps another little squeeze of lemon to brighten it up? When it tastes just right—bright and savory and full of flavor—scrape it into a bowl and set aside.

4 Assemble the crostini: Rub the remaining garlic clove on a toast, then spoon some beans on top, followed by a little dollop of pesto. Taste and adjust. A touch more salt, lemon, or garlic? Once you've nailed it, make the rest. Arrange on a platter and serve (if they don't get snapped up faster than you can make them).

Ingredient Notes

Pesto: Made here with parsley, but traditionally made with fresh basil, pesto is shockingly easy. That said, you can skip the pesto-making steps and use a favorite store-bought pesto, if you're hankering for a fast snack. But if you have the time and have never tasted homemade pesto, you've definitely gotta give it a go.

Beans: You can use pretty much any white, creamy variety—cannellini, great northern, butter, you name it. Do use canned beans that contain salt. Beans need time to absorb salt, so adding it to the *top* of the beans just isn't the same as starting with beans that have some salt already absorbed into their creamy centers.

Optional Prep

All of the elements—the bean puree, the pesto, and the toasts—can be made in advance. Doing so will allow you to assemble these in a jiffy! Store the bean puree and pesto separately and in the refrigerator for up to 3 days; after cooling completely, the toasts can be stored in a resealable bag on the counter for up to 1 day.

Variations

If you're in the mood for dipping, you can serve the bean puree in a bowl with a hearty drizzle of pesto on top and the toasts on the side.

We use parsley here for an earthy, herby twist on traditional Italian pesto, made with basil. That said, feel free to substitute basil or even arugula for the parsley.

GORGEOUS GREEN GODDESS DIP AND DRESSING

This is a terrific go-to dip or dressing for just about everything. It makes a killer dip for potato or tortilla chips, and might even change your mind about root veggie chips! It's delicious served with raw vegetables like sliced fennel, carrots, kohlrabi, radishes, cucumbers, and bell peppers. Same goes for veggies that are quickly blanched (boiled in salted water for a minute or so), like snap peas, green beans, cauliflower, or broccoli. You can toss it on salad greens or use it to hand-dip whole pieces of romaine. It's even terrific with fish or chicken tenders!

• • •

Makes about 1½ cups

Gluten free; for a vegan version, skip the yogurt

INGREDIENTS

Fresh parsley, about 2 to 3 bunches

Additional fresh herbs, about 2 to 3 bunches (any combination of cilantro, basil, dill, chervil, and/or tarragon)

Avocado, 1 very small Haas (or ½ medium or ¼ large)

Anchovy (optional), 2 or 3 fillets (these are super delicious, so we highly suggest using them; they can be substituted with a bit of anchovy paste from a tube, or even a teaspoon or so of fish sauce)

Garlic, 1 large clove

Plain yogurt, about 2 tablespoons (if you use Greek yogurt, you may need to add a bit of milk or water, or additional lemon juice and olive oil, to thin it out; you can also use mayo to avoid dairy; or, you can just skip this ingredient altogether and it will still come out delicious, minus a bit of creaminess)

Lemon juice, from 1 juicy lemon (regular or Meyer)

Red wine vinegar, a splash (can substitute sherry or champagne vinegar)

Olive oil, ¼ cup

Salt

Black pepper

Optional Prep

All of the ingredients except the avocado can be prepped and stored, covered in the refrigerator, up to 2 days in advance. That said, the dip keeps quite well for 1 or 2 days, so the whole thing can be made ahead.

Tip

All ingredient measurements in this recipe are approximate. Some anchovies are saltier than others, cloves of garlic can vary in size, and some herbs have a stronger and bolder flavor than others. Try these approximate measurements and then taste and adjust, taste and adjust, taste and adjust. Depending on your preferences, make a note (mental or physical) to try other ingredient combinations the next time.

1 Pick and wash your herbs: Herbs like parsley and tarragon need their leaves picked off because the stems are fibrous. Tender herbs like cilantro and dill can often be used with parts of their stems. (Taste a sprig; if the stems near the top are tender—which they usually are—you can include them. If they're tough and fibrous, just use the leaves.) Rinse and dry well (with a salad spinner or a clean kitchen towel). You should have about 2 cups total.

2 Blend it all together: Put everything in a food processor, including a pinch of salt and a crack or two of black pepper. Pulse a few times to chop and blend the dressing.

3 Taste and adjust: Use a spatula to scrape down the sides; this will help it blend evenly. Pulse a few more times, then taste and adjust. Need more salt? If so, add a pinch. (Just a pinch! You can always add more after the dressing is pulsed again; it's better to add it little by little.) If it's too salty, add more herbs and avocado. Does it need a bit more flavor? If so, add another anchovy fillet or ½ clove of garlic. And if it is too thick to use as a dressing or dip, add a little more olive oil and lemon juice, or even a few drops of water.

4 Serve: We like ours fairly smooth, but with pretty specks of green in it. You can make yours as chunky or as smooth as you like. Pulse until it's well combined and the desired consistency, then serve with fresh vegetables, toasts, or even chips.

ROMESCO DIP AND SAUCE

Okay, fine. This one's not really a dip and dressing like the Gorgeous Green Goddess Dip and Dressing (page 99) or the Creamy Goes-with-Everything Dip and Dressing (page 105). But like the others, it's so versatile—as a dip or sauce, in this case—we just had to include it.

Romesco is a sauce of Spanish origin, often eaten with seafood (great with grilled shrimp, tuna, or squid!), Crispy Smashed Potatoes (page 69), roasted vegetables, grilled meats, or even just-boiled eggs. Akin to the ubiquitous red condiment so popular in the U.S., it's sometimes called Spanish ketchup. There are many versions: some smooth like ketchup, some thick like tomato paste, and some chunky like this recipe. It's a very forgiving recipe that can easily be adapted to your preference or ingredient availability. Traditionally, toast or breadcrumbs are added to lend body and a sort of creaminess to the sauce, but it can be easily omitted if desired.

• • •

Makes about 2 cups

For a gluten-free version, omit the toast or use a GF kind; vegan

INGREDIENTS

Almonds, ½ cup raw (or substitute roasted)

Sweet red peppers, 2 large, such as bell or pimiento (or substitute a couple of jarred roasted red peppers)

Tomato, 1 large or 2 small (or substitute 4 or 5 sun-dried tomatoes, rehydrated in a bowl of hot water for 2 hours at room temperature or 1 to 2 minutes in the microwave)

Garlic, 1 large clove, chopped

Chili powder, 1 tablespoon

Smoky paprika (aka *pimenton*), 1 teaspoon

Cayenne pepper (optional), a pinch

Toast (optional), 1 slice, torn into small pieces (preferably rustic, country-style bread like levain or sourdough, but any type will do)

Sherry vinegar, 2 teaspoons (or substitute red wine vinegar, champagne vinegar, or similar)

Orange juice, about 1 teaspoon (preferably squeezed from a fresh orange!)

Salt

Olive oil, about ½ cup

1 **Roast the almonds:** Preheat the oven to 400°F. Place the almonds on a parchment paper–lined baking sheet and roast until they are light golden brown, about 10 to 12 minutes; they should have a pleasant toastiness when you bite into one. (Set a timer so you don't forget about them! They go from underdone to burnt faster than you can say "Shoot, the nuts!") Remove to a plate or wide bowl. They will become more crunchy as they cool. Keep the parchment paper on the baking sheet if it hasn't browned too much.

2 **Roast the peppers and tomato:** Increase the oven temperature to 450°F. Halve the peppers and remove the stem and seeds. Halve the tomato. Place both on the baking sheet; the tomato should be cut-side up. Roast for about 20 minutes, or until the peppers and tomato are browned and charred. Place the peppers in a bowl and cover with a lid or towel to steam for a few minutes. (This will make the skin easier to remove.) Once they're cool enough to handle, use your fingers or a knife to peel and discard most of the charred pepper skin; peel and discard the tomato skin.

3 **Blend it up:** Place the almonds, peppers, tomato, garlic, chili powder, paprika, and cayenne pepper (if using) in a food processor. Pulse a handful of times, until everything is chopped into small pieces. Then, toss the toast pieces into the food processor. Pulse a few times to incorporate the toast. Add the vinegar, orange juice, and a big pinch of salt and pulse a few times. Finally, drizzle in the olive oil as you pulse a few more times. The mixture should be very oily and fairly chunky. If you prefer it smooth, you can keep pulsing until it is smooth and uniform. Taste for seasoning. It should taste well-balanced and bold: sweet from the peppers and tomato and acidic from the vinegar. Add another pinch of salt or splash of vinegar to brighten it up, if necessary. Serve with grilled fish or meats, with fried or boiled potatoes, with blanched or fresh veggies, or with grilled or toasted bread.

CREAMY GOES-WITH-EVERYTHING DIP AND DRESSING

This is a great chip dip, vegetable dip, accompaniment to grilled meats (including our skewered recipes on pages 173 to 178), and even, with a bit of milk whisked in to thin it out, a terrific salad dressing. If you make it with Greek yogurt instead of sour cream, you can feel good about eating it, too!

• • •

Makes about ¾ cup

Gluten free

INGREDIENTS

Sour cream or plain Greek yogurt, ½ cup

Mayonnaise, ¼ cup

Chives, about 1 tablespoon finely chopped

Garlic, 1 clove, finely minced (or 1 teaspoon granulated)

Onion (optional), 1 tablespoon finely minced (or ½ teaspoon dried flakes or powder)

Lemon juice or red wine vinegar, about ½ teaspoon

Salt, a big pinch

Mix everything together in a small bowl and adjust the seasonings—especially the salt and acid (that is, the lemon juice or vinegar)—to taste. If possible, allow it to rest in the refrigerator for at least 30 minutes so the flavors can meld (come together). This is especially important if using dehydrated seasonings like granulated garlic or onion flakes, which need a little more time to rehydrate in the dip.

HERBY TOMATO SALAD
WITH SUPER SIMPLE VINAIGRETTE

When tomatoes are in season, they don't need much more than a super simple vinaigrette—olive oil, acid (think lemon juice or vinegar), and some salt. Herbs and red onion add color and complement the tomatoes' natural sweetness, and there you have it: the perfect summer tomato salad. It's lovely for lunch with a nice piece of crusty bread or as a side for grilled or fried meats, or even simply prepared fish.

• • •

Serves 4 to 6
Gluten free and vegan
Complexity: Simple

INGREDIENTS

Red onion, ½ small, sliced (see pages 30 and 31, for technique)

Salt

Red wine vinegar, a few tablespoons (or substitute 1 lemon or sherry, white wine, or even balsamic vinegar)

Fresh herbs, ½ bunch (basil and/or parsley would be great)

Tomatoes, a big bowlful (2 full baskets cherry tomatoes or 4 or 5 large heirloom tomatoes, or a combination, which is even better; you don't have to measure them, but if you want to, let's say 3 to 4 cups halved or wedged)

Olive oil, a few tablespoons

Cayenne pepper (optional)

Garlic (optional), 1 clove

Optional Prep

The onions can be sliced and macerated up to a few days ahead. Sometimes we make a big jarful and keep it in the fridge to use in a couple of different salads or as a pickle-y topping for meats and sandwiches. Same goes for the herbs; they, too, can be picked and washed a few days in advance, then stored in a fabric bag or a plastic bag lined with a paper towel. Best not to slice the tomatoes in advance, though, as they lose their succulence within an hour or so.

Tip

Remember: Taste and adjust—and season as you go! It's *(Serious) New Cook* Principle #2, and it's particularly important in a simple salad like this. Try a little experiment sometime: Make two batches of tomato salad, one where you salt the tomatoes *before* mixing them with the other ingredients and one where you don't. If you pay close attention, you'll notice a difference, we swear. Something magical happens when salt granules make direct contact with the juicy, freshly cut flesh of the tomatoes, and if you mix in the other ingredients first, that direct-contact magic can't happen in quite the same way. This is true of cucumbers, too, which become, rather freakishly, floppy and crispy at the same time after direct salting. So remember, to make magic in your cooking, season as you go, season as you go, season as you go.

Variation

If you want to make the salad heartier, you can add Homemade Croutons (page 113), blanched green beans, fresh cucumber, thinly sliced sweet peppers, or any other favorite vegetables.

1 <u>**Macerate**</u> **the onion:** Put the sliced onion into a small bowl and cover with a hefty pinch of salt and the red wine vinegar, then give them a quick massage with your fingers. Set aside to rest for at least 10 minutes.

2 **Prep the herbs:** Pick off the leaves and give them a wash and spin in a salad spinner. (Alternatively, you can give the herbs a rinse and then pick the leaves onto a clean towel to dry.) Roughly chop or tear them and set aside.

3 **Cut the tomatoes:** Using a very sharp <u>knife</u> (or perhaps easier is a little serrated knife), cut the cherry tomatoes through the stem spot. This makes for the easiest cutting and the prettiest halves. For larger tomatoes, core and cut them into large chunks. Give them a light sprinkle of salt, remembering that it's always best to season as you go. That's how you build interesting layers of flavor. Place the tomatoes, along with any tomato juices on your <u>cutting board</u>, into a large bowl.

4 **Assemble, taste, and adjust:** Add the onions and half of the macerating vinegar to the tomato bowl. Add the herbs and drizzle generously with the olive oil. Toss gently, then taste. Does it need another pinch of salt? Add it! More acid to brighten the flavor? Spoon in more of the macerating vinegar. Or is it too acidic? Add another drizzle of olive oil. Too salty? Add another handful of unsalted tomatoes or herbs. Like it spicy? Add a pinch of cayenne pepper or crushed, minced garlic. It should be juicy and bright, making it an ideal partner for crusty bread or a variety of meat dishes.

CHEF BRYANT TERRY'S
FENNEL AND CITRUS SALAD
WITH SIMPLE VINAIGRETTE

This recipe is adapted from vegan chef and food justice activist Bryant Terry's best-selling cookbook *Vegetable Kingdom: The Abundant World of Vegan Recipes*. Bryant, who has won an NAACP Image Award and a James Beard Award for his work, is also the author of several other cookbooks and the curator of the gorgeous, groundbreaking book *Black Food: Stories, Art, and Recipes from Across the African Diaspora*. Leah is lucky enough to know him through the strong community of folks in California's Bay Area who are working to create more healthy, sustainable, equitable food systems. This fennel and citrus salad is inspired by a dish prepared by his friend and fellow chef Monifa Dayo and a salad Bryant first tasted at a restaurant in Milan, where it was served as a last course. (Did you know that salads are often served at the *end* of the meal in Europe? Makes sense, since they aid digestion!) This salad brings together a terrific variety of flavors and textures. Part of its genius is that the main ingredients—oranges, fennel, and dates— are in season during the cold months, yet the salad screams sunshine.

• • •

Serves 4 to 6

Gluten free and vegan

Complexity: For a salad, this one is moderately complex. Chef Bryant Terry brings out extra flavor by infusing his olive oil **with the almonds and** macerating **the shallot in warm vinegar, but we've simplified things just slightly to make it a bit easier.**

INGREDIENTS

Fennel bulb, 1 small

Shallot, 1 large (or substitute ¼ small red onion)

Kosher salt, 2 teaspoons

Apple cider vinegar, ¼ cup

Navel oranges, 2 large

Cara Cara oranges, 2 large

Blood oranges, 4 large or 8 small

Extra-virgin olive oil or walnut oil, 2 tablespoons

Amber agave nectar, 1 teaspoon (or substitute white or light brown sugar)

Dijon mustard, 1 teaspoon

Black pepper, a few cracks

Sea salt, preferably light gray Celtic or flaky sea salt, for finishing

Dates, 4 large Medjool variety, or 6 to 8 of a smaller variety, pitted and chopped or torn into small pieces

Toasted almonds, ¼ cup, coarsely chopped (or substitute walnuts)

Fresh cilantro, a few sprigs, leaves left whole or chopped

Optional Prep

The dressing can be made several days in advance. Just complete step 4, adding all of the dressing ingredients (except for the orange juice, which you can add before serving) to a jar. In fact, you could make a double or triple batch and keep it in the fridge for other salads. If you use the leftover dressing for a green salad, don't forget to taste and adjust—*(Serious) New Cook Principle #2!* You may find you want to add a little squeeze of lemon juice to brighten it up even more.

Tips

Slicing fennel can be done more easily if you don't remove the core; this helps to hold the fennel "leaves" together as you work. Slicing can be done a number of ways: To use a sharp chef's <u>knife</u>, lay the flat (cut) sides down on a <u>cutting board</u> and very carefully slice the fennel as thinly as you can. If you have a <u>mandoline</u> slicer, you could use that instead, but do so with caution! No cook has ever *not* sliced off a bit of fingernail (at best!) at least once while using a mandoline. With a mandoline, it's easiest to hold the fennel's stem and begin slicing its top. A third option is to use a vegetable peeler, which produces paper-thin slices; it will just take a while! This technique works especially well if the fennel happens to be a bit dry or tough.

Chef Terry soaks the fennel slices in an ice water bath while preparing the rest of the salad. This can help the fennel crisp up even more than it is already, which may be especially useful if you're using a skinny bulb (which some Italian folk wisdom says indicates a female bulb), as opposed to a plump, succulent bulb (male). You can try this to make the fennel extra crispy and refreshing—just make sure you blot it dry before adding it to the salad; if you don't, the water will dilute the dressing.

1 **Prep the fennel:** Trim off the stems so that you're left with just the bulb, with no more than a ½ inch or so of stems at the top. Then, cut the bulb in half lengthwise. Trim off any tough, dry parts on the bottom (the root side), slice it thinly, and set aside (see Tips).

2 <u>Macerate</u> **the shallot:** Peel and mince the shallot, and put it into a small jar or bowl. Cover it with the kosher salt and the apple cider vinegar and give it a stir or shake. Set aside.

3 **Prep the oranges:** Finely grate the zest from 1 navel orange and set aside. Then, using a sharp <u>knife</u>, slice off the bottom and top of each navel and Cara Cara orange, creating 2 flat sides that will make it safer to cut. Working one at a time, place an orange on one of its flat sides on a <u>cutting board</u>, and carefully cut off the peel by running your knife along the curve of the orange so that you remove all of the peel and the white pith, leaving behind only the gleaming, juicy insides (see Tips). Then turn the orange on its side and slice it into rounds. Place the rounds into a medium bowl, and pour the accumulated juices from the cutting board into another bowl. Squeeze the peels into the juice bowl, eking out any delicious juice you can before discarding the peels. For the blood oranges, remove the peel just as you did for the navel and Cara Cara oranges. Slice out the individual segments (see Tip.)

4 **Make the vinaigrette:** To the macerated shallots, add ¼ cup of the citrus juice and the olive oil, along with the orange zest, agave, mustard, and cracked pepper. Whisk or shake until well combined. Then, taste and adjust, adding another pinch of kosher salt, if necessary. It should taste pleasantly sweet, salty, and tart, keeping in mind that the flavors will dilute, in a manner of speaking, when tossed with the rest of the ingredients.

5 **Compose the salad:** On a large platter or individual plates, arrange the orange slices and sprinkle lightly with the sea salt. Drizzle a tablespoon or so of dressing over the oranges. Arrange the fennel on top of the orange slices, while still allowing some of their pretty red and orange colors to peek through. Drizzle additional dressing over the fennel and then top with the chopped dates and almonds, along with the cilantro. Finish with a sprinkle of sea salt.

Tip   **Slicing oranges can be done using two primary methods.** Chef Terry uses both in this recipe. For the navel and Cara Cara oranges, you slice rounds, but for the blood oranges, you slice out the segments. You could stick with one technique or the other, but the segmenting technique is particularly nice if the membranes of the inner segments are tough or the orange has seeds you need to remove. To cut out the segments, first cut off all of the peel, following the instructions in step 3 of this recipe. Then, working over a bowl to catch the juices, hold the orange in your non-dominant hand and a small, sharp <u>knife</u> in your other. Carefully slide the knife along the sides of each segment, cutting it away from the membrane. After you have removed all of the segments, squeeze the remaining juices from the membrane that remains in your hand.

Chicory Salad
WITH HOMEMADE CROUTONS AND A BROKEN CAESAR VINAIGRETTE

This idea for a "broken" Caesar dressing came from Russell Moore, Leah's good friend, longtime chef at Chez Panisse, and now chef and owner of Kebabery in Oakland, California. (Check out his lamb skewer recipe on page 175!) While most cooks talk of "fixing" a broken vinaigrette, Russ saw intentionally breaking it as a brilliant way to take the components of an otherwise heavy, creamy-seeming dressing and allow them to shine on their own. Like many vinaigrettes, a classic Caesar dressing is whisked together until it is emulsified—traditionally with a raw egg yolk—resulting in a thick, cohesive dressing. In this broken version, no whisking is needed—just mix until combined, and you'll see that all of the individual flavors will come through. (This is why it helps to use the best anchovies you can!)

• • •

Serves 4

For a gluten-free version, use GF croutons

Complexity: Moderate. The first salad in this vinaigrette salad trio was super simple, with little more than salt, acid, and olive oil. The second salad was a bit more complex, though the vinaigrette was still pretty simple. Here, the salad itself is simple, but the vinaigrette is a tad more complex to make—and a lot more complex in flavor. Try all three salads and vinaigrettes, and you'll soon be making up your own signature ones!

INGREDIENTS

FOR THE CROUTONS

Bread, 3 or 4 slices (preferably a rustic, handmade loaf)

Olive oil, for drizzling

Salt, 1 or 2 sprinkles

FOR THE DRESSING

Anchovies, 4

Garlic, 1 large clove

Dijon mustard, ¼ teaspoon

Lemon juice, from half a juicy lemon or a whole drier one

Olive oil, 3 tablespoons

Parmesan cheese, packed ¼ cup grated

Black pepper

Salt

FOR THE SALAD

Chicory "lettuces," 2 small-to-medium heads (or substitute romaine lettuce, if you want to make a classic Caesar salad)

Mayonnaise (optional), 1 tablespoon

1 Make the croutons: Preheat the oven (or toaster oven) to 400°F. Tear or cut the bread into bite-size pieces and pile them up in the center of a baking sheet. Drizzle with olive oil and sprinkle with a pinch or two of salt. Mix with your hands to distribute the oil a bit, then spread them out in one layer. Bake for 5 to 10 minutes, checking them frequently and rotating the pan if they are browning unevenly. Once they start browning, keep a close eye on them. (They can go from barely golden to burnt very quickly.) Remove when golden brown.

2 Make the dressing: On a cutting board or in a mortar and pestle, mince and smash, or pound, the anchovies and garlic into a paste. Place the anchovy-garlic paste into a large bowl. Add the Dijon mustard, lemon juice, and olive oil, stirring well to combine. Then stir in the Parmesan, along with a couple cracks of black pepper. Taste and adjust, adding salt if needed.

3 Toss the salad: Tear the chicory leaves into bite-size pieces, then wash and thoroughly dry them. Add the chicory and croutons to the bowl with a pinch of salt and pepper. Using your hands, a large spoon, or some tongs, very gently toss together, being sure to scoop up the dressing along the bottom, until everything is coated with the vinaigrette. Taste and adjust with more lemon or salt. If your chicories are extra bitter, or if the dressing doesn't pack enough flavor, smear the mayo on the bottom of the bowl and gently re-toss the salad, distributing the mayo fairly evenly over the leaves. (In addition to the subtle creaminess mayo can add, it usually has a bit of sugar in it, which helps to round out the flavors and bring it all together.)

Optional Prep

The dressing can be made 2 days in advance and stored in the refrigerator. (If you do this, just make it in a jar. In fact, consider doubling the recipe. It's so good, you're going to want it again!) Before tossing it with the greens, be sure to let it come to room temperature—or run the jar under warm water—so the olive oil has a chance to reliquify.

Because chicories keep exceptionally well, prepping them in advance and storing them in the fridge is ideal. In fact, doing so can amp up their crispness and seems to bring out a hidden layer of sweetness. So, whenever possible, we like to wash, spin, and tear or cut ours, then store them in a glass container or a plastic bag along with a clean paper towel or napkin, which absorbs any excess water while maintaining the moisture in the bag. Doing so makes for quick and easy salad-making, especially if you also have a jar of dressing waiting in the fridge.

Variation

Sometimes you might want that thicker version of dressing, in which case you can simply whisk in a teaspoon or so of mayonnaise—or a raw egg yolk, if you are confident about its origin and freshness. And for die-hard Caesar salad fans, the croutons and dressing here can be used on romaine for a more traditional Caesar salad—perhaps the best you've ever tasted.

EGG DROP SOUP

This is one of our favorite soups, perhaps because it can be eaten for breakfast, lunch, or dinner! This is nothing like the weird, yellow, super cornstarchy stuff we used to see in (American) Chinese restaurants when we were growing up. Instead, it's silky and comforting, with well-balanced flavors and nutrients. We always use homemade chicken stock for this soup—it's easy to make, more flavorful than store-bought, and can be stored in the freezer to always have on hand. We've even provided a recipe!

• • •

Makes 4 cups or 2 bowls

For a gluten-free version use GF soy sauce or tamari

INGREDIENTS

Chicken stock, about 4 cups, preferably homemade (see page 40)

Ginger, 1 teaspoon finely grated

Soy sauce, ½ to 1 tablespoon (depending on how dark and salty yours is)

Cornstarch, 1 tablespoon

Eggs, 3 large

Toasted sesame oil, 1 tablespoon

Salt

Black pepper

Scallions, 2 or 3, thinly sliced (or substitute a small bunch of chives, chopped)

Variation

For a heartier version, you can add any of the following. Most can be added before whisking in the cornstarch, but toss in the shrimp and spinach at the very end, after the eggs.

Chicken, cooked, shredded or diced

Shrimp, raw or cooked

Peas, fresh or frozen

Asparagus, finely chopped or sliced

Snap peas, finely chopped or sliced

Shiitake mushrooms, sliced

Edamame, fresh or frozen, shelled

Spinach, washed and chopped

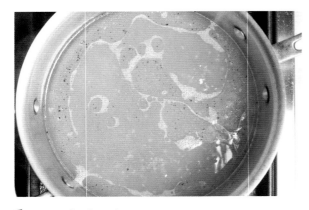

1 Heat the broth: Bring the stock and ginger to a boil in a medium saucepan over high heat.

2 Thicken the broth: In a small cup or bowl, thoroughly stir together the soy sauce and cornstarch. Whisk the cornstarch slurry into the boiling broth. Reduce the heat to medium and cook until the broth is slightly thickened, 1 to 2 minutes.

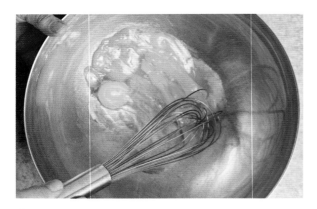

3 Whisk the eggs: In a medium bowl, lightly whisk the eggs, sesame oil, and ½ teaspoon salt. You want to break up the eggs, but it's nice to keep a tiny bit of separation between the whites and the yolks. Transfer to a liquid measuring cup.

4 Add the eggs and serve: Remove the saucepan from the heat. Pour the eggs into the hot broth in a slow stream, stirring gently but constantly to scatter the eggs as they cook. Taste and adjust the seasoning, adding a pinch of salt and crack of pepper, if needed. Ladle the soup into bowls, top with sliced scallions, and serve.

TOMATO BISQUE
WITH PARMESAN TWISTS

This soup—a bisque, more specifically—is at once comforting and bright. It's a smart and satisfying way to take advantage of summer's bounty, using juicy, sun-ripened tomatoes. (In the off-season, high-quality canned tomatoes do quite nicely.) It's smooth, thick, and rich—the defining features of a bisque—and is a dramatic improvement on tomato soup from a can. It's lovely on its own, but it's even better with some flaky Parmesan twists to dunk into it. Or, for the classic American combo, pair it with a grilled cheese sandwich.

• • •

Serves 4 to 6

For a gluten-free version, skip the Parmesan Twists or use GF flour and puff pastry; for a vegetarian version, use vegetable stock

INGREDIENTS

TOMATO BISQUE

Onion, 1 large, sliced

Olive oil, about 2 tablespoons, plus more for drizzling

Butter, 2 tablespoons unsalted

Salt

Garlic, 2 cloves, peeled and smashed

Tomatoes, 3 pounds, very red and very ripe, chopped roughly and cores removed

White rice, 2 tablespoons cooked, or 1 tablespoon uncooked

Chicken stock, 2 cups (preferably homemade, see page 40; or substitute vegetable stock or a combination of 1 cup chicken stock and 1 cup water)

Plain yogurt or crème fraîche (optional), a small spoonful per bowl, for garnish

Parsley, basil, or chives (optional), about 1 teaspoon finely chopped, for garnish

PARMESAN TWISTS

All-purpose-flour, 1 or 2 tablespoons, for dusting

Puff pastry, 2 small sheets or 1 large sheet (preferably a brand that uses all butter and no preservatives), thawed

Egg wash, made by mixing 1 raw egg with 1 tablespoon water, for brushing on top of the pastry

Parmesan, 3 to 4 ounces, finely grated (¾ cup; or use cheddar or Gruyère)

Variation

To make an even simpler version—or, to make it when tomatoes are not in season—use two 28-ounce cans of whole, peeled tomatoes in juice instead of fresh tomatoes. (Opt for salted San Marzano tomatoes, if possible; they are tastier and more fleshy, which will add body to the soup.)

To make a more sophisticated version, roast the fresh tomatoes in a roasting pan at 450°F for one hour, in lieu of adding fresh tomatoes to the pot.

TOMATO BISQUE

1 Make the bisque base: In a medium or large pot over medium heat, sauté the onion in the olive oil, the butter, and a hefty pinch of salt, until soft and translucent, about 8 minutes; if the onion starts to brown, reduce the heat. Add the garlic and continue to cook for another 2 to 3 minutes; avoid browning (because that makes garlic and onions bitter).

2 Add the tomatoes and rice: Stir in the tomatoes and rice, along with a hefty pinch of salt, and simmer over medium heat for about 10 minutes, until the tomatoes fall apart. Stir periodically to avoid sticking, and add a splash of water if all of the tomato juices evaporate. (Start the parm twists while this cooks.)

3 Add the stock: Pour in the chicken stock, and bring it up to a boil over high heat. Then, reduce the heat to medium and simmer for another 15 to 20 minutes, until the rice has completely softened and all of the flavors have melded.

4 Puree: Remove the pot from the heat and let it cool slightly. Set a medium strainer over another pot. Then, working with small batches at a time, ladle the bisque into a blender and puree until smooth. (When blending hot liquids, it is important that you fill the blender jar no more than one-third full; otherwise it will create a burn hazard, potentially blowing the top off and creating a huge mess in your kitchen.) Pour each batch of pureed bisque into the strainer set over the second pot, and use a spoon to press it through; the strainer will catch bits of tomato skin and seeds (to then be discarded), resulting in a smoother bisque (see Tip).

5 Finish and serve: Reheat as necessary while you taste and adjust. Add more salt, a pinch at a time, if needed. Add a bit of water if it's too salty. And add more stock if it's too thick. The consistency should be like a thin smoothie—thick enough to stick to your ribs (so to speak) but thin enough to sip. Ladle into cups or bowls and, optionally, top with a little drizzle of olive oil and plain yogurt or crème fraîche and a pinch of chives. Serve hot—alone, with a couple flaky Parmesan Twists, or with grilled cheese (classic!).

PARMESAN TWISTS

1 Start the Parm twists: Preheat the oven to 400°F. Line a large baking sheet with <u>parchment paper</u> and set aside. Flour your work surface, and roll out both puff pastry sheets to about ⅛ inch thick. Brush with the egg wash, then sprinkle on the grated cheese, gently pressing it in with lightly floured hands.

2 Cut, twist, and bake: Use a large, sharp, lightly floured chef's <u>knife</u> to cut the pastry into long strips about ½ inch wide. Cut straight down with the knife, rather than sawing or rocking. Transfer each strip to the lined baking sheet. As you set each one down, twist it into loose spirals (without stretching it out much). Bake for 15 to 20 minutes, until puffy and golden brown.

Green Tortilla Soup

This soup takes its cues from *sopa Azteca*, also known as *sopa de tortilla*, a popular Mexican soup known to many Americans as chicken tortilla soup. Unlike *sopa Azteca*, which uses a chicken and tomato broth, we make ours with chicken and green chiles. Many green chile varieties will work, but if you can get your hands on them, Hatch (a particularly special variety distinct to the Hatch Valley of New Mexico) and Anaheims are best. When Leah comes back from New Mexico, where her in-laws live, she always brings home some roasted green Hatch chiles and dried red ones. Made with the right peppers, this soup really captures those same flavors: savory, roasty, spicy, and the slightest bit sweet.

Green Tortilla Soup can be served as an appetizer or a meal, depending on the add-ins and garnishes you serve it with. Best of all, letting guests add their own garnishes makes it a fun DIY meal—and who doesn't love that?

• • •

Serves 4 to 6

Gluten free

INGREDIENTS

Green chiles, 2 or 3 fresh (Hatch, Anaheim, poblano, or jalapeño)

Tomatillos, 8 to 12

Garlic, 2 cloves

Chicken stock, 4 cups (preferably homemade, see page 40)

Onion, 1 large, diced

Olive oil, 1 tablespoon or so

Salt

Black pepper

Optional add-ins (see Variation)

Chicken, 2 to 3 cups, cooked and shredded (from a rotisserie chicken or poached—pun intended!—from a whole chicken when making stock)

Fresh cilantro, ½ bunch, leaves and tender stems washed and chopped

GARNISHES
Tortilla chips

Avocado, 1, diced

Lime, 1, halved

Tomato, 1 or 2, chopped (or a basketful of cherry tomatoes, quartered)

Radishes, 2 or 3, thinly sliced

Sour cream or plain yogurt, a little bowlful

Chili flakes or cayenne pepper (optional), a tiny pinch

Variation

For a heartier version, you can add any of the following after adding the stock but before adding the chicken. You want to allow them to cook until soft—then add the chicken. (The exceptions here are black beans and cabbage, which should be added just before serving.)

Corn, shucked and cut off the cob (or frozen)

Red bell pepper, diced

Zucchini, diced

Spinach or chard leaves, chopped

Green beans, cut into small pieces

Black beans, cooked (or canned, rinsed and well-drained)

Cabbage, thinly sliced

Tip

You can simpify this recipe. Just get your hands on a jar of high-quality roasted green salsa (which is typically made of roasted tomatillos, peppers, onions, and garlic) or a jar of roasted Hatch chiles. Skip steps 1 and/or 2, and simply spoon enough salsa or roasted chiles into the stock to give the soup body and loads of flavor. We don't recommend trying this with commercially made green salsa. Use only an all-natural, small-batch roasted green salsa (and not the tangy, fresh version!) or roasted Hatch chiles for this shortcut.

1 Prepare the chiles and tomatillos: Preheat the oven to 400°F. Cut the chiles in half lengthwise and remove the seeds. Remove and discard the paper husks from the tomatillos and rinse them under warm water. Cut them in half through the equator (as opposed to through the stem). Place the chiles and tomatillos on a parchment paper–lined baking sheet, cut-side down, and roast for 20 to 30 minutes, until they start to brown. Then, add the garlic cloves to the baking sheet and continue roasting for 5 more minutes. Transfer the chiles, tomatillos, and garlic to a blender. Add a splash of chicken stock, if needed to get the blade going.

2 Sauté the onion: In a large pot, sauté the onion in the olive oil over medium heat, until soft but not browned. Add the chile-tomatillo mixture, and season with salt and pepper to taste.

3 Heat the stock and chicken: Add the stock to the pot and bring to a simmer. Once simmering, add any add-ins you'd like (except the black beans and cabbage, which should be added at the very last minute), allow them to cook and soften for a few minutes, then add the chicken and bring up to a simmer again. Taste and adjust the seasoning with salt and pepper, keeping in mind that the garnishes will add more flavor and texture.

4 Serve: Ladle into bowls and serve the garnishes in small dishes so that guests can compose their own bowls.

Mains

BISCUIT-TOPPED CHICKEN POT PIE

This is a classic biscuit-topped chicken pot pie. (Okay, fine, maybe it's more accurately called chicken and biscuits, but it's a pretty similar concept!) To ensure you don't end up with an overcooked stew and an undercooked biscuit, we recommend you bake the biscuit separately. (It's a really good biscuit, too, so bake it up on its own any time!) You can keep the stew ingredients classic, as this basic recipe describes, or add additional vegetables you like. We love to add mushrooms, as well as fresh asparagus and snap peas when they're in season. Try our basic recipe first, then next time, add your personal touch by trying out some variations to see what you like best!

• • •

Serves 6

For a gluten-free version, substitute GF flour; for a vegetarian version, substitute vegetable <u>stock</u> and replace the chicken with more vegetables

INGREDIENTS

BISCUITS
All-purpose flour, 1¾ cups, plus more for dusting

Baking powder, 1 tablespoon

Sugar, 1 tablespoon

<u>Salt</u>, ½ teaspoon

Heavy cream, 1 cup

Butter, 1 or 2 tablespoons, melted, for brushing the tops

CHICKEN STEW
<u>Potatoes</u>, 2 large, peeled and cut into ½-inch cubes

<u>Salt</u>, 1 to 2 teaspoons, plus a pinch

Carrots, 2 large, peeled

Celery, 2 ribs

Butter, 3 tablespoons (or substitute or combine with <u>olive oil</u>)

<u>Onion</u>, 1 large yellow, white, or red, diced

Optional vegetables (see Variation)

All-purpose flour, 2 tablespoons

Chicken <u>stock</u>, 6 cups (preferably homemade, see page 40), warmed and lightly seasoned with salt

Chicken, 2 cups cooked shredded or diced (such as meat pulled from a rotisserie chicken or poached—pun intended!—when making stock from a whole raw chicken)

Peas, 1 cup, frozen

Fresh herbs, ½ cup, chopped (any combination of <u>parsley</u>, thyme, or tarragon)

Variation
You can substitute or add in countless vegetables, including mushrooms, snap peas, asparagus, green chiles, fennel, chard, spinach, leeks, turnips, pearl <u>onions</u>, and more.

Tip
Pot pie toppings can vary. Whether you're capping it off with biscuits (as we do here), pie crust (as in the recipe that follows), or <u>puff pastry</u> (following that one), pot pies are stews, baked (hmm . . . *usually*) with a pastry of some sort on top. You can't go wrong with that! Try our three recipes here, and then experiment by mixing and matching the stews and pastry toppings.

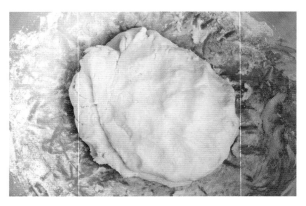

1 Start the biscuit dough: Preheat the oven to 400°F. Whisk together the flour, baking powder, sugar, and salt in a large bowl. Drizzle in the cream and mix with the fingers of one hand, lifting the flour up and around until it absorbs the cream. Once it starts to unify into a dough, flip it up and over a couple times, just until the dough comes together into a loose ball.

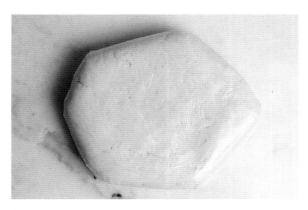

2 Form a dough disc: On a floured surface, pat the dough into a disc about ¾ inch thick, wrap it in plastic wrap, and refrigerate for 20 minutes.

3 Prep the vegetables: Place the potatoes in a medium pot with water to cover them by about an inch. Add enough salt to make the water taste like a nicely salted broth (about 1 to 2 teaspoons), and boil the potatoes until just tender, 3 to 4 minutes. Strain the potatoes and set aside. Meanwhile, dice the carrots and slice the celery. Similarly prep any optional vegetables you're adding in or using as substitutions.

4 Make a <u>roux</u>: In a large pot over medium heat, melt the butter and sauté the onion with a pinch of salt until almost translucent, 7 to 8 minutes. Sprinkle in the flour and stir for 1 to 2 minutes, until the flour mixture turns a light golden brown. It will look dry and weird.

5 Finish the stew base: A ladleful at a time, pour the warm chicken stock into the <u>roux</u>, whisking constantly as the mixture thickens. Once the roux is well-incorporated and no flour lumps remain, simmer on low for about 10 minutes.

6 Make the biscuits: Unwrap the biscuit dough and cut into 6 evenish shapes. (Use the remaining dough to make biscuits that you can enjoy with some jam for dessert!)

7 Butter and bake the biscuits: Brush the tops of the biscuits with the melted butter, and place on a <u>parchment paper</u>–lined baking sheet. Bake for 15 to 20 minutes, until the tops are golden brown. Set aside until the stew is ready.

8 Finish the stew: Add the vegetables and chicken to the pot (except for the peas, which cook super fast). Simmer over medium heat until the vegetables are tender, about 5 minutes. Add the peas and chopped herbs, and cook just until the peas are warmed through. Taste and adjust the seasoning. To serve, ladle into individual bowls and top with a biscuit.

PIE CRUST-TOPPED SALTEÑA POT PIE

All around Latin America, you can find delicious hand pies called empanadas, pocket pastries with variable fillings and crusts. In Bolivia, the most well-known are called *salteñas*. They are a marvel, with a buttery, slightly sweet crust enveloping a stew that hits all the right notes—spicy, salty, sweet, and even a bit tangy—all at once. Like a Chinese soup dumpling, the outer wrapping miraculously holds in the broth. Making that happen is pretty tricky, as is eating it. In Bolivia, a proper salteña-eater can devour the whole thing (with no utensils) without spilling a drop of broth. In fact, tradition has it that the first person to spill a drop of broth has to buy lunch for their companions!

Here we've taken the salteña filling and simplified the process, making a pot-pie version much like the one Leah's husband, Martín, ate growing up in Bolivia. His *abuela* called it *empanada en fuente*. We hope she'd appreciate our recipe for what we call Salteña Pot Pie.

. . .

Makes 4 to 6 individual pot pies

Equipment: 4 to 6 individual-serving-size, oven-safe ramekins or mini pie dishes (about 10 to 12 ounces each)

For a gluten-free version, use GF flour

INGREDIENTS

<u>Potatoes</u>, 2 large, peeled and cut into ½-inch cubes

<u>Salt</u>

<u>Olive oil</u>, about 1 tablespoon

Beef sirloin, 1½ pounds, diced (or ground beef)

Butter, 4 tablespoons unsalted

Turmeric powder, 2 teaspoons (see Ingredient Notes)

Onion, 1 large, cut into medium dice

Chili powder, ¼ cup

Oregano, 1 tablespoon dried or 2 tablespoons fresh

Ground cumin, 1 tablespoon

Beef or chicken <u>stock</u>, 4 cups (for homemade chicken stock see page 40)

Red wine vinegar, 4 to 6 tablespoons (or apple cider vinegar)

Sugar, 6 tablespoons, plus a pinch

Peas, 1 cup, frozen or fresh

Fresh <u>parsley</u>, ½ cup finely chopped

Raisins, ¼ cup

Black or green olives, ¼ cup, pitted

All-purpose flour, 1 or 2 tablespoons

<u>Pie crust</u>, 1, homemade (see page 33) or frozen store-bought, thawed

Hard-boiled eggs (optional), 2, sliced

Egg wash, made by mixing 1 raw egg with 1 tablespoon water, for brushing on top of the pastry

Ingredient Notes

Turmeric is a widely available substitute for annatto or achiote paste or powder, a seasoning made from the seeds of an achiote tree and commonly found in tropical cuisines (especially in Mexico and Central and South America). Like turmeric, it adds an intense (highly staining!) yellowish-orange color, along with a subtle peppery flavor.

Chili powder is a combination of seasonings that usually includes ground chiles and other spices like cumin, oregano, and paprika. These flavors all work well here, but if you can get your hands on pure New Mexican chili powder, that's better yet.

1 **Cook the potatoes and meat:** Preheat the oven to 400°F. In a medium pot, bring the potatoes to a boil in well-salted water and cook at a gentle boil until cooked through but still firm, 3 to 4 minutes. Drain and set aside. Add the olive oil to a large, straight-sided sauté pan or a heavy-bottomed stockpot, and lightly brown the meat in several small batches, seasoning with salt to taste as you go. Transfer the browned meat to a bowl and set aside. Reserve the pan (no need to clean it).

2 **Start the base:** Melt the butter with the turmeric in the reserved pan over medium-high heat. Add the onion, chili powder, oregano, and cumin. Stir to combine, and cook until the onion is tender, about 5 minutes.

3 **Finish the stew:** Stir in the stock, vinegar, sugar, potatoes, and meat. Bring to a simmer and adjust seasoning. Stir in the peas, parsley, raisins, and olives, and remove the pan from the heat.

4 **Prepare the pie crust:** On a lightly-floured surface, roll out the pie crust until ¼ inch thick. Then, cut rounds slightly larger than the tops of your ramekins or mini-pie dishes using a pastry cutter, scissors, or a sharp <u>knife</u> (if cutting on your surface is acceptable).

5 **Assemble and bake:** Set the mini pie pans or individual ramekins onto a baking sheet, then spoon in the stew. Lay a slice or two of boiled egg on top (if using). Top with pie dough and crimp the edges while pressing it into the tops of the dishes or ramekins (so they are pretty, but also so they seal in the stew). Brush the tops with the egg wash and sprinkle with a pinch or two of sugar. Bake for about 30 minutes, until the crust is a delicious-looking light brown.

Puff Pastry-Topped Mushroom Pot Pie

Puff pastry, which can be found in the freezer section of most grocery stores, is the simplest and, arguably, most impressive-looking way to top a pot pie. It's delicious and fun to eat. Here we've paired it with a luxurious mushroom stew—an elevated cream of mushroom soup that evokes a dish you'd have at a fancy French restaurant! The sweetness of leeks and fennel balances the woodiness of the mushrooms, and the spinach adds extra depth and color. The base is incredibly versatile, so feel free to experiment with the vegetables, as well as the mushroom varieties.

• • •

Makes 4 to 6 individual pot pies

For a gluten-free version, use GF flour and puff pastry; for a vegetarian version, use vegetable or mushroom stock

Equipment : 4 to 6 oven-safe bowls or large individual ramekins

INGREDIENTS

Olive oil, a few tablespoons

Leeks, 2 large, white and light green parts only, cleaned and sliced

Fennel bulb, 1, stems and fronds removed, cleaned and finely diced

Salt

Assorted mushrooms, 2 pounds, cleaned and torn or cut into bite-size pieces (maitake, shiitake, king trumpet, shimeji [beech], or any of the extra-special varieties, such as chanterelles, black trumpets, or morels)

Butter, 2 tablespoons

All-purpose flour, 2 tablespoons, plus more for dusting

Chicken stock, 4 cups (preferably homemade, see page 40), warmed

Puff pastry, one-half box (store-bought, frozen, preferably all-butter; see Variations), thawed

Heavy cream, ¾ cup

Fresh parsley, ½ bunch, washed, leaves picked and chopped

Fresh thyme leaves, 1 tablespoon chopped

Black pepper

Spinach, 2 cups baby or 1 bunch regular, washed

Egg wash, made by mixing 1 raw egg with 1 tablespoon of water, for brushing

Variations

The stew would be delicious on its own, over a nice crusty piece of toast, or even served over pasta or rice. If you want to take the velvety stew in a different direction, you can substitute or add in countless vegetables, including peas, snap peas, carrots, celery root, parsnips, and more.

Tip

Cleaning mushrooms varies by variety. Cultivated mushrooms like shiitake, king trumpet, shimeji (beech), and maitake—or the more common button, cremini, and portabellas—don't usually need to be rinsed. They can just get a close inspection and a light brushing, if necessary. Wild mushrooms like chanterelles, black trumpets, and morels, on the other hand, need to be rinsed in a few changes of water to loosen and remove dirt from their natural habitat.

1 **Cook the vegetables and mushrooms:** Preheat the oven to 400°F. Heat a hearty drizzle of olive oil in a wide-bottomed pot over medium heat. Put the leeks and fennel into the pot with a good pinch of salt and sauté until tender, about 8 minutes; avoid browning. Remove to a plate. Drizzle a little more olive oil into the pot and add one-third of the mushrooms with a pinch of salt. Sauté until tender and lightly browned, about 2 minutes. Transfer to the plate of sautéed vegetables and repeat twice more with the remaining mushrooms.

2 **Make a roux:** Add the butter to the same pot. When melted, add the flour and whisk until the mixture is just starting to turn golden brown, 2 to 3 minutes. Add the warmed stock in small ladlefuls, whisking in between each addition. When all the stock is added, taste the stew base and season lightly with salt, erring on the side of slightly less rather than slightly more. (The liquid will reduce and the flavors will concentrate as it cooks.) Simmer over medium heat for 7 to 12 minutes, until it is rich, velvety, and smooth. (Richer, more flavorful stocks need less time to concentrate, whereas lighter stocks need more time.)

3 **Prep the puff pastry:** Lightly dust a work surface with flour, then roll out the puff pastry with a rolling pin to a ¼-inch thickness. Using a sharp knife, cut it into squares a bit larger than the oven-safe bowls or ramekins you plan to use for the pot pies. Set aside.

4 **Finish the stew:** Add the sautéed vegetables to the thickened stew base. Add the cream, parsley, and thyme, bring to a simmer, and taste for seasoning, adding more herbs and salt, along with black pepper, as necessary to boost the flavor. Stir in the spinach, and taste and adjust the seasoning again. Turn off the heat. Place the oven-safe bowls or ramekins onto a baking sheet. Then, ladle in the stew, filling them ½ to ¾ inch from the rim.

5 **Top the pot pies:** With the puff pastry still lying flat, paint each square lightly with egg wash, avoiding the very edges. Then place the squares, egg-wash-side down, on top of each bowl. Gently pull the edges taut, so the pastry doesn't lie directly on the stew. Gently press the edges of the pastry to the bowl and gently brush the tops with egg wash. (Gentle business, this puff pastry work!)

6 **Bake and serve:** Bake for 20 to 30 minutes, or until puffed and golden brown.

SUSHI PARTY

Many people hear the word "sushi" and immediately think: raw fish. But really, in Japanese, sushi refers to vinegar-seasoned rice with toppings and garnishes. Those toppings can be raw fish, but they can also be other things, raw or cooked, including shrimp, vegetables, or egg. Little ovals of vinegared rice, topped with any number of things are called *nigiri*. Sushi rolls, more accurately called *maki*, are large rolls that have been cut to make beautiful little rounds. They can also be served as individual handrolls, called *temaki*. And unadulterated raw fish, eaten with no rice at all, is called *sashimi*. Whichever way you serve it, sushi makes for a delicious, fun, and wildly impressive party that is easier to prepare than you may think.

Maki is made most easily with a bamboo roller, but it can be made without any special instruments, as well. Kimbap (page 139) is the Korean version of maki. The rice is seasoned differently, but the rolling technique is the same. If you want to try your hand at maki, see the kimbap recipe for instructions. We like to make a few, cutting and arranging them on a platter for guests to enjoy alongside their DIY sushi.

Spicy tuna and spicy salmon are perhaps the most popular maki fillings in the U.S. You can make them yourself by mixing together a little Asian hot sauce (such as sriracha), a touch of mayo, and chopped raw fish (typically the bits left over after slicing out nice pieces of sashimi).

This recipe is mostly a how-to-assemble-and-serve guide. It's extremely flexible since you can basically put whatever you want on the rice. Some people like to keep it traditional, while others get very creative. (We draw the line at cream cheese, which graces the menu of countless sushi joints in the U.S.) Just be sure to start with ultra-fresh ingredients—*(Serious) New Cook* Principle #1: Use good ingredients!—and, if you'd like, use the Tip on the next page to get you started with some great combinations.

We like to serve it DIY-style so everyone can make their own. Some people like to try their hand at nigiri, or even maki, but mostly, we use little squares of seaweed to make two-bite temaki, providing the chance to try countless combinations. So remember *(Serious) New Cook* Principle #3: Experiment! And even more importantly, Principle #5: Have fun!

• • •

Serves 4 to 6

Gluten free

Ingredient Notes

Rice varieties like basmati, jasmine, and other long-grain white rice won't stick together enough to shape into sushi. Short-grain brown rice will work passably well if you use a little extra water and cook it a bit longer than usual.

Seaweed sheets come in several forms. To make *maki*, be sure to get unsalted *nori* sheets. The flaky, salted seaweed popularly sold in individual-size packages for snacking (or in larger sheets that you can find at Asian grocery stores) is too brittle for maki. However, it's delicious and works great for little *temaki* (handrolls). We put out both: nori that's been cut into squares and snacking seaweed that's already familiar to (and loved by!) most folks.

Tip

Favorite sushi combinations include: salmon-avocado-cucumber; tuna-scallion-mango, salmon-shiso-Meyer lemon; yellowtail-scallion-jalapeño; octopus-mango; spicy salmon-scallion; and avocado-cucumber

INGREDIENTS

Assorted veggies, a platterful (cucumbers, avocados, pickled Japanese yellow radishes, little red radishes, sprouts, carrots, shiso leaves, scallions, and/or jalapeños)

Assorted fruit (optional), 1 each (mango, nectarine, pineapple, and/or Meyer lemon)

Assorted fish, 1 pound total (wild salmon, tuna, and yellowtail— all popular and accessible types— as well as cooked octopus; be sure to only buy "sushi grade" fish from a reputable fishmonger)

Rice vinegar, about ¼ cup

Sugar, about 2 tablespoons

Salt, about 2 teaspoons

Rice, about 4 cups freshly cooked (from 2 cups uncooked) short- or medium-grain white rice (see Ingredient Notes)

Seaweed sheets, 2 individual packages per person or several packages of full-size sheets (see Ingredient Notes)

Wasabi, 1 tablespoon prepared (or use fresh root, finely grated)

Pickled ginger, about ½ cup, enough to make a few little piles for serving (available at many fish markets, Asian grocery stores, and large supermarkets)

Soy sauce or tamari, about ½ cup

1 Prep the vegetables and fruit: Cut any hard vegetables (cucumbers, carrots, radishes) into <u>matchsticks</u> ("julienned" pieces). Slice the fruit into thin-ish slices, with the exception of the Meyer lemon, which you should dice, rind and all. Arrange on a platter, cover with plastic wrap or a damp towel, and keep in the refrigerator until ready to serve.

2 Slice the fish: Use a very sharp <u>knife</u> to trim and slice the fish into fairly thin pieces about the length of your thumb. Trying not to mess around with the pieces of fish too much, lay them out on platters as artfully—or casually!—as you like. Cover with plastic wrap and keep in the refrigerator until ready to serve.

3 Season the rice: Briefly warm the rice vinegar, sugar, and salt in a small saucepan over medium heat, or in a microwave-safe bowl in the microwave, just enough to help the salt and sugar dissolve.

Gently scoop the freshly cooked rice (still warm) into a wide, shallow bowl. Drizzle the seasoned rice vinegar over it, using a wide spoon to gently scoop under the rice and turn it over to mix. Let it sit for a few more minutes before transferring to a serving bowl.

4 Prepare the accompaniments and serve: Set the table family-style with shared platters of fish, veggies and fruit, bowls of rice, plates of seaweed, little piles of prepared wasabi and pickled ginger, and little bowls of soy sauce for dipping. For anyone who wants to try making nigiri, provide finger bowls of water, which is needed to keep the rice from sticking to fingers.

KIMBAP

Like Japanese folks, Koreans enjoy raw fish, which we call *hwe*. That's not the only sushi(ish) similarity, though. Kimbap, which could be described as Korean maki, is a snack or light meal ubiquitous in Korea. In Korean, *kim* (pronounced *keem*) means seaweed and *bap* (pronounced *bop*!) means rice. The seasonings and fillings are different from Japanese maki, but the technique is similar. You place seasoned rice on a sheet of kim/nori, add fillings, roll tightly, and slice into pretty little rounds. Also similar to maki, contemporary kimbap fillings sometimes get very creative. (While many modern Koreans would disagree, we definitely draw the line at American cheese!) Here, we present traditional kimbap, which we used to make by the hundreds (okay, maybe not *hundreds* . . .) every weekend at our mom's Korean market when we were kids.

• • •

Serves 3 or 4 as a light lunch; 6 to 8 as a snack or appetizer

Gluten free; for a vegan version, skip the bulgogi and eggs

INGREDIENTS

Rice, about 4 cups freshly cooked (from 2 cups uncooked) short- or medium-grain white rice

Sesame oil, about 2 tablespoons, plus more for drizzling (preferably the aromatic, toasted kind available at Asian markets)

Salt

Neutral oil, for sautéing

Eggs, 2 large, beaten with a pinch of salt

Carrots, 2, peeled and cut into long chopstick-like strips

Black pepper

Spinach, 1 bunch, cleaned

Garlic, 1 clove, minced

Pickled daikon radish (optional), 1, cut into long chopstick-like strips (available at Asian markets; opt for a natural, preservative-free variety)

Bulgogi, ½ cup cooked (optional; page 191)

Kim/nori seaweed sheets, 1 package full-size sheets, typically 7 by 8 inches (unsalted)

Toasted sesame seeds (optional), for garnish

Optional Prep

Everything except the rice can be prepped in advance. Like Bulgogi Bibimbap (page 195), kimbap is a recipe that can be made quite easily if you already have *banchan* (Korean side dishes, which often include the prepared vegetables used here) in the fridge.

1 Prepare the rice: Gently spoon the hot rice into a large, wide bowl. Sprinkle the sesame oil and a generous pinch or two of salt over it. Use a wide spoon or paddle to scoop under the rice, flipping it over repeatedly to mix without crushing the rice. Taste, and add more salt, to taste.

2 Prepare the eggs: Heat a drizzle of neutral oil in a reliably nonstick <u>skillet</u> over medium-high. (If ever there is a time to use a pan with a nonstick coating, this may be it!) When it is very warm but not smoking, pour in the beaten egg in a single layer. (Ideally, it won't bubble and sizzle dramatically. If it does, the egg will still be usable; it just won't be as tender as it could be.) Turn off the heat and cover, allowing the egg to steam and cook through gently. When it is cooked, flip it onto a <u>cutting board</u>; reserve the pan. Use a large, sharp <u>knife</u> to cut the egg into full-width strips. (In other words, the center pieces will be very long and the sides will be short.) Carefully transfer to a platter, trying not to break the strips.

3 Sauté the carrots: In the same frying pan (if egg is stuck on it, clean it before continuing), sauté the carrots over medium-high with a little neutral oil and a pinch of salt and pepper. Cook until they are tender but not mushy, about 2 minutes. Set them next to the eggs on the platter, and set aside.

4 Prepare the spinach: Drop the spinach into a large pot of boiling, salted water for just 30 to 60 seconds, stirring to ensure even cooking. As soon as it is evenly limp and a uniform color, strain in a colander and rinse with a bit of cold water to cool slightly and stop the cooking. You don't want to rinse it until it's cold—just cooled-down enough to handle. Using your hands, pick up a handful at a time and gently squeeze out the excess water (just until it doesn't drip at all when you pick it up). Place in a medium bowl and add the garlic and a light drizzle of toasted sesame oil. Mix gently with your hands and taste a piece, adjusting the seasoning; if your water wasn't salty enough, you may need to add a pinch of salt. Add it to the platter next to the eggs and carrots.

5 Prep the other fillings: Line up the pickled radish and bulgogi on the platter, in roughly equal amounts. Fill a small finger bowl with clean water.

Tips

Remember _(Serious) New Cook_ Principle #2: Taste and adjust—and season as you go! While some cooks make kimbap with fresh, unseasoned fillings, we think doing it the way our mom taught us yields superior results. Seasoning each element individually builds flavors and complexity. So remember, taste and adjust, and season as you go!

A bamboo roller made for kimbap or maki helps to ensure even, tight rolls. It's not strictly necessary, however, as they can be rolled neatly by hand with a little practice, as we do here.

6 Roll the kimbap: On a clean, dry surface, set one piece of kim/nori. Use a spoon to place a couple tablespoons of rice onto the sheet. Dip your fingertips into water, then use them to carefully distribute the rice evenly around the sheet, leaving a 1-inch border along the top edge. Try not to smush the rice grains, instead using the very tips of your fingers to just scoot the rice around until you have an even layer. Next, place a narrow strip of each filling in a row about an inch or two from the bottom edge. Now the tricky part: Carefully lift up the bottom edge and flip it over the fillings, pinching it in the way you might do to tightly roll up a sleeping mat (like a camp mattress!) or towel. Continue rolling, moving your fingers along to keep even pressure, until you get to the top. Dip two fingers into the water and dampen the rice-free top edge before finishing the roll. Place seam side down on a clean cutting board. Then repeat with the rest of the kim/nori, rice, and fillings.

7 Slice and serve: Keeping the seam-side down, use a very sharp <u>knife</u> to cut each roll into approximately 10 rounds, each about ½ to ¾ inch wide. Arrange on a platter and serve. Alternatively, leave whole and eat as a giant handroll, a popular option for eating on the go. Arrange on a platter and, optionally, garnish with a pinch of sesame seeds before serving.

HAND-PRESSED RICE BALLS

These smart little snacks are perhaps most well-known in their birth-place of Japan, but they are also popular in Korea, owing to the history and cultural exchange between the two countries. In many Japanese and Korean markets today—in the US as well as in Asia—you can find these hand-pressed rice "balls," as they are frequently called, filled with all sorts of delicious bits and seasonings, wrapped in seaweed, and encased in a special cellophane wrapper that keeps the seaweed crispy while still holding together the rice. (Pulling off the wrapper without disturbing the rice takes a little practice, but once you get it, you'll be in awe of its clever design!)

• • •

Serves 3 as a light lunch or 6 as a snack

Gluten free; vegan if you omit the fish and meat fillings/toppings

Shaped into rice triangles, they are technically called *omusubi* in Japanese and *samgak-kimbap* in Korean. They can also be made into actual balls—in Korean we call the round or football-shaped versions *jumeok-bap*, meaning "fist rice," while in Japanese they are called *onigiri*. No matter the shape, these beautiful hand-pressed rice "balls" make a light meal perfect for eating on the go or packing in lunchboxes.

INGREDIENTS

Rice, 2 cups cooked short-grain white rice (or use leftover seasoned sushi rice—see page 137)

Nori seaweed (optional), 1 sheet (unsalted) plus more for crumbling

Your choice of fillings/toppings (see Ingredient Note), such as:

Salmon, cooked and broken up

Umeboshi plum pickle, chopped (available at Asian markets)

Fish roe, salted

Bulgogi (page 191), cooked and minced (or any other seasoned, cooked meat)

Kimchi, finely chopped

Salt

Sesame sprinkle (such as furikake; or plain sesame seeds)

Whole fresh sesame or shiso leaves (for wrapping)

Ingredient Note

You'll want somewhere between a pinch (as for fish roe or sesame sprinkle) and a small spoonful (as for bits of fish, pickle, bulgogi, or kimchi) for each rice ball you make. We often make a variety, so we use a spoonful here and a pinch there. It all depends on what you have and what you like. So, remember *(Serious) New Cook Principle #3: Experiment!*

Tip

Specially cut nori, often called *samhae nori* or *onigiri nori*, can be found in Korean and Japanese markets. Geniusly, it is sold in individually wrapped packages that keep the nori from touching the rice until you're ready to eat it, and they're often paired with onigiri molds for making perfect triangles. You kind of have to see it to believe it. Next time you're near a Korean or Japanese market, be sure to pop in and check them out.

1 Prep: If using leftover rice, reheat it in the microwave with a sprinkle of water until hot, 3 to 5 minutes. Place the hot rice into a medium bowl to cool to the touch. Cut the nori seaweed, if using, into strips about 2 by 6 inches. If you're using mix-ins (an especially good idea for something like chopped pickles or fish roe, which look pretty and taste better when they are well-distributed through the rice), gently stir them together with some rice in a small bowl, trying to avoid smashing the rice grains. (If you're making multiple types, use separate bowls.)

2 Start forming the rice balls: Use an onigiri mold, if you have one. Otherwise, dampen your hands with water and a pinch of salt in each palm; this ensures that the rice doesn't stick while giving it a light seasoning at the same time. Place one portion of rice (about ⅓ cup, if making medium triangles) in the palm of your hand.

3 Fill them (optional): If you're filling them, make a little indentation with your finger, spoon a little filling in the center, and cover with more rice.

4 Shape them: Use your fingers to shape the rice balls into triangles about 1 inch thick and 3 inches wide at the base of the triangle. If you're topping them (a great idea with tiny bits like sesame sprinkle or crumbled nori), put a few big pinches on top just before serving. If you're wrapping with nori, fold it around one side, creating a neat spot to hold on to the rice "ball" as you eat it.

CLASSIC BREADED AND PAN-FRIED CHICKEN BREASTS

Who doesn't love breaded and fried things? A good crispy breading creates a contrast with whatever it encases, whether it's a juicy chicken breast (the recipe here!), some tender, tasty vegetables (the recipe that follows!), or a flaky piece of fish (the third recipe in the trio). Once you know the standard three-step breading process, you may never buy the frozen stuff again. The process seals in natural juices while creating a crunchy outer layer. We like to make enough of these breaded and pan-fried chicken breasts to last several meals: hot the first night, packed with an ice pack for lunch the next day, right out of the fridge for a snack any time, or on some toasted bread with lettuce and mayo for a quick sandwich.

Served hot and juicy, Breaded and Pan-Fried Chicken Breasts pair perfectly with a cool salad—like any from our Vinaigrette Salad trio (pages 107–112)—and, if you're going all out, some Crispy Potatoes (pages 67–72). It's also great with some piping hot rice and a bowl of Japanese curry, chicken *katsu*–style. For an awesome chicken sandwich, pair it with some tangy coleslaw or a smear of mayo or pink sauce with some crispy lettuce. So good, so many ways. Just make 'em already.

INGREDIENTS

Boneless chicken breasts, 4 (about 6 to 8 ounces each)

Salt

All-purpose flour, about ¼ cup

Black pepper

Granulated garlic (optional), ½ teaspoon

Breadcrumbs, 3 to 4 cups (fresh white-bread crumbs are terrific, as are panko-style—but really, any style will work)

Eggs, 2 large

Neutral oil, at least 1 cup, for frying

Lemon wedges (optional), for serving

• • •

Serves 4

For a gluten-free version, use GF breadcrumbs and flour

Tip

Flattening chicken breasts helps to ensure even cooking. Try to get them reasonably flat and uniform in thickness. To do so, you can either pound them out with a flat mallet or slice off the top bit, leaving behind a uniformly thick cutlet. (The sliced-off bit makes a great little "nugget" you can bread and fry, or you can add it to stock to boost flavor.) The thickness of your cutlets will determine the cooking time. For full breasts just slightly flattened, about 6 minutes per side. For cutlets that have been sliced in half or pounded out quite thinly, more like 3 minutes per side. Note that thin cutlets are easier to cook, but are never as juicy. If one of your breasts is much thicker than the rest or doesn't seem to have browned as well as the others, leave that one on the heat for an extra 1 to 2 minutes.

Variation

Use the same technique—in fact, the same recipe—for any type of cutlet or fillet, including fish (as in the the third recipe in this series), thinly sliced steak, or boneless chicken thighs.

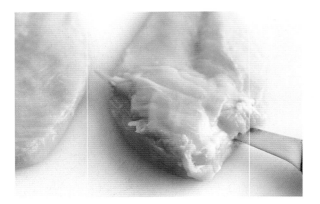

1 **Prep:** Lay the chicken breasts on a <u>cutting board</u> and flatten them by either pounding them out or slicing off the thickest part, leaving behind a nice, even piece (see Tip). Sprinkle some salt on each side. Put the flour into a medium bowl and season it with a few cracks of black pepper and the granulated garlic, if using. Put the bread-crumbs in another medium bowl. In a third medium bowl, whisk the eggs with a splash of water and pinch of salt.

2 **Bread the chicken:** Working with one piece at a time, dip each breast in the flour, shaking off any excess. Then dip it into the egg, allowing any excess to drip off. Finally, place it in the breadcrumbs, gently pressing on the breadcrumbs to form an even layer. Shake off the excess and place on a plate or baking sheet; continue until you've breaded enough to start frying a first batch. (You can bread the next batch while the first batch fries.)

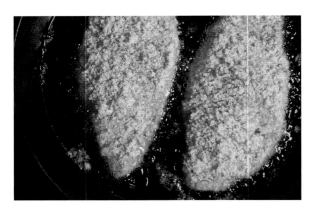

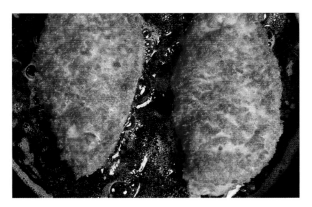

3 **Fry the first side:** In a large frying pan set over medium-high heat, pour enough oil to reach a depth of ¼ inch. After 30 to 60 seconds, drop in a tiny breadcrumb. If it sizzles right away, your oil is hot enough. Gently set each breast (or half of them, if your pan is not large enough to fry them all in one batch) into the hot oil and reduce the heat to medium. Fry until golden brown and cooked at least halfway through, about 3 to 6 minutes, depending on thickness. Maintain enough heat to keep a sizzle, but keep it low enough so the breadcrumbs don't burn before the breasts cook. Add more oil, as needed. Rotate them in the pan to ensure even cooking.

4 **Finish frying and serve:** When the edges of the meat turn from pink to white and the breasts have developed a nice, golden brown crust on the bottom, flip them and repeat. To check if they are done, transfer one cutlet to a cutting board, and cut it in half at its thickest section. If it is white all the way through, remove the cutlets to a cooling rack set over paper towels, allowing them to briefly cool and drain. If it is still more than the tiniest bit pink inside, cook for a bit longer and check again. As they rest on the cooling rack, they'll continue to cook, and the juices will redistribute, resulting in juicy, delicious cutlets. If you have a second batch, fry them while the first batch is resting. Serve with lemon wedges.

BREADED AND PAN-FRIED VEGETABLE PLATTER

Whether we're talking diner-style breaded mushrooms, burger-joint onion rings, Southern fried green tomatoes, or Italian fried fennel, breaded and fried vegetables are a wildly cravable way to get your five-a-day. Experiment with different vegetables and see what you like best. And definitely do what we do when we have a little breading left over: Dig through that vegetable bin in your fridge to see if there's a stray veg in there you could fry up! You may be surprised to find a new favorite.

• • •

Serves 4 to 6 as a side or appetizer

For a gluten-free version, use GF breadcrumbs. Can be made vegan by substituting vegan mayo or flax eggs for the eggs.

INGREDIENTS

Green tomatoes, 3 or 4 medium, sliced about ⅓ inch thick

Zucchini, 1 or 2 small, halved and sliced about ⅓ inch thick

King trumpet mushrooms, 3 or 4, sliced about ½ inch thick (or substitute any other type of mushroom you like)

Eggplant, 1 or 2 small (preferably one of the skinny, Asian-style varieties), halved

Salt

Black pepper

All-purpose flour, ½ cup

Breadcrumbs, at least 3 cups (fresh white-bread crumbs work especially well, as do panko—but really, any style will work)

Eggs, 2

Neutral oil, at least 1 cup, for frying

Flaky sea salt (or substitute any sea salt or kosher salt), for finishing

Fresh parsley leaves (optional), ¼ cup chopped, for garnish

Lemon wedges (optional), for serving

Aioli (see page 21), for serving (or use Creamy Goes-with-Everything Dip, page 105)

Tip

Other vegetables that are great to fry include okra, blanched cauliflower, sliced winter squash, sliced Asian sweet potatoes, blanched fennel, and boiled cardoons. When shallow-frying, as we do here, it's best to slice everything flat, so it's flippable. (This is as opposed to deep-frying, which involves as much as ten times more oil but allows odd shapes to float around and cook evenly.) Castelvetrano olives also work, since they are small enough to move around a pan with a lesser amount of oil. Fried onions are delicious, of course, though keeping the breading on them is tricky. If you love them, give it a try. See if you can come up with a strategy for slicing them in a way that helps the breading adhere!

This recipe leaves the flavors clean and neutral, with little more than salt and pepper, to allow the individual vegetable flavors to shine. If you'd like, you can try boosting the flavor by adding some seasonings to the breadcrumbs. Depending on what direction you want to take it, you could try grated Parmesan cheese, chopped fresh herbs like rosemary and sage, smoky paprika, chili flakes or marash pepper, or sesame seeds.

1 Prep the vegetables: Season the sliced vegetables with salt and pepper.

2 Prep your three-step setup: Put the flour and breadcrumbs into separate medium bowls. In a third medium bowl, whisk the eggs with a splash of water and pinch of salt.

3 Bread the vegetables: Working with one vegetable at a time, dip each piece first in the flour, shaking off any excess. Then dip it into the egg, allowing any excess to drip off. Finally, place it in the breadcrumb bowl, gently pressing on the breadcrumbs to form an even layer. Shake off the excess, and place on a baking sheet; continue until you've breaded enough pieces to start frying a first batch. (You can bread the next batch while the first batch fries.)

4 Fry 'em up: Into a large frying pan set over medium-high heat, pour enough oil to reach a depth of ¼ inch. After 30 to 60 seconds, drop in a tiny breadcrumb. If it sizzles right away, your oil is hot enough. Working with one vegetable type at a time (different vegetables cook at different rates), gently set the slices into the hot oil and fry each side over medium-high heat until they are cooked through but not mushy. (You can carefully taste one or prick one with a fork to test its softness/doneness.) Maintain enough heat to keep a sizzle, but keep it low enough so the breadcrumbs don't burn before the vegetables finish cooking.

5 Cool and serve: Once nicely browned on both sides and cooked through, remove to a cooling rack set over paper towels, or a plate lined with paper towels, to drain and cool briefly before arranging on a platter. When you have a platterful, add a sprinkle of flaky sea salt and a bit of chopped parsley, and serve hot with lemon wedges and a bowl of aioli or Creamy Goes-with-Everything dip.

BREADED AND PAN-FRIED WHITE FISH
WITH CHERRY TOMATO SALSA

Fish fillets are just begging to be breaded and pan-fried. Made with a nice, flaky white fish, they are tender and juicy, benefitting dramatically from being encased in a shell of crispy breading. In the summer, when tomatoes are delicious, try these hot fried fish fillets with our simple Cherry Tomato Salsa. You could also have them sandwiched between soft slider buns with some tartar sauce and lettuce for the best fish sandwich of your life. Or, try them in tacos, with a little guacamole and some tangy coleslaw. One recipe, lots of options.

• • •

Serves 4

For a gluten-free version, use GF breadcrumbs and flour

INGREDIENTS

FRIED FISH

Flaky white fish, 4 portions (about 6 ounces each) halibut, cod, or sole

<u>Salt</u>

Black pepper

All-purpose flour, about ¼ cup

<u>Breadcrumbs</u>, 3 to 4 cups (fresh white-bread crumbs are terrific, as are panko-style—but really, any style will work)

Eggs, 2 large

<u>Neutral oil</u>, at least 1 cup, for frying

CHERRY TOMATO SALSA

Red <u>onion</u> (or shallot), ½ small, finely diced

Red wine vinegar, ¼ cup (or substitute sherry or white wine vinegar or fresh lemon juice)

<u>Salt</u>

Cherry <u>tomatoes</u>, 1 pint, washed and cut in half from pole to pole (through the stem end)

<u>Olive oil</u>, ⅓ cup

Fresh herbs, ½ bunch total <u>parsley</u>, basil, cilantro and/or chives, washed and minced

1 Prep: Inspect the fillets for bones, using a pair of tweezers or pliers to remove any that remain. Season both sides with salt and pepper. Put the flour and breadcrumbs into separate medium bowls. In a third medium bowl, whisk the eggs with a splash of water and pinch of salt.

2 Prepare the salsa: <u>Macerate</u> the diced onion for at least 10 minutes in a small bowl with the vinegar and a big pinch of salt. Then, combine with the tomatoes, olive oil, and fresh herbs. Taste and adjust the seasonings, with particular attention to the amount of acid (vinegar) and salt.

3 Bread the fish: Working with one piece at a time, dip each fish fillet first in the flour, shaking off any excess. Then dip it into the egg, allowing any excess to drip off. Finally, place it in the breadcrumbs, gently pressing on the breadcrumbs to form an even layer. Shake off the excess, and place it onto a plate or baking sheet; continue until you've breaded enough fillets to start frying a first batch. (You can bread the next batch while the first batch fries.)

4 Fry 'em up: In a large frying pan set over medium-high heat, pour enough oil to reach a depth of ¼ inch. Let the oil heat, then gently set each fillet (or half of them, if your pan isn't large enough to fry them all in one batch; see Tips) into the hot oil and fry until golden brown, about 2 to 3 minutes per side. Maintain enough heat to keep a sizzle, but keep it low enough so the breadcrumbs don't burn before the fillets finish cooking. To check if they are done, remove one fillet to a plate and gently break it in half at its thickest section. If it is flaky and opaque, not floppy and translucent, it's done. Remove to a cooling rack set over paper towels, or a plate lined with paper towels, to drain. Serve immediately with a big spoonful of Cherry Tomato Salsa.

Tips

Cherry Tomato Salsa is similar to our Herby Tomato Salad (page 107). The main difference is that all of the salsa ingredients are chopped up pretty small, enabling it to work as a sort of sauce for the fish. You can also change things up a bit by adding other tasty, savory elements, such as diced Nicoise or kalamata olives, chopped capers, minced <u>anchovies</u>, diced fresh hot chiles, minced garlic, or a big pinch of cayenne pepper or chili flakes.

For the crispiest fry, always check your oil temperature before adding the ingredients you plan to fry. Drop in a tiny <u>breadcrumb</u>: if it sizzles, your oil is hot enough.

Keep the oil as clean as possible to avoid burnt bits. If you need to fry a second batch of fish, first use a slotted spoon or a mini-strainer to scoop out most of the loose crumbs that have been left behind in the oil.

Variation

Instead of—or, better yet, in *addition* to—Cherry Tomato Salsa, try serving the fillets with <u>aioli</u>, a classic garlicky mayonnaise, and a lemon wedge. Alternatively, whip up a homemade tartar sauce made of mayo, pickle relish, and lemon juice, for dipping, spooning over, or smearing on a sandwich.

FLASH-FRIED CUTLETS
WITH HERBY TOMATO SALAD

These super-quick, super-satisfying cutlets are as versatile as they are delicious. We always make a big batch with plans to eat them for lunch the following day, since they're excellent cold—but they never last that long! No matter how many we make, there never seem to be leftovers. Good thing they're so easy to prepare. We use a *much* easier-than-usual breading method inspired by *silpancho*, a popular Bolivian plate dinner consisting of a thin flash-fried cutlet over rice and potatoes, topped with a fried egg and some fresh salsa. Unlike three-step-breaded cutlets, the meat in silpancho is often pressed—or pounded, if using a thin slice instead of ground meat—directly into the breadcrumbs.

By using toasted breadcrumbs and pressing the meat superthin, you create a cutlet that can be fried so fast (flash-fried) it won't have a chance to become anything except crispy, moist, and tender, all at the same time. A weeknight staple in our houses, we alternate between serving them with a simple salad (like we do here) or as silpancho.

INGREDIENTS

<u>Breadcrumbs</u>, 4 cups (store-bought or toasted homemade)

Ground beef, 2 pounds (or substitute ground pork, turkey, or chicken)

<u>Salt</u>

<u>Neutral oil</u>

Herby Tomato Salad (page 107)

• • •

Serves 6

For a gluten-free version, use GF breadcrumbs

Optional Prep

The cutlets can be breaded up to 1 day ahead. Stack them on a plate with a piece of <u>parchment paper</u> or plastic wrap in between each one, then cover tightly and refrigerate until you're ready to fry.

Tip

For properly fried food, this recipe is shockingly easy. It's seriously the easiest breaded and fried thing you'll ever make. Nonetheless, frying requires a certain level of skill to get it done hot and fast without burning yourself or the food. Be sure to taste a piece from the first batch you fry. In addition to tasting for seasoning, you may realize you should cook the cutlets longer or shorter the next time.

1 Start making the cutlets: Spread a handful of breadcrumbs onto a flat-bottomed plate. Roll a ping-pong-ball-size portion of ground beef into a ball, and place it on top of the breadcrumbs. Pressing down with your fingers, flatten it out as uniformly as possible.

2 Flatten, coat, and season the cutlets: Flip over the pressed cutlet and continue flattening until you have a disc no more than ⅓ inch thick that is evenly coated with breadcrumbs. You may need to flip it over a couple times. Carefully set it aside on a baking sheet, and sprinkle each side very lightly with salt. Continue with the remaining ground beef and breadcrumbs.

3 Start frying: Pour enough oil into a large, shallow frying pan to just cover the bottom, and heat it over medium-high. After 30 to 60 seconds, drop in a breadcrumb. If it sizzles right away, your oil is hot enough. Carefully place the breaded cutlets into the oil; avoid overcrowding the pan. Keep the heat high enough to maintain a good sizzle. After frying for about 1 minute, use a flat spatula to peek at the bottom of one to see how it's browning. If needed, move them around so they brown evenly.

4 Finish frying: After the bottoms are nicely browned, carefully flip them over and continue frying until the second side is browned. Remember to adjust the heat as needed. Use your ears as much as your eyes. You don't want the pan smoking hot because the breadcrumbs will burn before the meat cooks, but you want to keep the sizzle going so they cook quickly without drying out. If it's taking longer than 1 or 2 minutes per side, increase the heat. Remove to a cooling rack set over paper towels, or a plate lined with paper towels, to drain.

5 **Continue frying:** In between each batch, use a spoon to carefully scoop out any burnt crumbs that accumulate in the pan, and add more oil, as needed, to keep the bottom of the pan covered. Repeat steps 3 and 4 until all of your cutlets have been fried.

6 **Assemble and serve:** To serve this family-style, arrange the cutlets on a platter and then spoon the Herby Tomato Salad on top. To serve plated, arrange one or two cutlets on each plate, then heap a spoonful of tomatoes on top. Any remaining salad—along with the delicious collected juices from the tomato and dressing—can be served in a small bowl at the table for extra spooning.

FLASH-FRIED CUTLETS, ASIAN-STYLE

This flash-fried cutlet puts our Bolivian *silpancho*-inspired technique to work in an Asian-style pork cutlet. It is reminiscent of Japanese *menchi katsu*, a breaded ground-meat cutlet sometimes eaten out of hand like a croquette. It can also be served sandwiched between two pieces of squishy white bread (a "sando") or with rice and shredded cabbage (as we do here). Kai, Cammie's son, is always trying to get his *katsu* curry fix, so he makes Japanese golden curry with his. Our recipe also takes some cues from *wanja-jeon*, Korean patties made with a combination of ground meat, tofu, and minced onion. They are surprisingly good cold and at room temperature, as well as blazing hot. The tofu and onion keep the patties tender and moist, while quietly cutting down on meat consumption. The result is a delicious and versatile cutlet that's particularly good served Asian-style.

• • •

Serves 4

For a gluten-free version use GF breadcrumbs

INGREDIENTS

Tofu, ½ block (7 ounces) medium or firm, liquid drained off

Ground pork, 1 pound

Onion, ½ medium, finely minced

Salt, ¾ teaspoon

Toasted breadcrumbs (preferably panko-style, homemade or store-bought)

Neutral oil, for frying

Green cabbage, 1 small head

Rice, a few cups cooked (preferably short-grain white rice)

Pink sauce (see page 33), for the cutlets (and the cabbage, if you like)

Ponzu sauce (see page 34) or sesame dressing (optional), for the cabbage

Variation

Frozen cauliflower "rice" (which is really grated or finely chopped cauliflower) can be used in place of the tofu. Just defrost it, then squeeze it out to remove as much of the liquid as you can. It's another great way to keep the cutlets moist and tender, while also reducing meat consumption.

Tips

Preseasoning the pork works in this recipe, since you're mixing it up with the tofu and onions anyway. (In other words, since you're mixing up the meat mixture, it's a good idea to get the salt mixed all around in there at the same time.) Also, these flash-fried cutlets are thicker than the silpancho-style cutlets in the preceding recipe; those are exceptionally thin and are made with ground beef straight out of the package, so there's no need to do any mixing or handle the meat before shaping them. If you were to season the meat as you press it into the breadcrumbs—which might be your instinct—you would run the risk of dropping salt into the breadcrumbs, making it saltier and saltier with each cutlet. That's why the thin cutlets in the preceding recipe are seasoned *after* they're formed.

Tasting and adjusting—*(Serious) New Cook* **Principle #2!—is tricky** when you're working with a meat, like pork, that can't be consumed raw. For that reason, we always fry up a tiny little tester when making things like these cutlets, meatballs, or even dumpling fillings. You can even fry it up before breading. That way, you can adjust the seasoning before it's too late to be properly incorporated.

1 Make the mixture: Use your hands to crumble the tofu into a medium bowl. Squeeze it out a bit and drain off the liquid it releases, blotting with a paper towel to absorb as much liquid as you can. Add the pork, onion, and salt and mix until combined (see Tips).

2 Start making the cutlets: Spread a handful of breadcrumbs onto a flat-bottomed plate. Roll a golf-ball-size scoop of the mixture into a ball, place on top of the breadcrumbs, and flatten it out into a thick disc with your hands.

3 Flatten and bread the cutlets: Working one at a time, flip each pressed cutlet over carefully and continue flattening until you have an evenly breaded patty about ½ inch thick (which is thicker than the silpancho-style beef cutlets in the preceding recipe). Carefully set it aside on a baking sheet.

4 Start frying: Pour enough oil into a large, shallow frying pan to just cover the bottom. Heat the pan over medium-high for approximately 1 minute. Test the temperature of the oil by dropping in a breadcrumb. If it sizzles right away, it's hot enough. Carefully place the breaded cutlets into the hot oil; avoid overcrowding the pan. Keep the heat high enough to maintain a good sizzle. If needed, move them around so they brown evenly.

5 Flip them: After the bottoms are nicely browned—1 to 2 minutes, depending on size—carefully flip them over and continue cooking until the second side is browned. Remember to adjust the heat as needed. Use your ears as much as your eyes. You don't want the pan smoking hot because the crumbs will burn before the meat cooks, but you want to keep the sizzle going. Each side shouldn't take more than 2 minutes to brown; if it's taking longer, increase the heat.

6 **Remove from the pan and cook the next batch:** Carefully remove one cutlet and break it open to see if the meat is cooked through. A tiny bit of pink is okay, since it will continue cooking for a minute as it cools. If it's more than a tiny bit pink or the meat still has a raw-looking texture, put it back in the pan briefly. When done, remove all the cutlets to drain on a cooling rack set over paper towels or a plate lined with paper towels. In between each batch, use a spoon to carefully scoop out any burnt crumbs that accumulate in the pan, and add more oil, as needed, to keep the bottom of the pan covered. Continue frying the rest.

7 **Prep the cabbage:** Remove the outer 2 or 3 layers of the cabbage, then quarter it through the core. Using a <u>mandoline</u> or very sharp <u>knife</u>, shred the cabbage into long shavings as thin as you possibly can. (If using a mandoline, keep the core intact—and be exceedingly careful! If using a knife, remove the core and lay the cabbage down flat.) Continue until you have a nice pile for each person.

8 **Serve:** Serve the cutlets with a scoop of hot rice, a pile of finely shredded cabbage, and some pink sauce and/or ponzu sauce.

Tips

Make a tester. These cutlets are very tender and may fall apart in the pan if you haven't squeezed out enough liquid from the tofu. The first time you make them, it's a good idea to fry up one tester before you bread them all. That way, if it doesn't keep its shape, you can address the problem before it's too late: making them a little thicker and more neatly formed can help, as can adding a few breadcrumbs and an egg to the mixture.

Quick-breading ground meat, like we do here, is a fast, easy alternative to the classic three-step breading process on pages 145–150. That said, because these pork cutlets are a little thicker (and, therefore, more tender and juicy) than ground beef flash-fried cutlets, three-step breading them would work extra well to seal in their juices, while ensuring a super-crispy outer layer. So, if you have the time, you could try using the mixture from this recipe with the three-step breading recipe. Experiment and decide: Is the more complex process worth the effort, or is the flash-fried process just as delicious, while being simpler and quicker?

FLASH-FRIED CUTLET SANDWICH WITH PICKLED ONIONS AND A FRIED EGG

If you like a good sandwich, you'll *love* this—our version of what's sometimes known as a Milanese sandwich in Italy, *torta milanesa* (in Mexico), or *trancapecho* (in Bolivia). You could make it with a thin, three-step-breaded cutlet (page 146), but the brilliant Bolivian *silpancho*-inspired technique for breading and flash-frying a ground meat cutlet (see page 154) can't be beat.

• • •

Makes 2 sandwiches, but the recipe can be easily scaled up

INGREDIENTS

Your favorite bun or roll, 2

Flash-Fried Cutlets (page 153), 2 or 4, depending on size (and appetite!)

Olive oil, for frying (or substitute butter)

Eggs, 2 large

Mayonnaise or pink sauce (see page 21), about 1 tablespoon

Lettuce, a few pieces romaine, butter, leaf, or iceberg, washed and dried

Macerated onions (see pages 29, 31, and 108), a couple of forkfuls

Salsa verde (see page 36), a couple of spoonfuls

1 Prep: Toast your buns, if desired. If your cutlets aren't just-fried, briefly reheat them in a hot pan or toaster oven.

2 Fry your eggs: Heat a drizzle of oil in a reliably nonstick skillet over medium-high. Fry your eggs the way you like them. We prefer ours crispy on the bottom and runny on the top, providing a mix of textures and creating a sort of egg-yolk sauce for the sandwich.

3 Assemble and serve: Spread a little mayo or pink sauce on the buns, then layer the cutlets, lettuce, egg, macerated onions, and salsa verde. Devour with several napkins on hand.

BRICKED CHICKEN

If you want a quick, juicy, crispy chicken dinner so good it will satisfy a fried chicken craving—without all the fuss, mess, or time—you want to make this Bricked Chicken. It's particularly delicious served immediately off the pan, when the skin is crackling and the meat is hot and juicy. But, it's also delicious cold, served on salads or sandwiches, or on its own.

Cooking under a brick—or, *al mattone* in Italian—is one of the oldest methods of cooking chicken. Its origins lie in the Etruscan civilization of ancient Italy (c. 500 BCE), where cooks weighed down whole birds in order to flatten them out to ensure even cooking and a crispy skin. We love the method for grilling whole chickens, but it also works really well for chicken thighs. To make things even easier, you don't even need a brick! A heavy pan wrapped in foil works best.

Serves 4 to 6

Gluten free

Equipment: A brick wrapped in foil, or a heavy skillet (such as cast iron wrapped in foil) that is a bit smaller than the frying pan you'll cook in.

INGREDIENTS

Chicken thighs, 6 to 8 bone-in, skin-on (or, a good butcher can debone the thighs for you—but be sure the skin stays; that's key!)

<u>Salt</u>

Black pepper

<u>Olive oil</u>, or substitute <u>neutral oil</u>

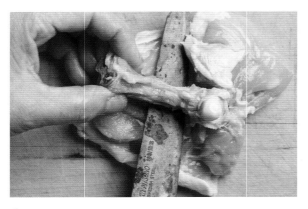

1 **Debone and season the chicken:** Lay one thigh on a <u>cutting board</u>, skin-side down. Feel around for the bone; there will only be one. Take a fairly narrow, sharp <u>knife</u> and carefully slide it along the length of the bone, exposing the bone as you cut the meat away from it. Then, slide the knife under the bone, starting in the center and cutting it free from the meat as neatly as possible. You may have to work around each end of the bone, cutting and wriggling it free from the meat. Save the bones for chicken <u>stock</u>. Season both sides of the chicken with a light sprinkle of salt and a little crack of freshly ground pepper.

2 **Pan-fry the first side:** Set a large <u>skillet</u> (not the brick/pan) over medium-high heat and drizzle in a couple teaspoons of olive oil. Once hot but not smoking—30 to 60 seconds—place the chicken thighs in the pan, skin-side down. (Unless your pan is enormous, you'll need to work in two batches.) Immediately place the foil-wrapped brick/pan on top of the thighs. You want there to be room for steam to evaporate off the skillet, so the brick/pan shouldn't cover the entire surface of the thighs in the skillet. (Move the brick/pan around periodically so it has a chance to flatten out each thigh equally.)

3 **Flip and finish the second side:** After the thighs are nearly cooked through—about 6 to 10 minutes, depending on size—remove the brick/pan. (You can tell they are ready to flip when about three-quarters of the flesh has changed to an opaque, whitish color, rather than dark pink). Flip the chicken and cook the second side without the brick/pan for another few minutes. When they seem done, you can stick an instant-read thermometer into the thickest part of the thickest thigh and see if it comes up to 165°F. Or, slice into one and check the color. If the meat is opaque (not pink and translucent, as it was raw), and the juices "run clear" (aren't bloody, that is), they're done. If not, pop it back in the skillet for another minute or two, then test it again.

BRICKED SALMON IN BROTHY RICE

Cooking poultry under a brick is reasonably common, since the weight helps flatten out an otherwise uneven piece of meat, but the technique also works well for skin-on fish, especially salmon, which has a fat layer that renders nicely under the weight. The result is a silky piece of fish with a spectacularly crispy layer of skin. Crispy salmon skin is prized in many parts of Asia, where it's served many ways, including with the fish itself, in sushi rolls, and even as snacks. Think of it like a fish-skin chip, or fish-skin bacon, only way more delicious than that sounds. We swear.

In this dish, we use the brick technique to cook up a lovely piece of fish that we like to serve with rice and a light broth. The recipe illustrates overlapping cultural and culinary traditions, and for us it conjures childhood memories: Part of our mom's true genius in the kitchen is looking in the fridge, seeing two leftover bites of one thing, one bite of another, and a little bit of something that might seem to us perhaps a touch past its prime, and then whipping it up into a brilliant lunch. (Like the time she used up the last bit of rice and the only things remaining in the fridge at the end of a vacation to whip up what became one of our favorite dishes. A few leftover green beans, a stray radish, the pickle juice and one remaining pickle in a jar, and a few stray pieces of romaine, and voilà—rice salad in lettuce boats!)

Along those lines, one of the most simple, comforting meals we grew up with was what we called "brothy rice." We'd just put some leftover rice, already-cooked veggies, a little leftover meat or fish, and maybe some kimchi or other little side dishes (*banchan*, in Korean) in a bowl, then pour some boiling water, tea, or a light broth over it all. To us, it's a hybrid of the Korean "dish" *sungnyung*, hot barley tea over the marvelously scorched rice (*nurungji*) stuck to the bottom of a rice pot toward the end of a meal, and the wonderful Japanese *ochazuke*, meaning "tea submerge" and popularly made with green tea. Our version here is more akin to a lovely ochazuke you might find at a good Japanese restaurant, made with a fine piece of salmon we've cooked under a "brick."

• • •

Serves 3 to 4

For a gluten-free version, use tamari or GF soy sauce

Equipment: A brick wrapped in foil, or a heavy skillet (such as cast iron wrapped in foil) that is a bit smaller than the frying pan you'll cook in.

Optional Prep

The salmon can be cooked up to 2 days in advance. The marvelous crispiness of the skin will be lost, but the fish will be equally lovely. To re-crisp the skin, you could remove it from the fish and broil it briefly in the oven or toaster oven.

Time permitting, you could also wrap the salted, *uncooked* salmon tightly in plastic wrap, and allow it to rest in the refrigerator for up to 2 days. This will gently cure it and enhance its flavor.

Variation

The basic idea behind our brothy rice (and Japanese ochazuke) is simply that you put rice and other good stuff—like cooked meat, fish, or veggies—in a bowl, then pour over some hot tea (cha) or broth (dashi), and top it with a sprinkle of something pretty and delicious like crumbled seaweed, sliced scallions, toasted sesame seeds, or chili flakes. Once you've got that basic concept down—and of course you do, it's so simple!—you're ready to invent all sorts of your own variations. And if you want to make it a balanced, one-bowl meal, you can try adding any or all of the following: sautéed spinach or other greens, crumbled crispy rice crackers, minced ume-boshi plums, pickled cucumbers, sliced radishes, a drizzle of soy sauce, and a drop of sesame oil or chili oil. If you have leftover cooked fish and want to try the brothy rice (aka "water rice" or ochazuke) without the show-stopping bricked salmon, go for it. You'll be embracing the dish's humble roots.

INGREDIENTS

Fresh salmon, 1 pound (preferably wild king salmon), cut into 3 or 4 individual portions

Salt (preferably sea salt)

Chicken broth, 4 to 6 cups (see page 40), or substitute dashi, green tea, barley tea, or similar

Soy sauce (optional)

Short-grain white rice, about 2 cups cooked (reheated, if necessary)

Seaweed-sesame sprinkle, a few pinches per bowl (a big pinch of crumbled toasted seaweed, a medium pinch of toasted black or white sesame seeds, and a tiny pinch of sugar and dried chili flakes—or use store-bought *furikake* or *shichimi togarashi*, two Japanese sesame sprinkles)

Chives, a very small bunch, cut into 1-inch pieces (or substitute thinly sliced scallions)

1 Season the salmon: Sprinkle a light, even layer of salt on both sides and all edges of the fish.

2 Prepare the broth: Heat your broth, then lightly season it with a pinch of salt and a small drizzle of soy sauce (for extra flavor). Taste the broth. It should be mild but pleasantly savory. If it's too salty, add a bit of water; too bland, add a bit of soy sauce. Keep warm (but not boiling) while you cook the fish.

3 Cook the fish: Heat a cast-iron skillet or other heavy-bottomed pan over high heat for about 1 minute; the pan should be very hot. Place the fish skin-side down, and set your foil-wrapped brick/pan on top, which will ensure that the skin crisps up from even, close contact with the pan. Reduce the heat to medium and cook for 2 to 3 minutes. (You may have to move the brick/pan around to ensure each piece of fish is equally flattened.) Remove the brick/pan to check the fish. Use a thin spatula to gently lift it and check the salmon skin, making sure it's not burning. It should be dark brown and crispy but not blackened. Also check the flesh, which should be opaque, indicating doneness on the outside. Flip the fish over, turn off the heat, and allow it to cook gently on the second side, uncovered, for 1 to 3 minutes more, depending on the thickness of the fillets. (High-quality salmon is delicious cooked medium, which means still light pink and somewhat translucent in the center, but it's also very forgiving—which is to say, delicious slightly undercooked and even slightly overcooked.)

4 Assemble and serve: Put a scoop of hot rice in the center of each bowl. Then, set a piece of salmon on top, skin-side up. Carefully pour in enough broth to fill the bowl about halfway, trying not to get the skin wet. Put a few pinches of the sesame-seaweed sprinkle on top, along with a few pinches of chives. Serve piping hot.

Bricked Duck Breast Lettuce Wraps

Though it takes a bit of time, this is a remarkably simple recipe, especially considering how delicious and impressive it is. We take a cue from one of our favorite indulgent dishes, Peking duck, which is eaten with hoisin sauce and sliced cucumbers and scallions in thin rice-flour crepes or fluffy *bao* buns (like the ones in our Soy-Braised Pork Belly Bao, page 187). But here we use simple-to-cook duck breasts and crisp lettuce wraps for a refreshing and interactive meal that works as well for a weeknight dinner as it does for a party. It's delicious—and who doesn't love a little do-it-your-way at the dinner table?

• • •

Serves 4 to 6, but it's easy to scale up or down. If the duck breasts are small, you could count on one per person; for average to large duck breasts, count on one-half to three-fourths per person.

Gluten free

Equipment: A brick wrapped in foil, or a heavy skillet (such as cast iron wrapped in foil) that is a bit smaller than the frying pan you'll cook in.

INGREDIENTS

Duck breasts, 4

Salt

Black pepper

Five-spice powder, about 1 teaspoon, plus a sprinkle (store-bought or homemade)

Scallions, 2 or 3

Cucumbers, 1 to 3, preferably a seedless variety (use 3 if they are small, like Persian cucumbers, or 1 if they are long, like English cucumbers)

Lettuce, 1 large or 2 to 3 small heads (try Little Gems, romaine hearts, Bibb lettuce, and green- or red-leaf lettuce, which are mild and crispy and big enough to use as wraps)

Fresh cilantro, 1 bunch (or substitute tender mint springs or radish sprouts)

Cooked rice, 2 to 3 cups (short-grain white rice and short-grain brown rice are especially delicious here)

Hoisin sauce

Asian hot sauce

Kimchi or other pickles (optional)

Variations

Try mixing it up by season and preference. In the spring and summer, we love it with all things fresh and crispy: green herbs, scallions, snap peas, cucumbers, lightly blanched or sautéed green beans. In the fall and winter, we sauté—in a little sesame oil and salt—thinly sliced vegetables, depending on what's in season: onions, zucchini, red bell peppers, or maitake mushrooms.

Optional Prep

All of the accompaniments—the greens, herbs, cucumbers, and sauces—can be prepped 1 day in advance and refrigerated, and the duck breasts can be scored and seasoned up to 1 day in advance, covered loosely and refrigerated. Duck breast is quite delicious served cold, as well, so really, you could cook this whole meal in advance, which makes it a spectacular recipe for entertaining! The only thing we'd be sure to serve piping hot is the rice.

1 Score and season the duck: Carefully score the fat side of each duck breast, which will allow the fat to render (melt off) while cooking. Using a sharp knife, slice a crisscross pattern on the fat layer without cutting all the way through to the meat. Then season both sides with a little sprinkle of salt, pepper, and the five-spice powder, patting the seasoning into it. Let the breasts rest in the fridge, uncovered, fat-side up, until ready to cook. (If you have time, allow them to sit in the fridge for 1 to 2 hours, so the flavors can permeate the duck more fully.) Unlike many meats, which cook better when allowed to come to room temperature first, duck breasts are best cooked straight out of the fridge. The colder temperature will slow down the cooking, giving the fat time to render without overcooking the meat.

2 Prep the accompaniments: Slice the scallions and cucumbers into thin strips. Wash and spin the lettuce leaves and cilantro sprigs. Arrange them on a platter with the scallions and cucumbers and refrigerate until ready to serve.

3 Start cooking the duck: Heat a large cast-iron skillet (or other heavy-bottomed frying pan) on medium heat. As the skillet heats up, gently set the duck breasts, fat-side down, onto it. (No need to fully preheat the skillet.) Place your foil-wrapped brick/pan on top of the duck, its weight flattening the breasts so the fat renders more readily and the meat cooks more evenly. After 2 to 3 minutes, reduce the heat to medium-low. As the breasts cook, move the brick/pan around so each piece gets flattened out equally. After 10 minutes, lift up the brick/pan and start checking for doneness. The fat should be deep golden brown and largely rendered off, leaving behind only a fairly thin, crispy layer. The meat may still look raw and dark pink on top, but it should feel fairly firm to the touch, and the edges should be starting to turn grayish brown.

4 Finish cooking: Remove the brick/pan and flip each breast, cooking the second side for an additional 4 to 6 minutes. If the breasts are thick and rounded, and the sides still look dark pink and raw, use tongs to roll the sides of each breast on the hot pan, cooking the outer edges briefly (see Tips). Small duck breasts should cook in about 15 minutes total; large breasts may take as long as 20 minutes total.

5 Rest, then slice: Remove the cooked breasts and place them fat-side up on a plate to rest for about 5 minutes. (Don't skip this step! The heat and juices need to redistribute, ensuring the breasts are more moist and evenly cooked. If you don't let it rest before slicing, the color will be less even and the juices will run out when you slice it.) Thinly slice on a <u>cutting board</u>. Ideally, the duck breast will be a medium-light pink all the way through (see Tips).

6 Serve: Arrange the sliced duck breasts on a platter and serve along with hot rice, your greens platter, hoisin and hot sauces, and, if you like, some kimchi or other pickles to be enjoyed on the side. To assemble the lettuce wraps, place a little bit of sauce in a lettuce cup, along with a little bit of rice, a slice or two of duck, and some herbs, scallions, and cucumbers.

Tips

As with steak, judging when the duck breasts are done will take some practice and experience. It will also depend on how rare or well-cooked you like them. Duck is traditionally served medium-rare, like red meat. If you find yours are too rare for your liking, you can always pop them back on the pan to cook them a little more. Also, some duck breasts are naturally more tender than others. Always taste your first cooked slice. If it's a little tough, be sure to slice the rest as thinly as possible. A sharp <u>knife</u> is key.

Rendered duck fat is a highly prized ingredient that can elevate many fried and sautéed dishes. Duck-fat fried <u>potatoes</u> are inexplicably delicious—significantly more savory and cravable than those fried in vegetable oil, but not at all "ducky" tasting. It can also be used in combination with vegetable oil to sauté Asian greens, especially when it has a hint of Asian flavors already, like the <u>five-spice-powder</u>-infused fat that renders off of these duck breasts. So, while it's still thin and warm, spoon or pour the rendered fat into a clean jar, and store it in your refrigerator until the next time you sauté some baby bok choy or napa cabbage. (It will keep for up to 6 months.)

Asian-Style Chicken and Vegetable Skewers

Skewered food, cooked over a fire, exists in countless cultures around the world. It's no wonder: It's a perfectly logical way to cook and serve dainty little pieces of meat and vegetables, it's infinitely variable, and it's fun to eat. This Asian-style skewer recipe is one of the simplest around. The ingredients are simply prepared, grilled nearly naked until lightly charred, then brushed with a simple citrus-soy glaze inspired by the flavors of Japanese ponzu sauce and Korean bulgogi marinade. Serve as an impressive appetizer or with rice for a complete meal.

• • •

Serves 3 or 4 as a meal;
5 or 6 as an appetizer

For a gluten-free version, use tamari in place of soy sauce; for a vegan version, skip the chicken

Equipment: Charcoal or gas grill; bamboo skewers

INGREDIENTS

CITRUS-SOY GLAZE
Mirin, ½ cup

Soy sauce, ½ cup (low-sodium, if you have it)

Brown sugar, 1 tablespoon

Meyer lemon or yuzu, 1 medium fruit, zest and juice (or substitute a lemon, lime, or orange, or ¼ cup any citrus juice)

Ginger, 2 or 3 slices fresh (each about the size of a quarter)

SKEWERS
Small peppers, 10 to 12, washed (shishito, Padrón, or Jimmy Nardellos—all flavor-packed and not-typically-spicy varieties that are great on the grill; or use mini bell peppers.)

Okra (optional), 10 to 12 small

Scallions, 1 bunch, white/light green parts only

Asparagus, ½ bunch, tough bottom ends trimmed (opt for fatter, rather than skinnier, shoots)

King trumpet mushrooms, 4 or 5, cleaned (or shiitake, chanterelle, or maitake)

Salt

Black pepper

Olive oil, a couple teaspoons

Chicken thighs, 1 pound boneless, skinless (or 1½ pounds bone-in; reserve the bones for stock)

FOR SERVING
Rice (optional), cooked short-grain white rice (or brown rice, if you prefer)

Lemon wedges (optional)

Spicy sesame sprinkle (optional), such a Japanese *shichimi togarashi*

Tip
When skewering very thin items like skinny asparagus spears, it can help to use two skewers in parallel, spaced a tiny bit apart. This makes them less likely to fall off and easier to flip.

Variations
You can skewer pretty much anything, but other particularly good options include fresh snap peas, zucchini, rectangles of tofu, little squares of mochi (Asian rice cakes), little hunks of bacon, and bacon-wrapped bundles of enoki mushrooms.

1 Prep for grilling and make the glaze: First, soak the bamboo skewers in warm water for at least 30 minutes (which makes them less likely to char or catch fire while grilling). Bearing in mind the amount of time your particular grill will need to preheat to medium-high, light it according to the manufacturer's instructions so it is ready to go when you are. Combine all of the citrus-soy glaze ingredients in a small saucepan; stir and bring to a boil over high heat. Reduce the heat to low and simmer for about 10 minutes, or until slightly thickened.

2 Prep and skewer the vegetables: Leave small peppers and okra whole. Cut scallions and asparagus into 1- to 2-inch-long pieces. If the mushrooms are thick, slice in half lengthwise. Depending on the size and shape of the vegetable, arrange a few onto one or two skewers (see Tip) but save the scallions for the chicken skewers. Brush lightly with olive oil, sprinkle with salt and pepper, and set aside until ready to grill.

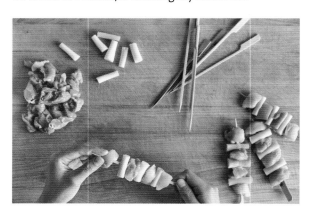

3 Prep and skewer the chicken: Cut the chicken into 1-inch chunks and skewer with a piece of scallion in between each piece. The onions will lend flavor and will help the chicken cook more evenly. Brush lightly with olive oil, sprinkle with salt, and set aside until ready to grill. (Put in the refrigerator if not using immediately.)

4 Grill and serve: Over medium-high heat, grill the skewers, turning over once or twice, until everything is lightly charred. Brush a light coating of the glaze on top, and continue cooking until the chicken is cooked through, about 3 to 5 minutes per side, depending on the grill's temperature and skewers' distance from the heat source. Check for doneness by removing one of the largest pieces of chicken, cutting or breaking it in half, and ensuring the interior texture and color is uniform. Be careful not to overcook. (The vegetables should still hold their shape, not become floppy.) Serve smoking hot!

CHEF RUSSELL MOORE'S
LAMB SKEWERS
WITH SPICY CARROT SALAD

We all have one—two if you're *super* lucky. A really great, totally unforgettable teacher. For Leah, that one was Russell Moore. She trained under Russ at Chez Panisse for many years, and so much of what she knows, she learned from him. Like us, Russ is half Korean, and maybe that's part of why we have similar palates and think about food in similar ways. But, it's possible Leah's palate and approach to food developed largely from his teaching. Russ never hesitated to take whatever time necessary to explain things when Leah had questions, and, above all else, he taught her that nothing is absolute. Ingredients and conditions constantly change, so you need to always taste and adjust—*(Serious) New Cook* Principle #2!—to roll with those changes. He also taught her the true value of maintaining the highest of standards when sourcing your ingredients—*(Serious) New Cook* Principle #1! Your food will simply taste better, and it will be better for your people and the planet.

After more than twenty-five years at Chez Panisse, Russ left to open a beautiful restaurant in Oakland, called Camino, featuring wood-fire cooking. Several years and one gorgeous cookbook later, he closed Camino and opened a little kebab shop called Kebabery. These lamb kebabs, related to the Middle Eastern kofta kebab, are Leah's favorite thing on the menu. We were thrilled when he offered the recipe, and charmed to read not strict instructions, but, true to his nature and his philosophy, little notes like "We serve them with a small spoon of pickled chili puree . . . you don't need to use chili if you don't want it, or you can use whatever you have on hand . . . we actually use a crazy combo of whatever we have on hand but just cilantro works fine! . . . You can skip the flatbread and lentils of course (ours is hella complicated!) or use pita." So, true to Russ's recommendations, make these kebabs and serve them how you like, with what you have. We can't resist his Spicy Carrot Salad, so we're including his recipe for that, as well. We also like to serve it with a dollop of plain yogurt and a pile of fresh parsley (which, you might be surprised to find, makes an instant "salad" when eaten together with the yogurt, carrots, and lamb).

• • •

Serves 4 to 6

Gluten free

Equipment: Gas or charcoal grill; flat bamboo skewers, soaked in water for at least 30 minutes

Ingredients

KEBABS

Ground lamb, 20 ounces (with some fat, but not crazy fatty because then they will catch on fire)

Yellow onion, ½ medium, grated on the medium holes of a box grater

Parsley, 2 bunches, washed, tough stems removed, 1 of the bunches roughly chopped

Mint, 1 bunch, picked and roughly chopped

Middle Eastern spices, 4 teaspoons (see Flavor Profiles, page 27)

Garlic, 4 medium cloves, minced

Sea salt, 1½ teaspoons

Olive oil, a small drizzle (or substitute neutral oil)

SPICY CARROT SALAD

Toasted sesame seeds, 1 teaspoon (white or black)

Caraway seeds, 1 teaspoon, toasted

Carrots, 3 large, peeled and grated on the medium holes of a box grater

Garlic, 1 small clove, minced

Medium hot chili flakes, big pinch (or substitute a smaller pinch of cayenne)

Olive oil

Salt

Lime, 1

FOR SERVING

Plain yogurt, a small bowlful

Chili flakes, for garnish (optional)

KEBABS

1 Make the meat mixture: In a large bowl, mix together the lamb, onion, chopped parsley, mint, spices, garlic, and salt using your hands. Combine thoroughly, but avoid overhandling the meat. If you smush it around too much, it will become tough.

2 Cook a tester: Make a small meatball from the meat mixture and flatten it (to cook faster). In a small frying pan, drizzle a bit of olive oil and cook the tester on both sides until done. Taste for seasoning. Does it need a little more salt? If so, sprinkle in some more and mix gently but quickly.

3 Form kebabs: Pressing a handful of meat around a flat bamboo skewer, form a sausage shape, then flatten it out just a bit. Repeat with all of the meat. They are best grilled rather quickly, so don't make them too thick.

4 Chill the kebabs: Chill them for 1 hour, if possible. (Meanwhile, make the Spicy Carrot Salad.) Weirdly, they work best if you cook them straight from the fridge, rather than bringing them to room temperature first (as you would do with many meats). If they are warm, they tend to overcook before they brown. Cold, they brown more nicely and stay on the stick better.

5 Grill the kebabs: Bearing in mind the amount of time your particular grill will need to preheat to medium-high (too hot will increase the chances of the kebabs catching fire), light it according to the manufacturer's instructions. When it's ready, grill the kebabs until they are nicely browned, just a few minutes per side. The kebabs are best cooked so they are browned on the outside but still a little pink inside.

SPICY CARROT SALAD

1 Prepare the spice mix: Roughly pound the sesame and caraway seeds (or roughly grind them in a spice/coffee grinder).

2 Make the salad: In a large bowl, toss the spice mix, carrots, garlic, and chili flakes with a good splash of olive oil, a big pinch of salt, and a couple squeezes of lime. Taste and adjust, with particular attention to the acid level and the seasoning, and let it sit for 30 minutes. Taste again and adjust accordingly. (Russ says, "I like it spicy, but it turns out a lot of people don't! I tend to not like it as limey as some folks. I'd rather get a lot of acid from the yogurt. But, what tastes delicious is really up to the person.") Serve with the kebabs, a big pile of the remaining parsley, a dollop of yogurt, and if you like it spicy, a pinch of chili flakes over everything.

SATAY SKEWERS
WITH PEANUT SAUCE

It's hard to pinpoint the precise origin of Southeast Asian satay, but many believe it evolved from the kebabs eaten by Middle Eastern traders in Indonesia in the early nineteenth century. There are many variations of satay, which today appears in numerous Southeast Asian cuisines. Most involve thinly sliced skewered beef or chicken that's marinated before grilling, then served with a spicy peanut sauce. Satays are a really nice combination of sweet, salty, and pungent. Plate the skewers on a platter with some peanut sauce for dipping and some crisp, refreshing pickled cucumbers on the side, and you've got a perfect party appetizer.

• • •

Serves 8 to 10 as an appetizer, or 4 to 6 as a full meal when served with rice and a side vegetable

For a gluten-free version, use GF soy sauce or tamari

Time: 90 minutes, including minimum marinating time of 1 hour

Equipment: Gas or charcoal grill; bamboo skewers, preferably long ones, soaked in water for 30 minutes

INGREDIENTS

MARINATED MEAT

Beef flank steak, about 1½ pounds, thinly sliced into narrow strips (see Tip), or use beef sirloin, London broil, chicken breasts or thighs, or tofu, if you'd like

Soy sauce, 2 tablespoons

Fish sauce, 2 tablespoons

Brown sugar, 3 tablespoons

Lemongrass, 1 to 2 stalks, white part only, cut into ½-inch lengths

Shallots, 3, peeled and halved

Ginger, 1 thumb-size knob, peeled and thinly sliced

Garlic, 2 large cloves

Limes, 2, juiced

Coriander seed, 1 teaspoon

Neutral oil, ¼ cup

PEANUT SAUCE

Peanut butter, ½ cup all-natural

Fish sauce, 2 tablespoons

Brown sugar, 1 tablespoon

Limes, 2, juiced

Garlic, 1 small clove

Hot chili (optional), ½ teaspoon chili flakes, finely chopped fresh chili, or small spoonful **Asian hot sauce**, such as sambal or sriracha

FOR SERVING

Quick-pickled cucumbers (see page 35), for serving (optional)

Optional Prep

The marinade and pickled cucumbers can be made and stored in the fridge up to 2 days in advance. (In fact, the pickled cucumbers will benefit from the extra time.) The peanut sauce can be made and the meat can be marinated (and kept in the fridge) up to a few hours in advance.

Tip

To make slicing raw meat easier, place it in the freezer for 30 minutes first. Then, on a large cutting board, position the flank steak so the grain (the muscle fibers) run parallel to the bottom of the cutting board. Beginning on the right side (or left, if you're left-handed!), use a very sharp knife to slice the meat in long, thin strips from top to bottom, cutting across the grain. This will make the meat easier to chew.

1 Make the marinade: Place the sliced steak in a large resealable bag or a medium bowl. In a food processor with metal blade or a blender, combine all of the mairnade ingredients and process until everything is finely minced and well combined, then pour it over the meat and stir to coat. Marinate, refrigerated, for 1 to 3 hours.

2 Make the peanut sauce: In a small bowl, combine the peanut sauce ingredients. Stir with a fork until well combined. If necessary to thin it out to a spoonable consistency, add a bit more lime juice or a splash of water.

3 Skewer the meat and grill: Preheat a grill to high heat, according to the manufacturer's directions. As it preheats, thread one piece of meat onto each long skewer, leaving a few inches on one end for a handle. Grill for 3 to 4 minutes per side, just until charred and lightly caramelized.

4 Serve: Place the skewers on a platter, and serve with the peanut sauce and pickled cucumbers (optionally), on the side.

BRAISED PORK SOFT TACOS

Braising—which is roasting in a bath of delicious liquid—is a super valuable technique to master. It's like a cross between poaching (cooking something fully submerged in liquid) and roasting (cooking something in hot air), with the benefits of both: food that is richly browned, yet moist and tender. It takes some planning and time, but most of the cooking is hands-off. A basic braised meat recipe like this one here is definitely something to have in your repertoire, as it will get you three-quarters of the way to several delicious meals for the week. You'll be able to whip up some great tacos, like we do here, or any number of sandwiches or pasta dishes, including the recipe that follows. You can also serve it over mashed potatoes, polenta, or rice, or fry it up alongside some eggs and hash browns.

• • •

Serves 3 to 4 with enough leftover pork for a second meal (such as the Braised Pork with Spaghetti on page 185) or 6 to 8 for one meal

Gluten free

Time: Overnight for preseasoning (highly recommended), a couple hours to rest at room temperature, and 3 to 4 hours of cooking time

Equipment: A Dutch oven, enameled braiser, or low stockpot—any medium-large, medium-height, oven-safe pan/pot with a lid

INGREDIENTS

Bone-in pork shoulder, 4 to 5 pounds (or substitute 3- to 4-pound boneless shoulder; see Ingredient Note)

Salt

Black pepper

Olive oil, about 2 teaspoons

Onions, 2 medium yellow, red, or white, peeled and sliced

Carrot, 1, peeled and sliced

Celery, 1 rib, sliced

Parsley stems, 1 bunch (save the leaves for another use)

Garlic, 5 or 6 large cloves, peeled and smashed

Bay leaf, 1

Orange peel (optional), a finger-length piece

Chicken stock, 2 cups (preferably homemade, see page 40), plus more as needed (or substitute water)

Red wine vinegar, ½ cup (or substitute white wine vinegar)

FOR SERVING

Corn tortillas, warmed individually in a pan with a bit of oil or steamed in a stack, wrapped in a damp cloth napkin

Coleslaw (or substitute diced white onion and chopped fresh cilantro)

Limes, 4 or 5, quartered

Hot sauce (optional)

Optional Prep

Because the timing of the pork can be difficult to judge, braising the pork ahead of time—even a day or two before you need it—then reheating it to finish your dish, whether it's to serve as tacos, like we do here, or with with spaghetti—can make things easier.

Tip

When braising, choose your spices thoughtfully. We braise this pork with minimal spice so the leftovers can be used in various preparations, like these tacos, arepa sandwiches (page 63), or pasta (page 185), each with slightly different flavor profiles. Alternatively, you can add a bunch of spices right off the bat to take it in a more specific direction.

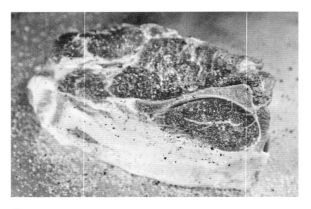

1 **<u>Preseason</u> the pork:** The night before you want to braise the pork, season it liberally with salt and pepper, and refrigerate it, covered. (A big resealable bag works well for this, as does a big bowl covered with plastic wrap.) The next day, take the pork out of the refrigerator 2 to 3 hours before cooking it.

2 **Sauté the mirepoix:** Preheat your oven to 350°F. Drizzle the olive oil into a braising pot over high heat, and add the onions, carrot, and celery (a combination called mirepoix) and sauté until just wilted, about 2 minutes. Add the parsley stems, garlic, bay leaf, and orange peel (if using), and give it a stir.

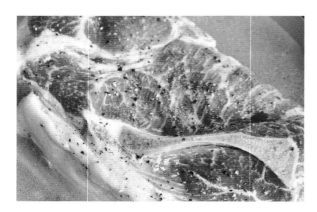

3 **Start braising:** Nestle the roast into the mirepoix, then pour the stock and vinegar around the roast. (Avoid pouring it directly onto the roast and rinsing off the seasoning.) Two-thirds of the roast should be submerged in liquid. If it isn't, add more stock or water. (You want to maintain close to this level of liquid throughout the cooking process.) Bring to a boil, then cover and place in the oven. Flip every 30 minutes or so. After about 90 minutes, remove the lid and continue cooking, uncovered. If the liquid cooks down to just halfway up the roast, add more stock or water to keep the meat moist. Keep cooking, flipping, and testing for doneness every 30 minutes.

4 **Finish the roast:** When the meat is golden brown, fork tender (see Tips), and you see it naturally separating from the bone, it's ready. Use tongs and/or a large spoon to remove the roast to a large platter or <u>cutting board</u>. Using a ladle, skim off and discard most of the fat that has risen to the top of the pot. (An old milk carton is a good place for this fat, as you don't want to pour it down the drain!) Set aside the braising liquid to use in your finished dish or to store with the leftover meat. It's like liquid gold—full of flavor—so keep it.

5 **Serve:** Chop, dice, or pull apart the meat—or use a combination method—and transfer to a warmed bowl. Ladle some of the hot braising liquid over it, then taste and adjust. Does it need another pinch of salt or crack of black pepper? You know what to do. Want it spicy? Add some ground chiles. Want it brighter? A squeeze of lime or even orange (use the one you stole the peel from!) would be nice. When it's delicious, serve in warm corn tortillas topped with a bit of tangy coleslaw and some lime quarters, or with a five-finger pinch of diced onion and fresh cilantro, and a side of hot sauce. Store any left-over pork in the reserved braising liquid (which you can strain through a mesh strainer in order to remove the vegetable pulp) in a sealed container in the fridge, where it will await your next dish.

Ingredient Note

Pork "butt" and "shoulder" are terms sometimes used interchangeably. In addition to the fact that butchers and cooks from different regions use slightly different meat-cut terminology, it's a little confusing because they both come from adjacent areas at the top of a pig's front legs/shoulders—not the hind or bottom as you might assume. Typically, a bone-in cut will yield a juicier, tastier, more tender roast, but it will take longer to cook. If you can't find a bone-in pork shoulder roast, you can certainly use a boneless one. Either way, we recommend trying to get the fattiest one you can, bearing in mind that most of the fat renders off during the long cooking time, leaving behind the tastiest, juiciest meat. In fact, if the boneless roast at the butcher shop happens to look very well-marbled (that is, with lighter colored streaks of fat running through the darker colored meat, like veins in natural marble), and the bone-in roast looks very lean, you might opt for the boneless.

Tips

Braising in electric pressure cookers or slow cookers is another great way to cook a big hunk of meat like this. It can yield the most reliably tender meat and, in the case of pressure cookers, will be done in a fraction of the time (about 15 minutes per pound, plus a natural release). Because all of the cooking is done with the lid on, it's important to first brown the outside of the meat in a frying pan or, if your device allows (as with an Instant Pot), right in the pot. Doing so will significantly deepen the meat's flavors and will mimic the browning that happens when braising in the oven.

Testing for doneness is important. Ideally, the roast will cook in 3 to 4 hours. It'll be easy to tell, too: When you stick a fork in it, the meat will be super juicy and so tender it will fall apart. If you stick your fork into the meat and it feels firm or tough, requiring some pressure to insert it, you know it needs more time—and possibly more liquid. Be sure to maintain enough liquid to submerge two-thirds of the roast. Total cooking time will depend on a variety of factors, including the cut of meat, how cold or warm it was when you started, and your cooking vessel.

SPAGHETTI WITH BRAISED PORK RAGU

It's hard to find something more comforting and satisfying than a big, hearty bowl of pasta—especially when it's as rich, meaty, and Parmesan-y as this one. This is almost like a Bolognese, which is a classic Italian meat ragu, but because it uses leftover braised pork shoulder, it's as quick as it is delicious. Basically, if you start with some delicious braised pork, you really can't go wrong. You'll have your pasta lovers (and who isn't one?) licking the bowl. Add this recipe to your repertoire, and you'll never go back to jarred sauce again.

• • •

Serves 4 to 6

For a gluten-free version, use GF pasta

INGREDIENTS

Spaghetti, 1 pound uncooked (or pasta of your choice)

Salt

Olive oil, 1 or 2 tablespoons

Onion, 1 small or ½ large red or yellow, sliced

Canned whole tomatoes in juice, one 28-ounce can (or substitute 5 or 6 delicious fresh tomatoes; see Tips)

Garlic, 2 cloves, minced

Braised pork, about 1 pound, diced or shredded, as well as about 1 cup of reserved braising liquid (see recipe on page 181)

Chili flakes (optional), a couple pinches

Black pepper

Fresh parsley, marjoram, or oregano, ½ bunch, leaves picked off and roughly chopped

Parmesan, grated, for serving

Variation

You could easily skip the tomatoes altogether and just add more braising liquid.

Tip

You can use fresh tomatoes instead of canned, if you have some good ones. Remember *(Serious) New Cook* Principle #1: Use good ingredients. That means, don't bother trying it with out-of-season, un-delicious tomatoes. You can also use fresh, frozen tomatoes (a great way to stock up when tomatoes are in season—just toss some whole tomatoes into a bag and freeze them!). Just add the whole tomatoes to the pan after you've sautéed the onions and garlic, then carefully pull off the tomato skins after a minute of cooking. They can then be crushed right in the pan—or "diced" with a pair of cooking shears or a sharp metal spatula—after they soften.

Tips

Reserve your pasta water—the starchy water left over after cooking your noodles. This is a valuable trick for many excellent pasta dishes. Sometimes, when you add the noodles to the sauce, they quickly absorb the liquids in the pan and would benefit from a little "loosening up"—especially if it's a "dry" sauce, such as sautéed vegetables and meat, without a lot of saucy liquid. Adding a bit of pasta water simultaneously loosens and thickens the sauce, in a manner of speaking. This can be useful when you're doing the final adjustments on a dish and is also super helpful for reheating (including when you want to dish out seconds and find that the pasta "tightened up" as it cooled). This particular recipe results in a lot of sauce from the tomatoes and braising liquid, but reserving a cup of pasta water is always good practice. So, if you use a colander to strain the cooked noodles, be sure to first scoop out a big cup of pasta water, setting it aside to use later, as needed.

Heat your bowls so your guests can enjoy their meal warm, from start to finish. The easiest ways to do this are to pop them in the microwave for a minute or two or run them under hot water (and dry them) before plating—or put them on a warming rack, if you're lucky enough to have one.

1 Cook the pasta: Heat a large pot of water over high heat, adding enough salt for it to taste as salty as seawater. (Meanwhile, start the sauce!) When the water comes to a boil, cook the pasta al dente (Italian for "to the tooth," which means tender but still a tad firm), or according to the directions on the package of pasta. Before you drain the pasta, scoop out at least 1 cup of pasta cooking water, in case you need it for the sauce (see Tips).

2 Make the sauce: Heat some olive oil over medium-high heat in a large sauté pan or stock pot. Sauté the onion until it is almost cooked through (translucent and tender, but not soft and mushy), 7 to 8 minutes. Meanwhile, scoop out the tomatoes using a slotted spoon (reserving the juice in the can) and chop them on a cutting board. After the onion is tender, reduce the heat to medium and add the garlic. Sauté for 1 more minute, stirring constantly and being careful not to let it brown. Then, add the diced tomatoes and cook it all down for a few minutes to concentrate the flavors before adding the reserved tomato juice.

3 Finish the sauce: After everything has simmered together for about 5 minutes, add the pork, along with a cup or ladleful of the braising liquid, a pinch of the chili flakes, and a crack or two of black pepper. Taste and adjust. Could it use a little more depth? If so, add another spoonful or two of the braising liquid. A little kick from additional chili flakes? A bit more salt and pepper? Add the fresh herbs and let simmer for a few minutes to allow the flavors to meld.

4 Finish the dish: Add the cooked pasta to the pan with the sauce. (If your timing is just right, you can scoop out the pasta and put it directly into the saucepan, saving you from washing a colander.) Stir it all together and taste one more time to adjust for seasoning. If it's not quite saucy and loose enough, add a bit more braising liquid or some of the pasta-cooking water (see Tips). Place into warmed pasta bowls (see Tips), grate some Parmesan on top, and serve immediately.

Soy-Braised Pork Belly Bao

On the streets of Taiwan, one of the most popular snacks is called *gua bao*, or pork belly bun. Made with fall-apart-tender braised pork, pickled mustard greens, and crushed peanuts, it's one of our all-time-favorite foods to eat when we visit Taiwan. Bao, which by itself refers to a bun typically filled with some kind of meat and garnishes, can be stuffed with any number of things. Bao have gained popularity in American cities like New York and Los Angeles, thanks to celebrity chefs Eddie Huang of Bao Haus and David Chang of Momofuku, among others.

This recipe draws on the traditional and the contemporary bao we love. Give it a try, then start dreaming up your own variations.

• • •

Makes 4 to 6

For a gluten-free version, use GF soy sauce or tamari

Time: About 2 to 3 hours (mostly unattended)

Complexity: Don't let the long ingredient list deter you. This recipe is reasonably simple.

Ingredient Notes

Folded Chinese steamed buns, also called folded *mantou* or *gua bao* buns, are exceptionally pillowy and slightly sweet. Shaped like an oval disc and folded in half, it is the same dough you might find on the outside of a fluffy Chinese barbecue pork bun. If you're lucky enough to have a Chinatown nearby, you can find them fresh at a Chinese or Taiwanese bakery, or frozen at many Asian supermarkets. If you're up for the challenge, you can definitely make them at home, too! It's worth looking up some instructional videos to get a sense of the texture expected at each stage, as working with yeast has a bit of a learning curve. It takes a little practice, but once you get the hang of it, you'll be whipping them up in a snap and inventing all sorts of new ways to eat them!

Dark soy sauce is a Chinese ingredient that is darker, thicker, and, due to the addition of sugar, a bit sweet, unlike regular soy sauce. As a substitute, you can use 1 tablespoon molasses or dark corn syrup, plus 1 tablespoon regular soy sauce (in addition to the ½ cup already called for).

INGREDIENTS

Pork belly, 1½- to 2-pound slab, uncut (preferably with skin on)

Salt

Black pepper

Five-spice powder, 1 tablespoon (store-bought or homemade, see page 26)

Neutral oil

Onion, 1 large or 2 small yellow or white, peeled and sliced

Garlic, 4 cloves, peeled and smashed

Ginger, 1-inch knob, peeled and sliced

Orange peel, 1½- to 2-inch strip, about a finger's width

Soy sauce, ½ cup

Sugar, about ¼ cup white or brown

Chinese cooking wine, ¼ cup (or substitute dry sherry or sake)

Dark soy sauce, 2 tablespoons

Folded Chinese steamed buns (folded *mantou* or *gua bao* buns), 4 to 6, store-bought (see Tip; or use soft potato buns or fluffy dinner rolls)

Hoisin sauce, a few teaspoons

Asian hot sauce (optional)

Cucumbers, 1 large or 2 small, fresh or quick-pickled (see page 35), sliced

Scallions, 2, sliced on the diagonal

Cilantro, 4 to 6 sprigs, washed and dried

Crushed roasted peanuts (optional), a few teaspoons (or substitute crushed roasted cashews or almonds)

1 Preseason the pork belly: Give the slab a light sprinkle of salt and pepper and the Chinese five-spice powder. Allow it to rest at room temperature while you do the next step, or up to 1 hour.

2 Sauté the aromatics: Add a light drizzle of oil to a lidded stockpot, high-sided frying pan, or braising pot set over medium-high heat. (It's best if it's just big enough to hold the pork belly plus 3 or 4 cups of braising liquid.) Sauté the sliced onion until wilted. Then, add the garlic and ginger, and sauté for another minute. Reduce the heat, if necessary, to avoid browning beyond light golden.

3 **Braise the pork belly:** Add the orange peel, soy sauce, sugar, cooking wine, and dark soy sauce, along with 2 cups water. Give it a stir and then a taste. It should be well balanced between sweet and salty. (In this dish, the braising liquid won't be consumed, so it should be assertively flavored.) Add a bit more water if it's overwhelmingly salty, or a bit more sugar or soy, for flavor and balance. Place the pork belly in the center, making sure the liquid comes at least two-thirds of the way up the sides. Add more water and/or soy, if needed. Bring it to a boil, then cover and reduce the heat to low. It will take, on average, 1½ to 2 hours (see Tip). Every 20 or 30 minutes, carefully turn the slab. Start checking for doneness after about 1 hour by sticking a fork or knife into the slab. If it goes in super easily, this indicates that the belly is very tender; remove from the heat and let it rest in the braising liquid for at least 10 minutes or up to 1 hour. (If you won't be using it by then, refrigerate, covered, until ready for use.)

4 **Prep the buns:** If you are using store-bought folded mantou buns, steam them for about 2 minutes or so, just until fluffy and soft. Alternatively, place them on a plate in the microwave, along with a ramekin full of water, and microwave on high for 30 seconds. (If you are using American potato buns, soft dinner rolls, or similar, skip this step.)

5 **Cut the meat:** One approach is to use a very sharp knife, cutting the belly into slices ¼ to ½ inch thick. Another approach—more commonly used in Taiwan, where gua bao originated—is to prep the buns first and then simply reach into the pot with a pair of tongs, pinching at the tender belly to grab some meat, causing it to fall apart into small, succulent pieces (assuming you cooked it long enough!) that get stuffed into the prepared bun.

6 **Assemble and serve the bao:** Open each bun, being careful not to split them in two. Spread a thin layer of hoisin sauce (and hot sauce, if using) onto each. Then place a slice or two (or a couple tongfuls) of meat inside, along with a few cucumber slices, a handful of scallions, and a sprig of cilantro. Sprinkle on a half teaspoon or so of crushed peanuts, if using, then serve immediately.

Tip

Cooking time may vary quite a bit, depending on a number of factors, such as how thick the slab is, how fatty or lean it is, how much braising liquid you use, and more. Err on the side of a shorter cooking time, if you'd like to slice the belly; and on the side of longer cooking time if you'd prefer the meat to be fall-apart tender. Both approaches are delicious, though first-timers might prefer falling-apart tender.

Variations

Thinly sliced bricked duck breasts (page 169), hot or cold, make a great substitute for the pork belly.

The braised pork belly is also exceptionally good served over rice.

CHEF SOHUI KIM'S
BULGOGI LETTUCE WRAPS

Bulgogi, which means "fire meat," is perhaps the most well-known and well-loved Korean dish—in Korea and around the world. This terrific bulgogi recipe is adapted from Chef Sohui Kim's cookbook, *Korean Home Cooking.* We love this recipe because it tastes just like our mom's. Chef Sohui says that's because Korean cooking has so much to do with *sohn mat,* or "taste of the hands," and since she immigrated to the U.S. from Seoul, South Korea, in the same era our mom did, their sohn mat—and, in turn, ours—is similar. Everything at Insa, Chef Sohui's popular Korean BBQ restaurant in Brooklyn, New York, highlights her incredible sohn mat. If you're in New York City, make it a point to visit. After (or even during) a delicious dinner, you can enjoy their ultra-stylish private karaoke rooms!

If you've never been to a Korean barbecue restaurant, do yourself a favor and go if the opportunity ever arises. It's super fun, and the food is usually amazing. Typically, you'll find barbecue grills built into the center of the tables, with high-powered vents sucking out the smoke above or around them. With the help of an adept server, you get to grill your meat right at the table, eating it the instant it's done, smoking hot and juicy. Bulgogi is one of the meats you can order, as is *kalbi*—beef short ribs, either roll-cut or flanken-style—the other Korean barbecue favorite. The marinades are similar, which means you can use Chef Sohui's marinade, substituting kalbi for the sirloin, to make another really classic Korean barbecue dish.

Since bulgogi means "fire meat," it's no surprise that one of the best ways to cook it is on a scorching hot pan set over a charcoal fire—or even skewered and grilled. That said, the more common way to make it nowadays is to cook it on the stove in a hot skillet, like Chef Sohui does here. Her method achieves a perfect bit of char on the meat, while also creating enough saucy drippings—delectably sweet and savory—to drizzle over the rice.

Bulgogi can be served any number of ways: simply with rice and fresh greens (as suggested here), in a rice bowl (see the bibimbap recipe, page 195), in Korean tacos (made famous by chef Roy Choi's Los Angeles food truck, Kogi), or even cold and straight from the fridge.

• • •

Serves 6 to 8

For a gluten-free version, use tamari or GF soy sauce

Tip

Although this recipe serves 6 to 8, if you're serving it for 4, you'll have leftover meat, which is great to use for Bulgogi Bibimbap (page 195), Kimbap (page 139), and more! The recipe can also easily be halved or doubled.

Optional Prep

The marinade can be made a few days early, and the meat can be marinated overnight (or a few hours in advance) and refrigerated, as long as you reduce or skip the Asian pear and underlined onion (see Tip). We often double or triple the recipe and then freeze some of the uncooked meat right in its marinade. To freeze, put the marinated meat into a large zip-top freezer bag, carefully press out all of the air, and seal it. Then, flatten the bag out evenly and lay it flat to freeze. That way, when you want a quick and easy dinner, it's a snap to defrost.

Tip

Slicing the meat thinly is the traditional way with bulgogi. Tender cuts like sirloin and rib eye are very forgiving, but tougher (though exceptionally tasty) cuts like skirt and flank require a little more attention to make certain you've sliced thinly and across the grain. The easiest way to get the job done is to partially freeze the meat first (an hour or two will do the trick) and use a very sharp butcher's or chef's knife. Inspect the steak to see which way the "grains," or muscley fibers, are running, and then cut across them. The shorter those muscley fibers are after you've cut them, the more tender the meat will be. Two other options: Pound the meat thin with a meat mallet or use ground beef! It's less traditional, but equally tasty.

INGREDIENTS

Sugar, ⅓ cup

Asian pear, ½ small or ⅛ jumbo (which is how big they are at Korean markets!), peeled, cored, and cut into bite-size chunks (or substitute 1 tablespoon mirin or 1 tablespoon apple juice)

Garlic, 2 medium cloves, peeled

Ginger, ½-inch knob, peeled and sliced (do not substitute ginger powder)

Sesame oil, 1 tablespoon (preferably toasted)

Black pepper, 1 teaspoon ground or freshly cracked

Onion, 1 small or ½ medium white or yellow, peeled and sliced thinly from pole to pole

Soy sauce, ¼ to ½ cup (depending on how strong yours is)

Beef sirloin, 2 pounds, sliced very thinly (or use rib eye, skirt steak, flank steak, or even ground beef; see Tip)

Neutral oil

Scallions, ½ bunch, cleaned and cut into 2-inch pieces

FOR SERVING (OPTIONAL)
Rice, about 4 cups cooked short-grain white rice

Leaf lettuce and fresh leafy herbs, washed and arranged in a big bowl or platter

Asian hot sauces (such as *ssam jang* or *gochujang* sauce, which can be found online or at Korean markets)

Tip **Natural tenderizers, like Asian pear and fresh onion**, for example, have special enzymes that work like magic meat tenderizers. That's handy in this recipe, and it's especially useful when you're working with tougher cuts of meat, like skirt and flank. One tricky thing, though, is that if you use too much or let it marinate too long—especially on tender cuts like sirloin—the proteins in the meat may begin to fall apart, resulting in an oddly mushy texture. Like many natural ingredients, how it reacts in a recipe depends on the specific variety of Asian pear or onion, as well as how ripe it is. So, keep in mind the cut of meat you're using, and pay attention to the texture of your bulgogi. That way, you'll learn how you might want to use a little more or a little less of these natural tenderizers next time. And if you prefer to marinate the meat a day or even a few days in advance, skip the Asian pear and onion when you blend the marinade. Instead, toss some sliced onion into it after blending, for added flavor.

1 Make the marinade: In a blender, combine the sugar, Asian pear, garlic, ginger, sesame oil, black pepper, one-fourth of your sliced onions, and ¼ cup soy sauce. Blend on medium speed until smooth, then taste and adjust: It should have a very pleasing sweet, salty, garlicky flavor. If it doesn't taste abrasively salty, add up to ¼ cup more soy sauce, a little at a time as you continue to taste it.

2 Marinate the meat: Place the meat in a bowl or resealable bag and pour the marinade over the meat. Let it marinate for 30 minutes at room temperature. Meanwhile, you can cook the rice and prep the lettuces and herbs, if you're serving it *ssam*-style (as traditional Korean lettuce wraps).

3 Cook the meat: Heat a skillet or grill pan over high heat. Coat the bottom with a little oil, just enough so the beef won't stick. Then, add a single layer of meat so as to not crowd the pan. (You don't want the meat to steam.) Cook until charred on one side, about 2 to 3 minutes. Then flip and cook it to your desired degree of doneness. (Koreans typically cook bulgogi well-done.) Pour or scoop the cooked meat and all of the cooking juices into a warm platter. Then, adding a bit of oil again, if needed, repeat until all of the meat is cooked. Transfer the remaining cooked meat to the platter.

4 Add scallions and onions, and serve: Once the meat is cooked, add a bit more oil to the pan and sauté the scallions and remaining sliced onions until they are soft and nearly translucent, about 3 minutes. Add them to the serving platter and gently toss together with the meat. Plate the bulgogi and serve immediately with hot rice and a platter of leafy greens and herbs. Or, serve in a rice bowl with fresh cucumbers, a bibimbap bowl (as in the recipe that follows), in corn tortillas for Korean tacos—or however you fancy!

BULGOGI BIBIMBAP

Two fundamental principles of Korean cooking are to season as you go, part of (*Serious*) *New Cook* Principle #2, and to balance flavors. Bibimbap illustrates these principles perfectly: Each element is prepared separately—each ingredient cooked for just the right amount of time and seasoned individually. And, all of the flavors—salty, spicy, sweet, and sour—are perfectly balanced. The traditional way to serve the dish is with everything arranged neatly in a bowl over hot rice. When it arrives at the table, you take your spoon and mix it all up, mingling the flavors into a delicious mess, the spicy *gochujang* sauce and yolky egg coming together in a marvelous sauce that enhances each bite. (Cammie has always refused this mix-it tradition, though, preferring to compose what's in each bite on her own. But shhhh . . . don't tell anyone!)

Interestingly, bibimbap is traditionally composed with elements you already have on hand—*banchan* (side dishes) or leftovers that have been prepared for prior meals. When that's the case, this is a super-simple meal! But to make it from scratch involves quite a few steps, making it somewhat complex. If you cook several Korean recipes over a couple days, you'll be rewarded with delicious meals that take a fraction of the time it would take to cook each from scratch. The bulgogi from the previous recipe and the vegetables here can be used in this bibimbap, as well as the kimbap (page 139). And, the vegetables here can be served as banchan (see Tip) alongside the bulgogi, creating a restaurant-worthy spread.

● ● ●

Serves 4

Gluten free (if the bulgogi was made with GF soy sauce or tamari)

INGREDIENTS

Carrots, 2 medium, peeled

Zucchini, 2 small or 1 medium

Neutral oil

Salt

Black Pepper

Garlic, 1 clove, peeled

Bean sprouts, about 2 cups

Spinach, 1 bunch, rinsed well

Sesame seeds (optional), a teaspoon or so, plus a sprinkle for serving

Toasted sesame oil, a few teaspoons (or substitute **neutral oil**)

Bulgogi, about 1 pound cooked (see previous recipe)

Rice, 4 cups cooked short-grain white rice, hot

Eggs, 4 large

***Gochujang* sauce** (optional, but highly recommended; see Asian hot sauces)

Optional Prep
Everything except the egg can be made in advance.

Tip

Temperature matters! Koreans are obsessed with hot foods being hot and cold foods being cold, while certain dishes are served at room temperature. We often serve foods in the very pots they're cooked in, like the special clay pots and bowls traditionally used for stews and soups, which keep the food blazing hot until the very last bite. On the other end of the spectrum, cold dishes—including some refreshing cold noodles in broth—are often mixed with ice to keep them cold to the end.

Bibimbap is an interesting case. The rice, meat, and egg must be piping hot, but the vegetables are often cold or room temperature. This is because it's a dish often made with *banchan*, which are the side dishes served at every meal, including sautéed vegetables like those used in this recipe. Banchan is often prepared in large batches, then brought out little by little for each meal. There's another version of this dish, though, called *dolsot bibimbap*. It's quite similar, except it is served in a blazing hot stone bowl. When it comes to the table, a raw egg yolk is placed on top. When you *bibim* it—or, mix it up like crazy!—the egg yolk cooks and all of the ingredients come together into a hot un-fried rice. Because the bowl is so hot, a layer of rice sticks to the sides of the bowl and grows dry and crisp. After you've finished eating what you can, hot barley tea is poured over the crispy rice and eaten like a toasty rice soup.

1 Cook the carrots and zucchini: Cut the carrots into matchsticks and the zucchini into half-moons. In a frying pan over medium-high heat, sauté each vegetable separately in a little neutral oil, with a little pinch of salt and a crack of pepper. Cook until tender, but not mushy, a few minutes each. Check for seasoning while they cook, adding a little more salt and pepper, if necessary. Set each vegetable aside (on one plate is fine). There's no need to keep them hot.

2 Prepare the bean sprouts and spinach: Mince the garlic clove, divide into two little piles, and set aside. Blanch the bean sprouts in a large pot of well-salted boiling water for 90 seconds, stirring to ensure even cooking. Remove the cooked sprouts to a heat-proof colander set in the sink, and quickly rinse under cold water to stop the cooking. (If you scoop the sprouts out with a strainer basket or large slotted spoon, returning the pot of hot water to the stove, you can cook the spinach in it without starting a new pot of water.) Using your hands, pick up a handful at a time and gently squeeze out the excess water (just until it doesn't drip when you pick it up). Place in a medium bowl and add one-half of the minced garlic, a sprinkle of sesame seeds, and a light drizzle of toasted sesame oil. Mix gently with your hands and taste a piece, adjusting the seasoning as necessary until it tastes satisfying. Set aside. Next, blanch the spinach for a quick 30 seconds, then drain, quickly rinse, and gently squeeze, just like you did with the bean sprouts. Arrange the spinach into a log on a cutting board, and chop it three or four times. Then, put it in a separate medium bowl and add the remaining minced garlic, a sprinkle of sesame seeds, and a drizzle of sesame oil. Add a pinch of salt, if necessary.

3 Reheat the bulgogi, if necessary.

4 Prep your bowls: Set out four large, wide bowls and add a scoop of rice to each. Then, working around the edges, arrange a little pile of each topping—bulgogi, zucchini, bean sprouts, carrots, and spinach.

5 Fry your eggs: Heat a drizzle of neutral oil in a reliably nonstick skillet over high heat. As soon as it's sizzly hot, add the eggs and sprinkle with salt. Fry sunny-side up or, if you prefer, over-easy, being careful not to cook the yolk through. (You need it to be runny so it can act as the sauce!) When they are done, carefully slide one onto each bowl of bibimbap.

6 Serve: Immediately serve each bowl topped with a dollop of gochujang sauce and a sprinkle of sesame seeds.

BULGOGI MEATBALLS

These meatballs are cute, simple, and delicious. They can be served many ways: as adorable little passed hors d'oeuvres, for dinner with rice or noodles and sautéed Asian vegetables, or with *ssambap*—Korean lettuce wraps with rice. They freeze up nicely, too, making for great quick meals or impressive lunches, so you might want to double or triple the recipe. This is not a traditional Korean recipe, but the flavors are true b*ulgogi*.

• • •

Makes about 40 small meatballs; serves 3 to 4 as a meal, 6 to 10 as an appetizer

For a gluten-free version, use tamari or a GF soy sauce and GF breadcrumbs

INGREDIENTS

Soy sauce, ⅓ cup

Brown sugar, ¼ cup packed light or dark

Garlic, 4 or 5 medium cloves, minced

Sesame oil, 2 tablespoons

Mirin (optional), 1 tablespoon

Unseasoned breadcrumbs, ⅓ cup (preferably panko, but you could use any white breadcrumbs or round butter crackers smashed to tiny bits)

Ground beef, 1 pound

Scallions, 2, sliced medium-fine (both the white and green parts)

Cornstarch, ½ teaspoon

Chives (optional), a tiny bundle, chopped, for garnish

Toasted sesame seeds (optional), a few pinches, for garnish

Chili flakes (optional), a few pinches, for garnish

Optional Prep

The marinade can be prepped in advance. If you want to make the meatballs in advance and freeze them for quick meals later, bake them at 400°F (rather than broil them), until just gently cooked through but not charred. (Start checking for doneness after about 8 minutes by cutting into one and looking for a uniform color and texture. The colder the meat is and the larger the meatballs are, the longer they will take to cook.) They can be cooled and frozen at that point. Before serving, thaw in the refrigerator and broil for a few minutes to reheat and char them a bit.

1 **Prep the marinade/sauce:** In a glass measuring cup (or small bowl), mix together the soy sauce, brown sugar, garlic, sesame oil, and mirin (if using).

2 **Mix the meatballs:** Preheat the broiler (or, if you don't have one, preheat the oven to the highest temperature setting). Pour half of the marinade into a large bowl (reserving the other half for the dipping sauce). Sprinkle the breadcrumbs on top, and give it a stir. Then add the ground beef and scallions, and mix it all together with clean hands. Try to combine the marinade, breadcrumbs, and meat as evenly as possible, but don't overwork it. Stop as soon as it's pretty well combined.

3 **Roll the balls:** Scoop up 1 tablespoon of meat and, using both hands, gently roll it into a ball. Don't smush or overwork it, but roll it just until it holds a nice, round shape. It should be between the size of a gumball and ping-pong ball, about 1 inch in diameter. Place on a baking sheet, and keep rolling! Leave about an inch in between each meatball.

4 **Broil the meatballs:** When the baking sheet is full, pop it under the preheated broiler. Check the meatballs after 6 minutes to see if they are browned. If they are browning nicely, carefully grab one with a pair of tongs and break it. If the inside is uniform in color and texture, it's cooked through. If it's not, give them a couple more minutes. Ideally, you'll get a nice char on the top without overcooking them.

5 **Make the dipping sauce:** While your meatballs are broiling, pour the remaining marinade into a small saucepan over medium-high heat. Make a cornstarch slurry by combining the cornstarch with 1 teaspoon of water in a very small bowl. Stir it into the reserved marinade and bring it up to a boil, stirring constantly. After it comes to a boil, reduce the heat to low, keeping it warm until you're ready to serve.

6 **Serve:** If serving as hors d'oeuvres for passing, stick a toothpick into each meatball and arrange them on a flat platter with a small bowl of the dipping sauce—or drizzle a little sauce over each one. If you're serving them at the table, pile the meatballs on a platter, with the dipping sauce and toothpicks on the side. If you're serving them as a main course, you can plate or serve them family-style with rice and sautéed Asian vegetables, sliced cucumbers, or a platter of crispy lettuces for wrapping. If using the optional chive, sesame seed, and chili flake garnishes, add them at the end.

Sweets
and
Treats

Meyer Lemon Pudding Cake Cups

This pudding cake can be made in a large soufflé dish, but baking it in individual dessert cups gives each eater the chance to discover the remarkable juxtaposition of airy soufflé on top and silky pudding on the bottom. Lemony-dessert fans, in particular, will rejoice. Meyer lemons, which have a distinctively tart-yet-sweet flavor and aroma, are divine here, but regular lemons work terrifically, too.

Ingredients

Butter, 3 tablespoons unsalted, melted, plus more for greasing

Sugar, ⅔ cup plus 2 tablespoons

All-purpose flour, ⅓ cup

Salt, ¼ teaspoon

Eggs, 4 large, at room temperature (warming briefly in a bowl or pan of hot tap water—perhaps alongside the milk—works well)

Meyer lemon zest, from 1 lemon (or regular lemon)

Meyer lemon juice, ⅓ cup, plus an extra squeeze for whipping the egg whites (depending on how juicy they are, that's about 2 to 3 Meyer lemons; regular lemons work, too)

Milk, 1¼ cups, slightly warmed (15 seconds in the microwave or a few minutes set in a pan of hot water will do the trick)

Powdered sugar, for dusting

• • •

Serves 4 to 6

For a gluten-free version, use superfine rice flour

Equipment: 4 to 6 ramekins, depending on size, or a 6-cup soufflé or baking dish (Taller, straighter sides will yield a more soufflé-like pudding cake.)

Tips

Warm eggs and milk are often specified in baking recipes because they help the batter ingredients combine more easily and result in a better rise and, ultimately, a more fluffy, airy baked good. The quickest way to make this happen is to measure the milk in a glass measuring cup and set it in a shallow pan of hot tap water. You can set the cold eggs right into the pan to warm up alongside the milk.

The ratio of pudding to cake depends at least in part on the height of your water bath. The hot water helps the pudding form on the bottom of the baking dish. So, if you prefer less pudding next time, use less water—and vice versa. (In fact, you could skip the water bath altogether if you want something more akin to a soufflé cake!)

1 Prep: Preheat the oven to 350°F. Lightly grease the ramekins by brushing melted butter over the bottom and sides. Set the ramekins in a high-sided roasting pan, which you will later fill with water, creating a water bath that will help develop the pudding.

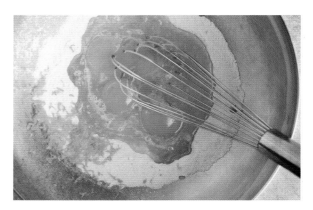

2 Make the batter: In a medium bowl, whisk together ⅔ cup of the sugar, the flour, and salt. Separate the eggs, placing the whites into a separate large bowl and adding the yolks to the flour mixture (unless you warm them in advance; see Tips), along with the melted butter, lemon zest, and lemon juice. Whisk until well combined, then add the milk and whisk just a few more times. Set aside.

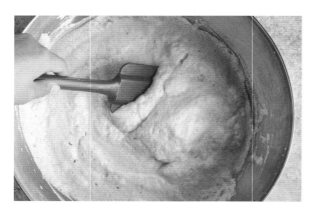

3 Whip and <u>fold</u>: Using a hand whisk or an electric hand mixer, beat the egg whites with a squeeze of lemon juice until fluffy. (The lemon juice will help them whip up nicely.) Gradually add the remaining 2 tablespoons sugar as you continue to beat to medium <u>peaks</u>. Use a spatula to gently <u>fold</u> the whipped egg whites into the batter in three separate additions. Fold just until no large streaks of white remain.

4 Bake: Pour the mixture into the buttered ramekins, about three-quarters full. Carefully pour warm tap water into the roasting pan, creating a water bath that comes halfway up the sides of the ramekins (see Tips). Bake for 20 to 25 minutes, or until just set. It should jiggle like set Jell-O when you gently wiggle a ramekin. Immediately remove the ramekins from the water bath, using tongs and/or hot pads; be careful to avoid the hot water. Dust with powdered sugar, if desired, and serve.

COCONUT RICE PUDDING CUPS

Rice pudding is one of those desserts that is enjoyed in many cultures around the world. It's no wonder: It's totally satisfying—at once filling and light—and it's highly adaptable to different palates. In some cultures, including many in Latin America, rice pudding with cinnamon is popular. In some parts of South Asia and the Middle East, it's often made with rose water and cardamom. And in Southeast Asia, you're likely to find coconut rice pudding. That's where this recipe takes its cues from, pairing creamy coconut milk with fresh berries in what is, to us, a classic combination.

• • •

Serves 4 to 6

Gluten free

INGREDIENTS

White rice, ½ cup uncooked (preferably short or medium grain, though any variety of white rice works; see Tips)

Vanilla bean, 1 pod, split lengthwise (or 1 teaspoon vanilla extract; see Tips)

Whole milk, 2 cups

Coconut milk, one 13.5- to 14-ounce can

Salt,

Egg yolks, 2 large

Sugar, ⅓ cup

Raspberries, 1 pint (or strawberries, blackberries, diced mango, or any other topping that sounds yummy to you)

Tips

The type of <u>rice</u> used for rice pudding varies as much as rice itself. Here, we use short- to medium-grain white rice—the variety most commonly found in East Asian households (like ours). You could use any type of white rice, though, including basmati or jasmine, which are both exceptionally aromatic. You could even use black rice, which pairs particularly well with the coconut; just know that you'll need to double or triple the initial cooking time for black rice, depending on the specific variety.

Vanilla beans impart an aroma and flavor unsurpassed by vanilla extract. The beans (also called pods) are long, thin, and somewhat sticky and dry. Use kitchen shears or a sharp <u>knife</u> to split them in half lengthwise, then use the back of a knife to carefully scrape out the thousands of teeny-tiny seeds that line the inside of the pod. Typically, the whole pod is steeped along with the seeds so that maximum flavor can be extracted; the pod is removed before serving, leaving behind only the pretty little vanilla bean flecks. If you use vanilla extract instead, it is best to add it toward the end (along with the egg yolks, in this recipe) so that the flavor doesn't have much chance to evaporate.

1 Cook the rice: Rinse the rice (which is a good practice for nearly any type of rice) in a fine-mesh strainer under cool, running water until the water runs clear, indicating the surface starch and any impurities have been rinsed away. Combine the rice with ½ cup water in a medium saucepan, and bring to a boil over high heat. Reduce the heat to low, cover, and continue cooking for 15 minutes, until most of the water is absorbed.

2 Add the milks: Remove the cover and scrape the vanilla bean seeds into the saucepan. Add the vanilla bean pod, along with the milk, coconut milk, and a pinch of salt, stirring well to break up the rice and combine the ingredients. Increase the heat to high. When it reaches a boil, reduce the heat to low and simmer, uncovered, for another 10 minutes, stirring frequently to ensure the rice doesn't stick to the bottom.

3 Add the egg yolks: In a medium bowl, whisk together the egg yolks and sugar (and vanilla extract, if using in place of the vanilla bean). Temper the egg mixture by stirring in small amounts (a big spoonful at a time) of the hot rice mixture. Keep adding small amounts until it's all combined. Then, carefully pour the combined mixture back into the saucepan and bring to a simmer over low heat, stirring constantly. Once it is simmering, cook for 1 to 2 more minutes, stirring occasionally.

4 Let it rest: Transfer the pudding to a bowl. Place a piece of plastic wrap directly onto the surface of the pudding to prevent an icky dry layer from forming. Let it rest for 5 to 10 minutes, allowing the flavors to meld as it sets slightly. (You can refrigerate it at this point, if not serving immediately.)

5 Serve: Remove and discard the vanilla bean. Stir the pudding, then spoon the mixture into individual serving bowls, top with fresh <u>berries</u>, if desired, and serve.

Buttermilk Panna Cotta Cups

This is, hands down, the easiest fancy dessert ever. It tastes like a luxurious pudding with the subtle tang of a perfect cheesecake. No one will believe it's basically milk Jell-O. Top it with some fresh berries, sliced tropical fruit, or berry compote (see our recipes on pages 53–57), and it'll seem like you splurged on dessert at a fancy restaurant. So, impress the heck out of your friends and family—we won't tell them how easy it really is! Or, make it for yourself. It's guaranteed to put a smile on your face, too.

• • •

Serves 4 to 6, depending on your ramekin, jar, or cup size

Gluten free

Time: 15 minutes, plus a minimum of 3 hours chilling time

Equipment: 4 to 6 little ramekins, jars, or cups (which don't need to be oven-safe)

INGREDIENTS

Unflavored gelatin, 1½ teaspoons (that's a little more than half a standard gelatin packet)

Heavy cream, 1 cup

Sugar, 7 tablespoons

Vanilla bean, ½ pod, split lengthwise with kitchen shears (or use 1 teaspoon vanilla extract, though you will miss the lovely little vanilla bean specks)

Buttermilk, 2 cups (or substitute half-and-half, or a combination of regular milk and more heavy cream for a total of 2 cups)

Your choice of toppings, a few spoonfuls (Any Berry Compote or Fresh Berry Compote—pages 53 and 57—or fresh berries or diced mango, for example)

Optional Prep

These need to be made at least a few hours in advance and will keep well in the fridge for up to 4 days. Hold off on topping them until serving.

Tip

If you would like to unmold the panna cotta onto a plate to serve, you'll need to brush a little neutral oil onto the inside of each ramekin before pouring in the cream mixture. To serve, set a plate directly on top of each ramekin, and flip! You'll have delightfully jiggly little mounds of sweet cream, perfect for a drizzle of berry compote.

1 Prepare the gelatin: Place 2 tablespoons of room temperature water into a small bowl and sprinkle the gelatin on top.

2 Warm the cream mixture: Place the cream and sugar in a small saucepan. Scrape out the vanilla bean seeds and add to the saucepan, along with the pod. Bring to a simmer over medium heat, then remove from the heat and add the gelatin mixture (and vanilla extract, if using in place of the vanilla bean). Whisk until the gelatin dissolves. Cool to room temperature.

3 Add the buttermilk: Stir the buttermilk into the cooled cream mixture. Then, pour the mixture through a fine-mesh strainer set over a bowl or large glass measuring cup, straining out the vanilla bean pod and any lumps.

4 Fill the ramekins: Pour the mixture into small ramekins, jars, or cups.

5 Chill: Cover each container with plastic wrap and chill in the refrigerator for at least 3 hours, until set. Serve with a dollop of berry compote, a few fresh berries, or a bit of diced mango.

Homemade Ice Cream

Ice cream is awesome—and even more so when you make it yourself. While there are many different approaches to ice cream making, all you really need is one good one, and that's what we present here: a solid recipe for making smooth, rich, creamy vanilla ice cream—which you can then turn into an infinite number of *other* flavors. Classic strawberry your thing? We got you covered. Always wonder why it's hard to find raspberry ice cream? We got you. Or are you more of a crazy candy bar and potato chip ice cream kind of person? Maybe you only like butter pecan when it's so fresh the nuts are still crunchy. Or you have a genius combination you've been wishing someone would make for years. Here's your chance. Master this basic homemade ice cream recipe, then go crazy. You can stir in just about anything your heart desires. Or, keep it simple for a classic bowl of vanilla ice cream—or to use in the not-to-be-missed recipes that follow.

• • •

Makes about 1 quart (more, depending on your stir-ins)

Gluten free

Time: 30 minutes, plus at least 7 hours for chilling

Equipment: Ice cream maker, the bowl frozen for 24 hours minimum (or see Tip for a no-special-equipment option)

Ingredients

Vanilla bean, 1 pod (or 1 teaspoon vanilla extract)

Heavy cream, 2 cups

Whole milk, 1 cup

Sugar, ⅔ cup

Salt, ½ teaspoon

Egg yolks, 4 large

STIR-IN SUGGESTIONS
Strawberry puree (1 quart strawberries pureed in a blender with ⅓ cup sugar)

Any Berry Compote (page 53) or **jam**, ¼ to ½ cup

Pounded black sesame seeds or **Asian black sesame seed paste**, ¼ cup or so

Crumbled soft brownies or **cookies**, 3 to 5, depending on size

Chocolate chips or **candy bars**, chopped, ½ cup or more

Toasted nuts, chopped, ½ cup or more

Peppermint candies, chopped, ½ cup or more

Decaf instant coffee (1 to 2 tablespoons) or **matcha** (2 to 3 tablespoons), whisked up in a tiny bit of cream, then stirred into the custard right before straining

Tip

If you don't have an ice cream maker, you can "churn" by hand! Just pour the chilled base into a large bowl and freeze for about an hour. At that point, briefly "churn" it every 30 minutes or so, either with an electric mixer or by hand. When it reaches soft ice cream stage, after 3 to 4 hours, add your stir-ins, then scrape it out of the bowl and into a freezer-safe container, cover it, and freeze until hard (like your favorite packed pint).

1 **Start the ice cream base:** Using kitchen shears or a sharp <u>knife</u>, split the vanilla bean in half lengthwise and scrape the fine black seeds into a small saucepan. Add the vanilla bean (the whole pod), cream, milk, sugar, and salt. Warm the mixture over medium heat, stirring occasionally, until the sugar has dissolved, 2 to 3 minutes. Remove from the heat.

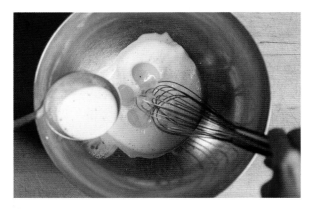

2 **Start tempering the yolks:** Put the egg yolks into a large bowl. Begin whisking as you pour one ladleful of the hot cream mixture into the bowl, continuing to whisk until well combined. (This is called tempering, and it's necessary when combining hot liquids with egg yolks; the gradual mixing allows a creamy mixture to develop, instead of scrambled eggs in cream.)

3 **Add more cream:** Whisk in another ladleful of hot cream.

4 **And a bit more:** Keep whisking in cream until about half of it has been added.

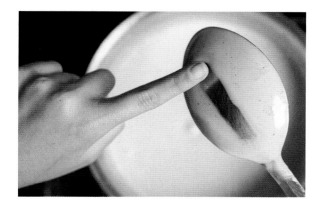

5 Make the custard: Whisk the bowlful of tempered yolks into the saucepan with the remaining cream mixture. Cook over low heat, stirring constantly with a wooden spoon until the mixture "coats the spoon." (That means when you lift the spoon out of the custard and run your finger across it, it's thick enough to leave a clear trail. Be patient and pay attention, as this might take as long as 10 minutes, and it goes from "not ready" to "over" pretty quickly.) What you have now is custard.

6 Strain the custard: To ensure a smooth, rich ice cream, strain the custard through a medium-fine sieve set over a large bowl to remove any lumps that may have formed. Scrape as much of the vanilla bean through the strainer as you can, then put the vanilla bean pod back into the strained mixture to add an extra boost of vanilla flavor.

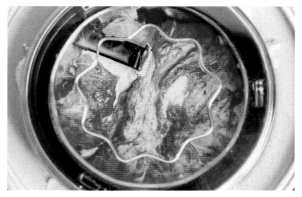

7 Chill and churn: Cover the bowl with plastic wrap and chill in the refrigerator for a minimum of 4 hours (or up to 2 days). Alternatively, quick-chill it over an ice bath by setting the bowl in a larger bowl filled with lots of ice and a little water. Stir constantly until very cold, at least 10 minutes. When cold, remove and discard the vanilla bean pod, and churn according to the directions for your ice cream maker.

8 Add your stir-ins: When your ice cream has reached soft ice cream stage (about 20 minutes in an ice cream maker), add your choice of stir-ins—with the machine still running—and continue mixing for 1 minute more. Use a wooden spoon to help combine, if necessary, then scrape the ice cream into a container and freeze for at least 3 hours before serving.

MOCHI ICE CREAM

We're not sure what's more fun, making or eating these sweet little mochi ice cream balls! Cammie's daughter, Noie, has been making them since she was in elementary school. Back then, they were *very* messy, but very delicious. Years (and lots of practice!) later, she still enjoys making them—but now she turns out pristine, adorable little clouds of mochi, filled with everyone's favorite ice cream flavors. We all agree that strawberry is particularly great in them, but we also favor black sesame and matcha (in keeping with the Asian roots of the recipe), as well as coffee and chocolate. (Because: coffee. And chocolate. Duh.) So, grab (or make!) your favorite pint and have some fun—*(Serious) New Cook* Principle #5—turning out these little clouds of happiness.

• • •

Makes 12 mochi

Gluten free

Time: 30 minutes, plus at least 5 hours total chilling time

Equipment: A 1½-inch "disher" (aka cookie scoop or mini ice cream scoop; a 3½- to 4-inch pastry cutter (or a glass or bowl with a similar diameter); microwave-safe plastic wrap or silicone bowl topper

INGREDIENTS

Ice cream, 1 pint of your favorite flavor—or a little of several different flavors

Sweet glutinous rice flour, 1 cup (available online or at Asian markets; *Shiratamako* works best, *Mochiko* works fine)

Sugar, ⅓ cup

Cornstarch, about 1 cup, for dusting (or substitute potato starch)

1 Form the ice cream domes: Using a small disher/scoop, quickly scoop 12 domes of ice cream and place them on a parchment paper–lined baking sheet. (Alternatively, get crafty with two spoons! Try not to use your fingers, which will melt the ice cream; see Tips.) They should be about the size and shape of half a ping-pong ball. Freeze until solid (at least 3 to 4 hours).

2 Make the dough: Combine the sweet rice flour, sugar, and 1 cup water in a large microwave-safe bowl and cover with microwave-safe plastic wrap or a silicone topper. Microwave for 1 minute, then use a dampened silicone spatula (or spoon, if you don't have one) to stir the rice flour mixture, breaking up any lumps that have formed. Re-cover the bowl, nuke it for 1 minute more, and stir again. Cover one last time and nuke it for a final 30 seconds. The dough should have changed uniformly in texture, becoming somewhat translucent; if it hasn't, stir one more time and nuke it again for 15 seconds.

3 Roll out the dough: Place a large piece of parchment paper on your counter and sprinkle ¼ to ½ cup of cornstarch all over it. Using your dampened spatula, scoop out the dough and plop it right onto the cornstarch. Sprinkle another handful of cornstarch on top, then start patting it out to flatten, adding more cornstarch to sticky parts as needed. Use a rolling pin to flatten the dough evenly to ¼ inch thick.

4 Cool and cut the dough: Place the mochi (parchment paper and all) on a flat platter or baking sheet and chill in the fridge for 15 to 20 minutes, allowing the dough time to firm up. While the dough chills, tear off 12 squares of plastic wrap and set aside. Remove the dough from the fridge and use a 3½- to 4-inch pastry cutter or a small bowl to cut out 12 discs.

5 Form the mochi: Working quickly, pick up a dough disc and dust off any excess cornstarch, then set it in the palm of your non-dominant hand. Take one scoop of ice cream from the freezer and place it in the center of the circle, dome down (leave the remaining ice cream domes in the freezer until ready to use). Wrap the dough around the scoop of ice cream, layering and pinching it together on the flat side. Next, place the mochi ice cream ball in the center of a piece of plastic wrap, dome down, and twist the plastic wrap around it, tightly sealing it up so that it won't unravel. Shape it into a nice, smooth dome, then place it back in the freezer. Repeat with the remaining discs of dough and ice cream balls. Let them set in the freezer for about an hour.

6 Thaw slightly, then enjoy: Remove your mochi ice cream from the freezer 5 minutes before eating, so it has a chance to soften enough to bite into. Enjoy—and share, *(Serious) New Cook* Principle #4!

Tips

A cookie or mini ice cream scoop makes forming the ice cream domes much easier and neater, though it is not required. Ideally, the scoop should form 1½-tablespoon domes, flat on the bottom and round on the top.

Keep it cold! It's essential that your ice cream be frozen hard, both when you're scooping the centers and wrapping them. Remember that the back of the freezer is usually colder than the door, and every time you open the door, the temperature jumps up, adding to the total freeze time needed. Also note that warm hands melt ice cream! If it's hot in your kitchen, or if you just generally run hot, rinse or soak your hands under cold water before forming the mochi balls. Just be sure to dry them well first.

(Double) Dalgona Coffee Milkshakes

Coffee lovers, this might just be the best milkshake you've ever had.

You may be familiar with dalgona coffee, the inconceivably frothy whipped coffee drink, but you may not know that its name actually refers to a traditional Korean candy often called dalgona. It's made with nothing more than sugar and baking soda (and sometimes a bit of water)—no coffee at all! You make it by melting some sugar, then mixing in a pinch of baking soda, which causes it to froth up magically. It's quickly poured onto a flat surface to harden, creating a sweet treat enjoyed throughout Korea. Street vendors press it into flat little lolli-pops often called *ppopgi*, and others (in cultures around the world) let it set up into honeycomb candy, cracking it to bits after it has cooled. It's exceptionally crunchy and sweet, with a hint of burnt caramel—or slightly burnt coffee!—flavor. Whipped dalgona coffee, then, got its name because the color and texture of each, mid-stir, is nearly identical, and the flavor is freakishly similar.

While a dalgona coffee is usually served as a coffee whip spooned over hot or cold milk, we take it to the next level in this dalgona coffee milkshake. It's fun and easy to make, but if you're up for a challenge, try making a *double* dalgona coffee milkshake, with real dalgona candy, on top of dalgona coffee whip, on top of a milkshake. The candy adds a spectacular crunch, contrasting sharply (literally!) with the smooth, creamy dalgona whip. Making the candy at home is quick, but might take a few tries. It cooks slowly at first, then goes from amber to burnt faster than you can blink. It also takes some practice to melt the sugar without letting it crystallize. (Science geeks, get to it!) Luckily, each try will only take you five to ten minutes, so if you have the sugar to spare and welcome a new challenge, experiment away. Otherwise, take the easier route and whip up the simple version (without the dalgona candy, skipping step 1) of this addictively delicious dalgona coffee milkshake.

Makes 2 large milkshakes

Gluten free

Tips

Sweetness is expected in a milkshake, of course, but because dalgona coffee whip is half sugar and dalgona candy is all sugar, we love to add ice to this milkshake. It tempers the sweetness just a tad and makes it reminiscent of an iced coffee.

Decaf instant coffee, which is available widely, is our go-to for coffee desserts like this. There's nothing worse than enjoying dessert only to regret it later when you're lying in bed staring at the ceiling for hours on end. High-quality instant coffee can be found in regular supermarkets, Korean markets, or ordered online and/or through serious small-batch coffee roasters.

Variation

For a dalgona coffee, skip the ice cream and serve the dalgona whip over a glass of cold milk with ice, atop a mug of hot milk, or in a teacup with a bit of hot water.

INGREDIENTS

Dalgona candy (optional; see instructions for the extra challenge recipe!)

DALGONA WHIP

Decaf instant coffee, 2 tablespoons

Sugar, 2 to 3 tablespoons (3 tablespoons whips more nicely, but folks without a serious sweet tooth may prefer to use 2)

Hot water, 2 tablespoons

VANILLA MILKSHAKE

Ice

Vanilla ice cream, 2 scoops (preferably homemade, see recipe page 211)

Cold milk, about 1 cup (whole, lowfat, or skim all work fine)

✳ Optional Extra Challenge ✳ Make dalgona candy: Set a piece of parchment paper on a large plate or baking sheet, and set aside. Place ¼ cup sugar and 2 tablespoons filtered water in a small saucepan over medium heat; do not stir. (Minerals or impurities in the water or on your utensil will cause the mixture to crystallize.) Keep a close eye as it melts and boils, watching for it to change color just the slightest bit. (The mixture has to come to a boil and continue boiling for a few minutes, which is tricky because you don't want it to burn!) As soon as you notice the melted sugar starting to turn gold, remove it from the heat and, as rapidly as you can, stir in ¼ teaspoon baking soda until it becomes a frothy blob, around 5 seconds. *Immediately* dump it onto the parchment in one big pile, and allow it to cool and harden (a few minutes, if you nailed it). Once it's rock-solid, whack it with something to break it into small pieces. (If it smells more than a little bit burnt, it is! Ditch it and try again.)

1 Make the dalgona whip: Combine the coffee, sugar, and hot water in a large bowl. Whip it, preferably with a hand whisk, until your arm feels like it's going to fall off and the mixture becomes thick, glossy, and marvelously viscous—think firm peaks of marshmallow fluff or Swiss meringue. (You could use a hand mixer on medium, but where's the fun in that? Plus, whipping it too fast results in foamy, rather than superfine, bubbles.) Set aside.

2 Make the milkshake: Fill two large glasses about one-third full of ice. Add a scoop of vanilla ice cream to each, and pour in enough cold milk to cover it—the glass should be no more than two-thirds full. Stir it together briefly, breaking up the ice cream just a bit. Then, spoon the dalgona whip over the ice cream. If you nailed the extra challenge and have some dalgona candy, add a small handful to the top. Serve with a spoon for mixing and devouring.

SCOTT PEACOCK AND EDNA LEWIS'S
APPLE CRISP

A good fruit crisp should be in every cook's repertoire. It's quick and easy to prepare, and it's infinitely adaptable. Here we have a classic apple crisp recipe adapted from *The Gift of Southern Cooking*, a treasure of a cookbook written by Miss Edna Lewis and her dear friend and co-author, Scott Peacock.

Often referred to as the Grand Dame of Southern Cooking, Miss Lewis was born in Freetown, Virginia, a farming community established by formerly enslaved people, including her grandparents. She left Freetown for the North during the Great Migration, eventually settling in New York City, where she was a political activist and accomplished seamstress known for her African-inspired dresses, before becoming partner and chef of Café Nicholson, a stylish and popular French cafe in midtown Manhattan. She went on to chef at numerous other restaurants, including the historic Gage & Tollner, a Brooklyn steakhouse that had been open since 1879. As its highly acclaimed chef in the late 1980s and early 1990s, Miss Lewis reinvigorated the restaurant, redesigning the menu to include numerous Southern dishes and drawing extensively on local ingredients from the New York City farmers' markets and Manhattan's iconic Fulton Fish Market—which illustrates *(Serious) New Cook* Principle #1: Use good ingredients! Incidentally, Gage & Tollner closed in the mid-2000s due to economic difficulties in the neighborhood, but it was reopened to much fanfare in 2021 by a team including Chef Sohui Kim—who also contributed a guest recipe for this cookbook (see page 191). The new menu includes many of Miss Lewis's specialties.

In addition to political activism, dress-making, and cheffing, Miss Lewis worked as a pheasant farmer, cooking teacher, and cookbook author. One of her most famous books, *The Taste of Country Cooking*, is well-known for celebrating the rich culinary traditions from her childhood in Freetown. It established Miss Lewis as one of the preeminent voices of Southern and African American cooking—and, moreover, of American food itself.

• • •

Serves 6 to 8

For a gluten-free version, use GF flour

Equipment: A 9 by 13-inch baking dish or roasting pan. However, if what you have is smaller, you may have extra apples and topping, which you can bake separately in a ramekin or other small baking dish.

Ingredient Note

Different apple varieties cook up *completely* differently. Some, like easy-to-find MacIntosh and heirloom-variety Gravenstein (our fav!), will fall apart when you cook them. Others—like Pink Lady, Fuji, Granny Smith, and Golden Delicious—hold their shape. A good apple pie needs both "bricks" (nice whole slices of apple) and "mortar" (the stuff that holds together those apples when you slice it)—which you get either by mixing fall-apart apples with hold-their-shape apples, or by adding cornstarch or flour to hold things together.

Crisps and crumbles, however, are typically served scooped into a bowl, rather than sliced, so the "mortar" is less important. (In fact, we happen to prefer it when sweet-tart apple syrup mingles with the apples and topping!) But even if you don't need to mix your apples for texture, you can do so for flavor. Some apples have really nice, balanced flavors, while others need a little extra help from lemon juice and sugar to achieve the right balance. (A few—like supermarket-popular Red Delicious—need a *lot* of help. We suggest avoiding those!) It's all about experimenting— (*Serious*) *New Cook* Principle #3!— figuring out what you like, and above all, tasting and adjusting— (*Serious*) *New Cook* Principle #2!

Scott Peacock, a James Beard Award–winning chef, met Miss Lewis when he was in his twenties and she in her seventies, and they began an enduring friendship that shaped his understanding of his own culinary heritage as a Southern chef. We are humbled that he shared this recipe for their Warm Apple Crisp, one of the last recipes he and Miss Lewis cooked together before her passing in 2006.

Crumble, crisp, or cobbler? They are all fruit desserts baked with some sort of nicely browned topping. A cobbler typically gets a biscuit-topping, which absorbs the sweetened fruit juices beautifully. The terms "crisp" and "crumble" are perhaps more debatable. Many folks use them interchangeably. We rather like the theory that a crumble topping is made primarily with flour, butter, and sugar that's been squished together to form nice little crumbs on top, while a crisp has added ingredients like nuts or oats to give it a little extra crisp. But Scott Peacock and Miss Edna Lewis call this Warm Apple Crisp, and we won't argue with that. Indeed, it's warm, appley, and crisp! Whatever you call it, if you start with delicious fruit, it's hard to go wrong.

INGREDIENTS

Apples, 9 medium (any delicious variety—see Ingredient Note)

Granulated sugar, 1 cup plus 2 tablespoons

Salt, ¾ teaspoon

Lemon juice, from ½ lemon

Butter, ¾ cup (12 tablespoons) unsalted, cut into small pieces and refrigerated

Unbleached all-purpose flour, 1 cup

Brown sugar, 2 tablespoons (preferably dark brown, but light works, too)

Ground cinnamon, ½ teaspoon

Vanilla ice cream (preferably homemade, see page 211)

1 **Prepare the filling:** Preheat the oven to 350°F. Peel and core the apples, and cut them into ⅓-inch-thick slices. Toss them in a large mixing bowl with 2 tablespoons of the granulated sugar and ¼ teaspoon of the salt. Add the lemon juice and toss to combine.

2 **Assemble the apples:** Rub about 1 tablespoon of the butter on the sides and bottom of the baking dish, then dump in the apples, spreading them out evenly. Use a spatula to scrape out every ounce of the apple syrup that has accumulated in the bowl. The apples may come nearly to the top of the pan, but make sure there's at least ½ inch of room for the topping. Top the apples with about 3 tablespoons of the butter and set aside.

3 **Make the topping:** In a large mixing bowl, whisk together the flour, brown sugar, and cinnamon with the remaining 1 cup granulated sugar and ½ teaspoon salt. Add the remaining 8 tablespoons cold butter pieces to the flour mixture. Using your fingers, toss the butter around to coat in flour. Then, pinch little pieces of the butter between your fingertips, creating flour-coated bits that resemble dry oatmeal. You want to butter all of the flour while preserving as many tiny butter bits (the "oats" you hope to see) as you can. If the mixture breaks into pieces that are smaller—more like sand—add a couple more tablespoons of butter.

4 **Top and bake:** Sprinkle the topping over the prepared apples. If it is primarily loose and sandy, take little handfuls and squeeze it together, creating small clumps. Distribute the topping (bits or clumps!) evenly over the apples. Set the baking dish on a parchment paper–lined baking sheet in order to catch any drippy juices, then bake in the center of the oven for 45 to 60 minutes, until you see apple-syrupy bubbles appearing on the edges of the baking dish and that the topping is crisp. Serve warm, on its own or with a scoop of vanilla ice.

BLUEBERRY COBBLER

If there's one dessert that's emblematic of the Fourth of July, it's blueberry cobbler. And it's no wonder. The classic dessert is jam-packed
with mounds of one of America's most prized native fruits: blueberries.
In season just in time for the holiday, blueberries shine brightly in a
classic cobbler. They need little more than a bit of sugar to transform
into a sweet mess of mini-orbs just waiting to burst in your mouth.
Simple, tender biscuits on top draw up some of the juices, flavoring
them like a smear of jam. Perfect on its own, a little drizzle of cream
really takes it over the top.

• • •

Serves 6 to 8

For a gluten-free version, use GF flour

**Equipment: A 9 by 13-inch baking dish
or 6 to 8 individual ramekins**

INGREDIENTS

BLUEBERRY FILLING

Blueberries, 5 cups, washed

Sugar, ⅓ cup

Lemon zest, from 1 lemon
(the yellow parts only!)

Cornstarch, 2 teaspoons

BISCUIT TOPPING

All-purpose flour, 1¾ cups

Sugar, 2 tablespoons

Baking powder, 1 tablespoon

Salt, ½ teaspoon

Butter, 4 tablespoons unsalted, very
cold and cut into small cubes

Heavy cream, 1 cup, plus an optional
drizzle for serving

1 Make the filling: Preheat the oven to 350°F. In the baking dish, toss the blueberries with the sugar, lemon zest, and cornstarch until evenly combined. (If baking in individual ramekins, mix in a bowl, then evenly distribute them among the ramekins.) Set aside.

2 Make the biscuit dough: Thoroughly whisk together the flour, sugar, baking powder, and salt. Toss in the cubes of butter and pinch them around in the flour until you have a bunch of pea-size bits of butter among the flour. Drizzle in the cream. Mix with a spoon just until the flour bits and cream are incorporated. Then, use your hands to toss and mix, lifting the flour from the bottom and turning it all over, just until the dry ingredients are moist and it naturally comes together into a shaggy, messy, loose ball (avoid clumping and smushing it into a ball). Set aside.

3 Assemble the cobbler: With lightly floured hands, gently form small, fairly loose discs of dough (about the size of hockey pucks—though soft and fluffy, unlike hockey pucks; see Tips), and arrange them over the berries. There should be some space in between the biscuits, giving the blueberries space to breathe and the biscuits space to grow.

4 Finish the cobbler: Set the baking dish on a parchment paper–lined baking sheet in order to catch any drippy juices, then bake until the biscuits are golden brown and the juices are bubbly and syrupy all around and in between them, 40 to 45 minutes. (The blueberries in the center will cook more slowly than the ones on the edges, so you'll end up with a nice mix of bursting and whole berries.) Serve hot or cold, with an optional drizzle of cream.

Tips

These biscuits are the bomb! You can use the biscuit recipe alone, too. Just bake them on a baking sheet at 425°F for 12 to 15 minutes. They are buttery and tender—versatile enough to eat on their own with a little jam or honey, alongside some fried chicken, under some milk gravy, or topped with some Fresh Berry Compote (page 57) and whipped cream for an awesome strawberry shortcake.

Biscuit-shaping techniques depend on preference. For a cobbler, we like the super-quick, easy-going method we describe here. Some people like to just plop the dough by the loose spoonful right onto the blueberries, though we favor a basic cutting method, like the one we use in our Biscuit-Topped Chicken Pot Pie (page 125)—another versatile biscuit recipe, by the way, that's interchangeable with this one (it's just slightly more involved and comes out slightly more flaky). If you have pastry cutters or a just-right-size glass, you can cut out classic rounds, of course. Any way you shape 'em, though, avoid handling the dough too much if you want your biscuits to be tender (and who doesn't want that?).

Most blueberries need nothing more than sugar and a smidge of lemon zest, but always taste yours first, part of (Serious) New Cook Principle #2: Taste and adjust. Count yourself lucky if you have a mix of super sweet and slightly sour ones. They'll add complexity to every spoonful. You can also build some complexity with a bit of extra sugar or a squeeze of lemon juice, if the blueberries need it.

Nectarine-Plum Crisp

You can only get terrific stone fruits—peaches, plums, and nectarines, for example—well into summer, during peak growing season. Knowing that the types available off-season tend to be mediocre, at best (and grown too far away!), we don't touch the stuff until it starts appearing at our local farmers' markets. When it does, it's a marvel—particularly in the warm, sunny parts of the country where there's often a staggering selection of organic, locally grown varieties. We eagerly buy bagfuls, knowing they'll get devoured fresh, be transformed into the most delicious jams, and make their way into baked goods that just scream summer—like this Nectarine-Plum Crisp! The simple crisp topping provides a great contrast for the juices of summer. Serve it hot or cold, alone or with a dollop of <u>whipped cream</u>. Just enjoy it while you can.

• • •

Serves 6 to 8

For a gluten-free version, use GF flour and oats

Equipment: A 9 by 13-inch baking dish or 6 to 8 individual ramekins

INGREDIENTS

Nectarines, about 3 large

Plums or pluots, 2 or 3 large plums, or as many as 8 to 10 small ones (any juicy variety; not the Italian prune plums)

Granulated sugar, ½ cup

All-purpose flour, ¾ cup

Light brown sugar, ½ cup packed

Salt, ½ teaspoon

Butter, 6 tablespoons unsalted, cold and cut into small pieces

Quick-cooking oats, ¾ cup (or substitute whole rolled oats; see Tips)

Pecans, ½ cup, chopped (or substitute walnuts)

Tips

A food processor is a perfect tool for crisp topping, and it's especially ideal if you're using rolled oats instead of quick oats. Blitzing rolled oats in a food processor a few times will enable them to crisp up more quickly, like quick oats. It will also make quick work of cutting in the butter, turning it into perfect-size bits for the topping. Simply complete step 2 in a food processor, and if you use rolled oats, be sure to give it all a few extra pulses at the end.

As with the other crisps and cobblers—and all of the recipes you make!—remember these *(Serious) New Cook* Principles: #1—Start with good ingredients. This crisp is only incredible when made with incredible plums. #4—Share. Crisps are comforting and delightful, so spread the love! And #5—Have fun! Always.

1 Prep the fruit: Preheat the oven to 375°F. Cut the nectarines and plums into ⅓-inch-thick slices. They don't have to be pretty or perfect, so just cut around the pit if it's not a freestone (a variety whose fruit pulls right off the pit neatly). You should have about 5 cups total. We prefer slightly more nectarines than plums, but use what you've got! Place them in a large mixing bowl and sprinkle ¼ cup of the granulated sugar over them, tossing to coat. Dump into a baking dish and set aside.

2 Make the topping: In a medium bowl, whisk together the flour, brown sugar, the remaining ¼ cup sugar, and salt until combined. Add the cold butter and use your fingers to coat the butter in the flour. Then, pinch little pieces of the butter between your fingertips, creating flour-coated bits that resemble dry oatmeal. Add the oats and pecans and rub it all together to combine.

3 Top the crisp: Sprinkle the topping over the prepared fruit. You want it to be at least a bit clumpy, so if it is completely loose and sandy, take some small handfuls and squeeze them together to form some little clumps.

4 Bake it: Set the baking dish on a parchment paper–lined baking sheet in order to catch any drippy juices, then bake for 45 to 60 minutes, until it is golden brown on top and has been bubbling around the edges for at least 5 minutes.

ALMOND POLENTA PLUM CAKE

Whether you call it a snack cake, snacking cake, tea cake, torte, or something else, what really matters is that this is a really satisfying, totally unadulterated cake. No need for frosting or other embellishments, snack cakes can be enjoyed any time of day. This Almond Polenta Plum Cake is no exception. Made with wholesome ground almonds and cornmeal, and packed with sweet, juicy plums, it's simply irresistible.

• • •

Serves 6 to 8

Gluten free

Equipment: A 9-inch springform pan (or substitute an 8 by 8-inch or a 9 by 9-inch baking dish)

INGREDIENTS

Butter, 1 cup (16 tablespoons) unsalted, melted and cooled

Plums, 10 to 12 small plums (Santa Rosas are especially good here), or 6 medium-large plums or pluots (avoid Italian plums, which are drier, and go for tart, complex-tasting ones, if possible; ask a seller for recommendations; see Ingredient Note)

Eggs, 4 large, at room temperature (warming briefly in a bowl or pan of hot tap water works well)

Vanilla extract, 1 teaspoon

Almond extract, 1 teaspoon

Almond flour, 2 cups (aka ground almonds)

Light brown sugar, 1 cup packed

Fine cornmeal, ¾ cup

Baking powder, 1 teaspoon

Salt, ½ teaspoon

Granulated sugar, 2 tablespoons, plus more as needed

Ingredient Note

This recipe relies heavily on *(Serious) New Cook* Principle #1: Use good ingredients. It is a simple—as in, easy and simply delicious—recipe, so starting with delicious plums is essential. If it's not summertime, or you can't get terrific plums, employ Principle #3: Experiment! See what other delicious fruits might work as a substitute. Nectarines? Cherries? Pineapple? Berries? (Use enough to partially cover the top, leaving space in between the fruit so you end up with some deliciously browned cake, as pictured.) You can even make it with no fruit at all—just warm, tender almond polenta cake.

Tip

Baking measurements are sometimes given as volume, as we do here, and sometimes given as weight, which is more precise. For simplicity, we offer only volume. Brown sugar should be packed into the cup when measured because it often clumps, making it hard to scoop evenly. White sugar and most flours, including the almond flour and cornmeal in this recipe, should not be packed. Using a measuring cup, loosely scoop it and level it off with the straight side of a knife for an even measurement.

1 **Prepare for baking:** Preheat the oven to 375°F. Grease the sides and bottom of your springform pan with a teaspoon or two of the melted butter. Then, cut a round of parchment paper that's a bit larger than the diameter of the pan, and place it on the bottom of the pan, right on top of the butter.

2 **Cut and pit plums:** Starting at the stem end, carefully run a sharp knife around each plum, all the way through to the pit, cutting it in half. Then, twist the halves. If it's a freestone variety (a type of stone fruit), it will twist and split in half easily, and the pit will pop right out. If it's a clingstone, on the other hand, use a small sharp-edged spoon, a grapefruit spoon, or a small paring knife to carve around the pit to remove it.

3 **Make the cake:** In a large bowl, whisk together the eggs, vanilla extract, almond extract, and remaining melted butter until combined. In another large bowl, whisk together the almond flour, brown sugar, cornmeal, baking powder, and salt. Dump the dry ingredients into the wet ingredients and whisk until just combined. Pour the batter into the prepared pan.

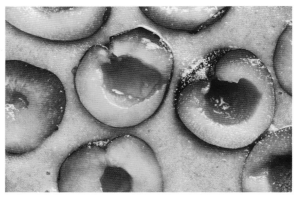

4 **Top and bake:** Place the plums, cut-side up, on the batter. Sprinkle about 1 tablespoon of the granulated sugar on the plums. Bake for 30 minutes. Then, remove the cake and sprinkle the plums with another tablespoon sugar. Bake for another 10 minutes, then check the plums. If they are dry or watery, rather than syrupy and bubbly, sprinkle another 1 tablespoon sugar on top. Bake until the plums have started to caramelize and the cake is nicely browned—or a toothpick inserted into the middle of the cake comes out clean—about 45 to 55 minutes total. Cool for 10 minutes before popping open and removing the side of the pan. Slice and serve warm.

CLAIRE PTAK'S
CLASSIC CUPCAKES

Claire Ptak might be best known for the show-stopping Royal Wedding cake she baked for Meghan Markle and Prince Harry, Duchess and Duke of Sussex. She was a renowned baker long before that, as the pastry chef at Chez Panisse, where she and Leah were friends and colleagues, and later, as the chef and owner of Violet, London's most beloved bakery. Her numerous cookbooks—and a peek through the window at Violet—reveals her tremendous range. In addition to breathtaking special-occasion cakes, she's famous for her blondies, whoopie pies, rustic snacking cakes, and, of course, cupcakes. Here's her recipe for raspberry cupcakes, made with a perfect lemon sponge and the most raspberry-licious frosting you'll ever have.

. . .

Makes 12 to 16 cupcakes, depending on the size of your tins. (If you have just one 12-cup tin, you can bake up any leftover batter in ramekins, which may take a couple extra minutes in the oven.)

Equipment: A cupcake tin and liners (or grease the tin with butter and dust with flour, if you don't have liners); a piping bag and decorating nozzle or a gallon-size resealable storage bag with one tip cut off (optional)

INGREDIENTS

LEMON SPONGE CAKE

All-purpose flour, 2 cups

Baking powder, 2 teaspoons

Butter, ½ cup plus 1 tablespoon (9 tablespoons) unsalted, very soft, but not melty

Sugar, 1 cup (preferably superfine sugar, though regular granulated will do)

Salt, ½ teaspoon

Eggs, 3 large, at room temperature (warmed briefly in a bowl or pan of hot tap water works well)

Milk, ½ cup plus 1 tablespoon (preferably whole milk)

Lemon juice, 4 teaspoons freshly squeezed

RASPBERRY FROSTING

Raspberries, about 1 cup fresh

Powdered sugar, up to 4 cups, sifted

Butter, ⅞ of a cup (14 tablespoons) unsalted, softened

Milk, 1 tablespoon (preferably whole milk)

Lemon juice, 1 teaspoon freshly squeezed

Kirsch (optional), ½ teaspoon (kirsch is a cherry liqueur; if using, reduce lemon juice to ½ teaspoon)

Fresh berries (optional), 12 to 24, for garnish

Optional Prep

The cupcakes can be made the day before serving and stored, covered, at room temperature. The frosting can be made up to 5 days in advance and stored in an airtight container in the refrigerator; bring to room temp and re-whip before using.

Tip

A whole cake can be made with this recipe, if you prefer. Either bake it in an 8-inch square pan (for what's often called a "sheet pan" cake) or two 6-inch round cake pans (for a layer cake). Just be sure to first butter the pans, then dust them with flour. If making a layer cake, you can spread a layer of raspberry jam or frosting in between the two layers.

Tips

Buttercream frosting can be fickle. The temperature of your ingredients needs to be just right in order for everything to emulsify. Otherwise, you'll end up with a weird, unusable mess instead of a lovely, fluffy buttercream. If you see this starting to happen as you're whipping it together, there are usually ways to rescue it: If the raspberry puree just won't incorporate and the buttercream looks a bit saucy and "broken," slowly whisk in more powdered sugar until it takes shape. If it seems warm and soupy, set the bowl on ice packs or wrap it with ice-cold wet towels while you whip it. If it's lumpy and "broken," feels quite cool, and still won't come together, it may need a bit of warming with warm (not hot) wet towels or, better yet, a hair dryer blown at the outsides of the bowl.

Piping bags make frosting fun. To use, attach a tip, fold over the sides of the bag, and then carefully spoon in some icing no more than ⅓ full. Flip the sides back up, carefully press out the air, and twist the top of the bag, preventing the icing from squirting out the wrong end and providing the pressure needed to come out the right end. Carefully squeeze the frosting on top of each cupcake in whatever decorative pattern you like, such as a zigzag, a circle, a mound, or several little "kisses." Experiment—(*Serious*) *New Cook* Principle #3—with different tips, if you have them, to see which shapes you like best. And most important, have fun with it— (*Serious*) *New Cook* Principle #5.

1 Prep: Preheat the oven to 350°F. Line a cupcake tin with paper cupcake liners and set aside.

2 Start the cupcake batter: <u>Sift</u> or whisk together the flour and baking powder in a medium bowl and set aside. Put the softened butter and the sugar in a large bowl or the bowl of a stand mixer. Use an electric hand mixer or the paddle attachment on a stand mixer to cream them on high until almost white and fluffy—*at least* 5 to 6 minutes with a hand mixer or 3 minutes in a stand mixer. Keep at it until it's very pale yellow and doubled in volume. (This is the trick to a fluffy cupcake with a fine crumb.)

3 Finish the batter: To the creamed butter mixture, add the salt and eggs, one at a time, mixing on medium until fully incorporated. Then add half of the flour mixture, and again mix on medium until just combined. Next add the milk and lemon juice, and mix until combined. Finally, add the remaining flour mixture, and mix until just combined.

4 Bake the cupcakes: Spoon the batter into each cupcake liner to two-thirds full, and bake until they just start to brown and look set, 16 to 20 minutes. (Stick a wooden skewer or a thin <u>knife</u> into the center of one to check; if it comes out clean, they are done.) Remove from the tin and set on a wire rack to cool completely before icing them.

5 Make the frosting: Puree the raspberries with 2 tablespoons of the powdered sugar. Set a fine-mesh sieve over a large bowl (or the bowl of a stand mixer) and press the puree through it, straining out the seeds. Set the strainer aside, then add 2 cups of the powdered sugar and the butter and milk. Using an electric hand mixer or the paddle attachment on a stand mixer, beat together on the lowest setting possible for 3 minutes. Scrape the sides down with a spatula, then add an additional 1½ cups of powdered sugar and continue to mix on the lowest setting possible for another 3 minutes. The frosting should be light and smooth, but still have enough body to hold its shape. (In other words, it needs to be thick enough to frost a cupcake!) If it seems too soft, slowly beat in up to another ½ cup powdered sugar. Finally, beat in the lemon juice and kirsch (if using) until everything is well incorporated. If the frosting still seems too soft (and/or if the temperature in your kitchen is very warm), refrigerate it for 3 minutes, then stir with a spatula. Repeat as necessary until the consistency is ideal for frosting.

6 Frost the cupcakes: Using your piping bag or a gallon-size resealable storage bag with one corner tip cut off, frost your cupcakes (see Tips). Alternatively, use a spoon to simply smear some frosting on top! Then, share—(*Serious*) *New Cook* Principle #4—and enjoy!

Chocolate Air Cake

This cake is a marvel. It's at once intense and delicate. Our recipe is based on Chez Panisse's Chocolate Pavé, a long-standing favorite. It's traditionally baked in a square pan—hence "pavé," which means paving stone in French. But, quite unlike paving stones, this cake is light as air! We like to bake it in a 9-inch springform pan, which lends a certain formality, making it perfect for serving as a simple birthday cake or an elegant weekend dessert. If you cook it a little less, you'll have a molten cake—a wildly popular dessert back in the 1990s!—though we prefer it cooked through, resulting in something closer to a soufflé.

• • •

Serves 6 to 8

Gluten free

Equipment: A 9-inch springform cake pan (or an 8-inch square pan); parchment paper, cut to fit the bottom of your cake pan

INGREDIENTS

Butter, ¾ cup (12 tablespoons) unsalted, cut into large chunks, plus a bit more for buttering the pan

Dark <u>chocolate</u>, 7 ounces, bars or chips (minimum 60% cocoa)

<u>Salt</u>, ¼ teaspoon

Eggs, 5 large, separated

Sugar, ¾ cup

<u>Powdered sugar</u>, for <u>dusting</u>

<u>Whipped cream</u> (see page 41) for dolloping

1 Prep: Preheat the oven to 350°F. Butter the sides and bottom of a 9-inch springform pan. Line with the circle of <u>parchment paper</u>, then smear a bit more butter on top of the parchment. (You can use your fingers to do this.)

2 Melt the chocolate: In a medium pot, bring about 2 inches of water to a gentle simmer over medium heat. Put the butter and chocolate in a large bowl set on top of the simmering pot of water (a technique called a water bath). Melt the butter and chocolate, stirring occasionally with a wooden spoon or heat-safe silicone spatula, until completely smooth (about 5 minutes). Stir in the salt. Remove the bowl from the heat.

3 Start the batter: While the chocolate and butter are melting, put the egg yolks and ½ cup of the sugar into a large bowl or the bowl of a stand mixer with whisk. Using an electric hand mixer or the stand mixer, whisk on high until it turns pale yellow and begins to form "ribbons," about 5 to 7 minutes (see Tips). Pause to scrape down the sides of the bowl periodically.

4 Whip the egg whites: Whip the egg whites until they become foamy (see Tips), and then slowly sprinkle in the remaining ¼ cup sugar. Continue whipping until soft <u>peaks</u> form.

5 Add the chocolate to the egg yolk mixture: Make sure your chocolate-butter mixture is no longer hot. If it is, let it cool on the counter. Once it's just warm, whisk it into the egg yolk mixture until well incorporated.

6 Finish the batter: Gently <u>fold</u> one-third of the fluffy egg white mix into the chocolate–egg yolk base. Using a rubber spatula, gently fold, from the bottom up to the top, until few white streaks remain. Then add in another one-third of the egg whites, gently folding until almost fully incorporated. Finally, add the rest of the egg whites and fold until no streaks remain and the color is uniform. Pour the mixture into the prepared baking pan.

7 Bake the cake: Bake for 40 minutes, then gently jiggle the pan to check to see if it is just set in the center. When you think it is set, remove it from the oven and let it cool on a cooling rack (see Tips). Serve with a dusting of powdered sugar and whipped cream.

Tips

The "ribbon" stage describes when sugar and egg whites are whipped together to a particular thickness: when the mixture is thick enough that drizzling it back and forth as it drips off the whisk creates "ribbons" that remain visible for a couple seconds before "melting" back into the mixture.

Whipping egg whites by hand is a good idea, as it provides a more stable whip, which helps the cake rise better. That said, stand mixers and electric mixers are easier—just start on medium-low until foamy, gradually increasing the speed to medium-high until you've reached the level of <u>peaks</u> required.

Despite how fussy and delicate soufflés are, they usually re-puff when reheated. This cake is very similar to a soufflé. So, when you first remove it, don't turn off your oven immediately. After 5 minutes, if it has sunken dramatically, put it back in the oven quickly (and gently) for another few minutes.

TRICOLOR MATCHA FRAPPÉ

Forget overpriced cafe drinks, this frappé is as delicious as it is gorgeous! (Not to mention the fact that when you make it yourself, you know exactly what's in it—and this one's got only the good stuff.) A strong blender makes quick work of pulverizing the ice into a slushy treat, though it's excellent enjoyed simply over ice, if you prefer. The fresh strawberries mingle with the creamy matcha, making a delightful treat.

INGREDIENTS

Ice

Milk, 1 cup

Sugar, 2 tablespoons

Matcha, 2 teaspoons, plus a pinch for dusting (see Ingredient Note)

Strawberry puree, from 1 cup fresh strawberries blended with 1 tablespoon sugar and a few pieces of ice

Whipped cream (optional), for topping

• • •

Makes 2 tall glasses

Equipment: A blender, preferably a high-powered, bullet-style one (though any type will work)

Ingredient Note

Matcha is a high-quality green tea that's been ground into a fine powder, making it suitable for whisking (or blending!) with water or milk, rather than steeping. It is believed to have powerful health and cognitive benefits. Though it has less caffeine than coffee, matcha often has more caffeine than other teas, cup for cup, because you consume the leaves themselves. So, drink it responsibly (and not too late in the day!).

1 Make the matcha frappé: Put a big handful of ice, along with the milk, sugar, and matcha, in a blender and pulse until well crushed and blended.

2 Compose: Divide the frappé between two glasses and top each with strawberry puree and a dollop of whipped cream, if using. Dust with matcha and serve immediately with a straw or long spoon.

GRAPE TEA SLUSHY

Grapes and oolong tea combine to make a surprising summertime slushy. A style of tea that falls somewhere in between green and black, oolong is clean-tasting yet full of complexity. It pairs brilliantly with black grapes, which tend to be very sweet with a subtle hint of bitter from a substance called tannins found just under the skin. Black tea grape slushies topped with slightly salty whipped cream cheese are a wildly popular type of "cheese tea" in Asia, often found at bubble tea shops. Might sound odd, but all the flavors mingle together in a way that's remarkably sweet, savory, and satisfying. At home, we usually stick with just grapes and tea (and frankly, any varieties work, though black grapes and oolong are especially great together!), but when the mood strikes, we'll add a little dollop of salted yogurt whipped cream to the top for something just a little different.

• • •

Makes 2 tall glasses

Equipment: A blender, preferably a high-powered, bullet-style one (though any type will work)

INGREDIENTS

Black grapes, 2 cups seedless, cold

Oolong tea, 2 cups brewed, chilled

Ice, about 1 cup

Sugar (optional), 2 to 3 teaspoons, depending on how sweet your grapes are

Yogurt whipped cream (optional), see page 41, for topping

Sea salt (optional), for topping

Whole peeled grapes (optional), a handful, for garnish

Ingredient Note

Oolong is considered a low-caffeine tea, like green tea, with significantly less caffeine than coffee or black tea. The overarching classifications of tea—green, oolong, black—are based on the length of time the tea leaves have been oxidized, a process that dries them, makes them darker, and increases their caffeine content. Oolong is oxidized just slightly more than green, giving it a slightly darker hue and just slightly more caffeine.

1   Blend: In a blender on high speed, blend the grapes, tea, and ice until the ice is pulverized and the grape skin specks are uniformly small. Taste it and decide whether to add sugar before blending the slushy a bit more.

2   Top and serve: Transfer to glasses and, if desired, add a few peeled grapes and give each drink a small dollop of yogurt whipped cream and a tiny sprinkle of sea salt. Serve immediately with a straw or long spoon.

LEMON-APPLE FIZZ

Nothing beats a cold, fizzy, homemade drink when you want a refreshing thirst-quencher. This Lemon-Apple Fizz is about as refreshing as it gets! Sweet, bright, and herbaceous, it's topped off with a splash of soda or seltzer that adds to the refreshing zip, each tiny bubble really bringing out the flavor.

• • •

Makes 2 medium or 3 small glasses

Equipment: A blender, preferably a high-powered, bullet-style one (though any type will work)

INGREDIENTS

Lemon, 1 large and juicy or 2 if small and/or dry-ish (Meyer lemon is especially good in this!)

Apple juice or cider, 2 cups

Honey, 1 tablespoon (or substitute sugar or agave)

Fresh basil, 3 leaves (or use fresh mint)

Ice

Seltzer, club soda, or sparkling water, a splash per glass

1 Prep the lemon: Slice two nice rounds of lemon and set aside to use as a garnish. Then, squeeze the remaining lemon into a blender. (One good way to strain out the seeds is to squeeze it over a small strainer—but you can use whatever you have, including your fingers!)

2 Combine: To the lemon juice, add the apple juice, honey, basil leaves, and a handful of ice.

3 Blend: Pulse until the ice is crushed and the basil specks are uniformly small. Taste it, remembering that it will get diluted a bit with the soda. If it's too sour, add a bit more apple juice or honey; if it's too sweet, add a bit more lemon juice and ice. Re-blend.

4 Serve: Fill your glasses with ice and add the lemon–apple juice blend, stopping ½ to ¾ inch from the top. Garnish each with a slice of lemon. Top with seltzer, club soda, or sparkling water. Clink glasses with a friend— *(Serious) New Cook* Principle #4: share!—and enjoy. Cheers!

Special Menus ———

Logic, flow, balance, and—of course—maximum yumminess are the key characteristics of a great menu. Whether it's a single dish or multiple courses, think about how all the flavors, textures, colors, and shapes will work together on the plate and in your mouth. Some tips to remember: If the vegetables all ripen in the same season and come from roughly the same region of the planet, the meal is more likely to feel and taste naturally cohesive. Try balancing rich elements with refreshing ones, sweet with salty, oily with acidic, soft with crunchy. Imagine yourself eating each course in conjunction with the following courses to get a better sense of how different dishes go together. Also try to balance more complex, time-consuming dishes with quick and easy ones that can be made ahead.

A Birthday Party

- Grape Tea Slushy or Lemon-Apple Fizz (page 239 or 240)
- A vegetable platter with Gorgeous Green Goddess Dip and Dressing or Romesco Dip and Sauce (page 99 or 101)
- Classic Breaded and Pan-Fried Chicken Breasts (page 145) with Vegetables (page 147)
- Classic Cupcakes (page 231)

Mother's Day Brunch

- Prosciutto-Wrapped Asparagus Spears or Fennel and Citrus Salad (page 89 or 109)
- Bricked Salmon in Brothy Rice (page 163)
- Meyer Lemon Pudding Cake Cups (page 203)

Father's Day Dinner

- Prosciutto-Wrapped Melon Wedges (page 85)
- Biscuit-Topped Chicken Pot Pie or Spaghetti with Braised Pork Ragu (page 128 or 185)
- Chicory Salad with Homemade Croutons and a Broken Caesar Vinaigrette (page 112)
- Buttermilk Panna Cotta Cups with Any Berry Compote (pages 208 and 53)

Korean Dinner

- Mom's Frittery Bindaeduk Pancakes (page 75)
- Bulgogi Lettuce Wraps or Bulgogi Bibimbap (page 191 or 195)
- (Double) Dalgona Coffee Milkshakes (page 217)

Fancy Dinner

- Radish and Miso-Butter Crostini (page 93)
- Frittery Shrimp and Scallion Pancakes (page 80)
- Bricked Duck Breast Lettuce Wraps (page 169)
- Chocolate Air Cake (page 234)

Sushi Party

- Sushi Party (see page 135)
- Mochi Ice Cream (page 215)

Packable Lunches

- Classic Breaded and Pan-Fried Chicken Breast (page 145)
- Flash-Fried Cutlets (page 153)
- Tomato Bisque (page 117)
- A vegetable platter with Gorgeous Green Goddess Dip and Dressing (page 99)
- Fennel and Citrus Salad (page 109)
- Hand-Pressed Rice Balls (page 142)
- Kimbap (page 195)
- Prosciutto-Wrapped Stuffed Dates (page 83)
- Buttermilk Panna Cotta Cups (page 208)
- Coconut Rice Pudding Cups (page 205)

Study Break Snacks

- Any Crostini (pages 91–96)
- Chips with Creamy Goes-with-Everything Dip (page 105)
- Pillowy Silver Dollar Pancakes (page 55)
- Savory Puff Daddy Minis (page 50)
- (Double) Dalgona Coffee Milkshakes (page 217)
- Sweet and Cheesy Handmade Arepas (page 64)
- Egg Drop Soup (page 115)

Index

Acknowledgments

Cammie & Leah

We offer our deepest gratitude to the many people who have been part of this journey.

Foremost, to our mom, the remarkable Kum Su Kim, for everything: For the fearlessness with which you have taken on life, showing us what it means to be strong and brave and bold. For your boundless love and support and generosity. For your help with so many of these recipes. For the countless amazing meals you've cooked—and continue to cook!—for us, providing endless inspiration and nourishment. You're the best cook we know, Mom.

To our dad, Bruno Puidokas, for creating our earliest food memories: Foraging for mushrooms and *gosari* and wild berries. Tending a garden. Savoring the delicacies shared among your eclectic circle of Italian and German hunter-butcher friends. Cultivating our palates with your brazen love of stinky cheese, wild mushrooms, cured meat, tinned fish, and pickled everything. We wouldn't be who we are without you, Dad.

To Molly DeCoudreaux, our brilliant photographer, for your keen eye and tireless work, as well as your support and friendship. To our agent Danielle Svetcov and our book designer Debbie Berne, along with the entire crew at Rizzoli, especially associate publisher Jim Muschett and editor Tricia Levi, for your patience and your work ushering this book through with two novice cookbook authors—during a global pandemic, no less!

To Cal Peternell for your support and enthusiasm, and for the lovely foreword to this book. To Black Wing Clay for your amazing pottery, and Rule & Level for your dreamy props (and for being so great to work with). And to all of our recipe testers and feedback-givers, young and old, experienced and new. Thank you!

To the incredible guest chefs who contributed recipes: Sean Sherman, Alice Waters, Bryant Terry, Russell Moore, Sohui Kim, Scott Peacock (with Edna Lewis, in spirit), and Claire Ptak. We're thrilled to introduce a new generation of cooks to your brilliance!

Leah

To Martín, for inspiring me. And for loving me.

To Oscar, for lovingly questioning all that I say, do, cook, and eat. And to Fina, for being my sweetest, most honest food critic.

To Cammie, for everything! From sharing this lifetime of sisterhood, friendship, and motherhood together to your parenting wisdom, and the beautiful words you strung together to write this book.

To my Quiroga family, for your boundless love and support.

To Cal Peternell, Russell Moore, and Gilbert Pilgram, for being the best teachers and mentors, as well as friends. To Alice Waters and the entire Chez Panisse family, for providing a wonderful place to learn and grow (up).

To Carlotta, Indigo, and Olivia Orta, for your help in the early stages, and to Olivia Rathbone, for your recipe testing and for all that you do on the farm. And to the dear friends who have dined at my table, for your loving company, conversation, and support. You continue to nourish my soul.

Cammie

To Kai and Noie, two fine young cooks already, for your endless input and work on this book, from taster to recipe tester to critic to model. Your enthusiastic collaboration and unwavering support mean the world to me. You never cease to inspire me. I'm so proud of you both.

To Edgar, my best friend and partner in everything, for always believing in me. I adore you.

To Leah, foremost for being my big sister and friend. And, for taking this journey with me! You've taught me so much. I wouldn't be who I am without you.

To the Lin family, for your love and support—and for all the great eats and side-splitting laughs.

To all of Kai's and Noie's friends, for your feedback and enthusiasm. To my NYU students for helping me keep my finger on the pulse with your always-terrific feedback and encouragement. And to my friends, for your enthusiasm and support (including Cynthia and Amy, for never tiring of tricky grammar and syntax queries).

254

About the Authors

Leah and Cammie are sisters who grew up in an immigrant family in the Midwest. Their Korean mom's cooking (and to be clear, she can cook EVERYTHING, not just Korean food!), their German-Lithuanian dad's gardening, hunting, and foraging, and the food traditions of an eclectic circle of family, friends, and neighbors—many immigrants themselves—shaped their early palates.

Leah graduated from Cornell University before pursuing her true passion, cooking. She attended the Culinary Institute of America, which led to an externship at Alice Water's iconic Berkeley, CA, restaurant, Chez Panisse. She went on to work there for over ten years, quickly working her way up to head chef—one of the youngest ever to hold the post. Her experiences there refined and shaped not only her palate, but also her commitment to local, organic, sustainable foods. She eventually left Chez Panisse to start a family and run a small farm in Sebastopol, California. Through her extended family, her palate and her cooking repertoire have grown to include New Mexican and Bolivian flavors and techniques, as well.

Cammie is an avid home cook who got her start cooking in commercial kitchens (or rather, got her start as a little girl in her mama's kitchen!) but pursued her vocation as a teacher and writer. She is an award-winning educator with over twenty years of experience teaching young adults—first as a New York City public school teacher and now as a professor at New York University, where she teaches courses in first-year writing, critical service learning, and food writing. She lives and cooks with her family in Brooklyn, New York. Through traveling, cooking, and eating with her extended family—joyous food-lovers, too—her repertoire has also grown to include Taiwanese cuisine, with perhaps a bit of Hawaiian and Central Pennsylvanian.

These powerful influences are reflected in their palates, their daily cooking, and the diverse collection of recipes and cooking techniques in this book.

First published in the United States of America in 2022 by
Rizzoli International Publications, Inc.
300 Park Avenue South
New York, NY 10010
www.rizzoliusa.com

Foreword: Cal Peternell
Photography: Molly DeCoudreaux

Publisher: Charles Miers
Associate Publisher: James Muschett
Editor: Tricia Levi
Design: Debbie Berne
Managing Editor: Lynn Scrabis

Guest chef contributions on pages 77, 91, 109, 175, 191, 221,
and 231 were provided with their consent.

Printed in China

2022 2023 2024 2025 / 10 9 8 7 6 5 4 3 2 1

ISBN: 978-1-59962-165-4
Library of Congress Control Number: 2022934943

Visit us online:
Facebook.com/RizzoliNewYork
Twitter: @Rizzoli_Books
Instagram.com/RizzoliBooks
Pinterest.com/RizzoliBooks
Youtube.com/user/RizzoliNY
Issuu.com/Rizzoli